# GOD, PUT OUT ONE OF MY EYES

## ALSO BY ARLENE SWIFT JONES

*The Insisting Thistle* (poetry)
*Deenewood, A Sequence* (poetry)
*Pomegranate Wine* (poetry)

# GOD, PUT OUT ONE OF MY EYES

## A Cyprus Memoir, 1962-1965

## Arlene Swift Jones

Antrim House

Simsbury, Connecticut

Library of Congress Control Number: 2010928677

ISBN: 978-0-9843418-0-1

Printed & bound by United Graphics, Inc.

First Edition, 2010

Captioned photographs by Arlene Swift Jones et al.
with thanks to Kristin & Robin Jones for locating so many of them

Cover photograph (of Mehmet with flock) by Arlene Swift Jones

Author photograph by Frank Jones

Book design by Rennie McQuilkin

Antrim House
860.217.0023
AntrimHouse@comcast.net
www.AntrimHouseBooks.com
21 Goodrich Road, Simsbury, CT 06070

# DEDICATION

I dedicate this book to the Cypriots—Greek and Turkish alike—who perished in the Cyprus inter-ethnic wars.

I also include persons no longer with us, especially my husband, Frank Jones.

Others are: Ambassador Taylor and Edith Belcher; Ambassador Tuvia and Georgia Arazi; Richard Welch; Meriden Bennett; Colonel and Mrs. John Sale; Robert and Maureen Pendleton; Kemal Rustem; Sabri Tahir; Nahim Bey; Mehmet; Kadir Tarik; Chief Justice Mikalakis and Dolly Triantfyllides; George Polyviou; Michael Petris; Glafkos Clerides; Savvas Polydorou; and Ireni. What we all have had in common is a love for Cyprus and equal grief over its fate.

I cannot go without mentioning Karakoumi and Charlie Boy, now dust among the stones.

# PREFACE

I lived on Cyprus immediately before and during the early years of hostilities between Greek and Turkish Cypriots, 1962-65, just after the island gained independence in 1960. The story I am about to tell takes place not long after that of Durrell's *Bitter Lemons* and is about my family's experiences during the time my husband served as CIA Station Chief at the American Embassy in Nicosia. We were beguiled by the charm of the island, its hospitality, its mythology so mixed with its history in the cradle of the world's civilization; but the whole family was forced to face political and military realities, culminating in civil war on the island. This experience became a rite-of-passage for us, embroiled as we were in the vast and murky politics governing the Eastern Mediterranean, where fear dominates and dramatizes ethnic conflict and personal reactions to total warfare on a small, seemingly paradisical island.

Arlene Swift Jones
Bloomfield, CT
June 5, 2010

# FOREWORD

There is beauty and barbarity in the Paradise Lost of Cyprus described in Arlene Swift Jones' narrative. Mountain eagles soar gracefully and scream against a tempest, the wine-dark sea releases strange sharks, and a noble old fig tree is home to a serpent of sorts. The same beauty and barbarity coexist in local rituals: an Easter Monday feast, a Greek wedding... Always war is latent in the uneasy peace between minority Turks and majority Greeks. When hostilities do break out, unpredictable losses invade. The author's lovable cook, undone by war and ethnic hatred, turns to drink; beloved family animals starve, caught up in the midst of strife; the Archbishop of Cyprus cuts a Christmas cake for blind children on the same night when he hands out guns to teenage terrorists; and the author herself learns that she is capable of murder. In the end, there is only grief in the perpetuation of historic ethnic hatred which feeds upon itself. One is reminded all too forcefully of present-day conflicts in the Balkans, the Holy Land, and the Near East. And yet in the courage of the author, who fights to keep her family together; in the innocence of her children; in the love and nobility of soul shown by both Turks and Greeks, matching the glorious setting in which they live; and in the primitive but pristine passion of traditional island ceremonies, there is the hope that the human spirit is capable of rising above the horrors so vividly described in *God, Put Out One of My Eyes.*

# TABLE OF CONTENTS

# A Greek Proverb

*One day God approached Janni, a Greek peasant farmer working in his fields, and said to him: "Janni, you are a very good, honest, God-fearing man. And I want to reward you by granting you one wish. Anything you desire shall be yours... But remember that Charity is a gift to be shared, and I will reward your neighbor, Mehmet, with twice what you ask for." Janni scratched his head carefully. Finally, he replied:*

**God, put out one of my eyes!**

# GOD
# PUT OUT
# ONE OF MY EYES

# NICOSIA, SEPTEMBER 1962

The plane lifted off from Athens into nothing but blue, the sky indistinguishable from the sea, without even a cloud to mark our movement. We were a silver speck, suspended like an astronaut in an indigo vastness. Suddenly, a citadel of white, green-faceted, licked gently by a sapphire sea. One entire jewel contained within an eagle's shining eye borne by droning silver wings, circling inwards and landing on bleak baking barrenness. Nicosia retreated inwards from that sea and wilted in the summer sun.

We had been assigned directly from Warsaw without home leave between posts, our family of three girls and my CIA husband. We were anticipating sunny beaches, fresh fruits and vegetables year-round. Poland had offered us cabbage, potatoes, cauliflower and carrots. And surveillance. And beef which was only fit for boiling. *Stuka Miesa,* over and over. Or the tenderloin of beef, which in this case came from a tired old cow, with its darkened blood and yellowed strings of fat swishing around in a pan at the Polish diplomatic meat shop, also meant for ranking Communist party members. For years after we left Poland, our youngest daughter, Kristin, refused grilled lamb, sautéed veal, and rare roast beef. She wanted "meat that sticks in your teeth."

Poland was grey, cold. The wounded buildings huddled like shadowy elephants, or hulks of abandoned ships. We lived in one, fortunate to have several rooms for one family. It came with its embedded microphones, which precluded our having any real conversations. My husband and I, if we wanted to talk about anything controversial, went for walks, and often were followed by the identifiable black Mercedes sedans. We never, of course, discussed his work. So much of his life was anathema to me: we were reduced to discussing the weather, the children, the maids, and the cook. Things in my life I swore I would never discuss. But there I was, in my pseudo-diplomatic life, where the ladies would go to another room after dinner and talk about exactly those things. The men would retire to smoke and drink cognac or port. And talk.

Cyprus was to be a vacation, indulged in with sea and the great blue sky enveloping the big rocky stone that was Cyprus, at the end of a great body of water, with its history of endless conquests and religions and cultures since the beginning of time. It contained remnants from every period of early history and was the first place where Christianity was preached. I was thrilled.

We descended from the plane onto the burning tarmac and were met by a tongue-lick of fire. Then the scorched land which produced it, a desert bowl empty of everything but flaming heat. The cool green jewel seen from the air had disappeared—our first mirage. Eyes met and cried out; our answers were to touch each other's hands, my children and I. A new country, a new home. Frank, my husband, was already absorbed in welcome by a departing colleague and his childless, aging wife. Her eyes read us coldly.

Arrived. September, 1962.

We are Frank Jones, sent to Cyprus by President Kennedy, who wants more intelligence on what he thinks will be a Middle East explosion; we are Arlene and our three daughters, ages 9, 7 and 6, all blonde, all happy to get to the sun after three years in a grim climate, a grim country: Communist Poland where the sun, figuratively and actually, rarely shone. Their names are Jeannie, Robin, and Kristin.

Driving from the airport, skirting a portion of the town (was it a city?) our eyes confirmed the barrenness. We could not see a weed, a blade of grass—nothing but baking earth, now and then a lonely olive tree, fighting with the earth for water. Nothing green. Where was the much-praised beauty of this island? Shuttered houses sulked, withdrawing from the sun.

In front of the Ledra Palace Hotel there were short palm trees, caked with dust. Voices rose from closed interiors, and all the words were strange; no sound was familiar to our ears. "Greek," we said.

Cyprus had been a British Crown Colony from 1878 until 1960, when the island became independent for the first time in its ancient history. So English was spoken by nearly all its citizens. Over the years the island was bartered and sold, given, as it was to Cleopatra by Anthony, conquered again and again through Crusade after Crusade, pillaged, burned, occupied, Christianized, paganized, the cults of Aphrodite and the Virgin vying for popularity among the varied population. The Lionheart was married here. But I would later learn: *We are pure Greek*, the Greek Cypriots vowed, when they were conquered by Turks in 1571. What languages had been spoken here! Aramaic must have been one of them, for it was here that the Gospel of Christ was first preached by Saul, reborn as Paul when he accepted Christianity.

We slept and dreamed of green, of grass, of trees, of water sounds in streams, of rain, and awakened into rooms dim from drawn shades. We stumbled blindly into the sunshine of a perfumed Jasmine garden where we breakfasted with the entwining vines and the bees. But where are we? Who?

Again, a new home, I say. I must find a house that will make a home. We can only fill it with ourselves.

We do. Within walls, under this scorching sun, are cool, shuttered interiors, ritual sugared fruits in a jar, brought on a tray with a spoon. And a glass of cold clear water. Welcome, they say: the houses, the fruit, the offering hands. Welcome.

And the houses appear. The first one, temporary, was owned by a large German Shepherd dog named Mustapha. He helps himself to the chops on the table waiting to be cooked for dinner. He considers them his and I do not argue. He is waiting for his master who isn't returning to Cyprus. Mustapha does not know that, and we cannot bear to tell him. But Mustapha does know that he is lucky. There are dozens of homeless, masterless, pariah-like dogs (he was once so) because no one has the heart to kill new puppies, and the shepherds always guard their lambs. Sheep seem to graze on stones, but they are nourished. Mustapha is better nourished. I will learn later that folklore has it that if dogs cross their legs lying down, they belong to a Christian. If they do not, they belong to a Turk. Mustapha must have been very confused, I thought, having a Turkish name but belonging to a Christian.

This former bachelor house will be our home until I can find another. In Cyprus the American Embassy expects their staff members to find their own houses, unless they are fortunate to have one acceptable from their predecessors. We didn't. As fond as I was of their house, it would not accommodate a family with three children.

The second house, a week-end and summer house, we did inherit, just outside of Kyrenia overlooking the Mediterranean Sea. I would have been content to forgo the capital, Nicosia, with all its diplomatic dinners and cocktails, and live there. Not acceptable, says Frank...

As it overlooks the Mediterranean Sea, it is overlooked by the entire Kyrenia mountain range, including its most prominent feature: Pentedacylos—five steep points, known by all Cypriots as the five fingers, thrown by a rejected lover at the queen; others say by the hand of a god. The hills rise to them and are full of olive and carob trees and bushes and vineyards and eucalyptus and acacia and geraniums and cyclamen and shepherds. The house is two hundred years old, with dark wooden beams, whitewashed walls two feet thick of mud brick and plaster, and a center courtyard, containing a fishpond overgrown with wild geraniums. Cactus climbs and clings to the old walls, their brilliant colors a shout of defiance to the burning sun. One cactus is different, is shy as a goddess and opens its ten-inch pearly trumpet only to the night, each bloom lasting one night only. Is it Aphrodite's flower, or Aphrodite herself? She was "born" in Cyprus, springing out of a sea shell in the crystal waters off the sun-drenched beach of Paphos.

The courtyard contains a crumbling oven nesting under a grape arbor. There is a bathroom in what used to be the stable and still has the donkeys' trough and rings for tying. One of three bedrooms has a platform two steps high, drawers underneath: the family sleeping space in an old Turkish farmhouse. There is a fireplace on the lower level. The courtyard opens through a small old beam-supported doorway onto a large patio which looks simultaneously at the sea with one eye and the mountains, including the village of Bellapais, with the other: Bellapais, and the now-ruined abbey built by Lusignans in the 1100-1200's, as a monastery, and brought to ruin during the Venetian rule. There Lawrence Durrell found his ancient house, but a sturdier house than our sea house. His was built to withstand time. But how much time, considering what time was to Cyprus?

In Kyrenia, a mile away, there is a grocer, British-trained in that he sells Boveril and Golden Syrup and chutney and Worcestershire sauce, and delivers. Across from him is a local farmer's market which sells everything you can't buy from the grocer. Locally-cured olives of diverse varieties, and halumi, a white sheep's cheese kept in brine and served *au naturale* with mint leaves, or fried. Additionally there is Sabri, who found Durrell's house and can provide anything else one can't find. But I don't know that yet. Durrell wrote about him in his book, *Bitter Lemons,* which describes the four years of what the British referred to as the "troubled times" when the

British, with the aid of the Cypriot Turks, fought the Greek Cypriots and Greeks to prevent *enossis,* or Union with Greece.

The house is eighteen miles from Nicosia, on a road winding over the Mesaoria Plain to the mountains. The Plain side is a desert, pockmarked as the moon's face, totally barren in September, but I am told that in spring it is a green carpet of wheat, changing to gold. The sea side of the mountain is another world: white roads twisting through silver olive trees, defined by the taller and darker green color of the carob, and further defined by the random and prolific fig tree, the veritable Adam of them all. There are banana and orange trees, the banana tree very small and cultivated in sheltered spots, wind-free.

# KARAKOUMI

The world was so *delicious* in Cyprus: the sense of freedom, the fact that we didn't have that inevitable black Mercedes behind us or around the corner, or somewhere within our vision; the constant sun with its sky of blue compared to its gray inconstancy in Poland; the fruits we had been denied in colors of orange, purple, yellow, green—a rainbow tempting as Eve's apple. We would receive no punishment for eating them, nor cause others pain, except for remembering friends still in Poland. I hoped such fruits would always be such a miracle, but like most things one gets used to them and doesn't remember a time without them.

Now we were brimful with the first blush of love. Every rock, every dry bone of the parched land, seemed so much more holy and true than the green forests of Poland, as though the earth were trying to explain itself to us by showing its bones, like Adam and Eve before the fall—naked, and unashamed.

We decided that we should buy a pony. We had already decided that, as soon as we found the sea house. Cyprus was sun, warmth, and outdoor-ness: in the sea, on the sea, by the sea, year-round. We had been in Cyprus only a month and had already discovered that we could keep a pony, heretofore mythical, in a downstairs room of the Kyrenia cottage in the shade of a fig tree overlooking the sea. I wondered if the pony should have a better view of the sea than we, as though animals or the farmers cared about a view, unless they were romantics.

"The pony will be here all week, Mommy, and should be able to see the sea!" Kristin said. Frank and I smiled, our eyes beginning to develop crinkles at the corners after what had been years of eyes with none. To find a pony, we'd have to depend upon Nahim Bey, owner of our sea house. And perhaps

Sabri, such a great friend and rogue, as Durrell called him, who had found Durrell's house, and negotiated all the reconstructions. He ran a milk bar in Kyrenia.

Easy, said Nahim Bey, who seemed to procure everything. His car was full of things procured: bits of string, old pails of paint, bottles, wheels. "One never knows," he said. A Bentley full of junk.

Nahim Bey was fat. "It's his stomach," Kristin said. "He's so big," from Robin, who was so little. "I don't like him," Jeannie said, drawing away from a man with stains on his clothes.

"You may not like him, but what would we do without him?" Frank asked. "He owns our wonderful house, found Yashar, and now he will help us find a pony."

"I'll go," Jeannie said, tempted in spite of the grease spots on Nahim's suits. "Me too," Kristin agreed. "Let's get in the back," from Robin. "The back back!" Jeannie directed. And they did, sitting cross-legged on the floor of the Taunus station wagon. Nahim Bey was in the front because he couldn't get in the back seat of a two-door car. But Yashar had to go too, as small as Nahim was big, Yashar already engaged by Nahim to care for the unfound pony and to cut the overgrown vines and brush around his house, at our expense.

Trusting our knight errant—he was a little Quixotic, except for his size—we were off to unknown villages. "Turn here, turn there, turn left, now right." He never said "One mile north towards the mountains you will find..." We expected to go off each bend in the road until we passed it, or were upon it. The girls were buzzing with their little knowledge of Cyprus: "Is it Kasaphani? Is it Kyrenia? Is it Morphu? Is it Larnaca? even though Larnaca was on the southern coast. They tried every village name they had ever heard of.

"Is it Tarragona?" asked Kristin.

"Silly. That isn't even in Cyprus. That's in Spain." But

we had been in Spain, south of Barcelona on the Playa de San Salvador for three summers, and had gone to Tarragona. And in Geneva Robin had asked, after crossing Lac Leman by ferry, "Mommy, is it Africa?" Land on the other side of a body of water must be Africa, as it had been in Spain where she had forever asked when on the beach: "Where do the boats go, what is on the other side?" But no one of us could answer her questions now: "But where are we going? When will we reach there? How far is it?"

As though one could go very far in Cyprus with seven people in one car on a Sunday morning. "But you see," Nahim pronounced very slowly and confidently, "I have made arrangements," and the word "arrangements" had something mystical and expectant about it. It restored our confidence.

"Ah!" the girls said, smiling secretly, loving sort-of-secret things which they thought better than my "We'll see," which my mother had always said to me and which, though I didn't find it an answer, I repeated to my children. My silence indicated to them that we were willing to "wait and see." And Frank's silence said "I am driving," meaning he, too, was willing to wait and see.

And then we came to a village called "Karakoumi" and in its outskirts, which meant 50 meters from the café, was a rider on horseback. On a poor scraggly horse if we ever saw one. Our quiet but horrified looks said that in unison. There was an exchange of words between Nahim and the rider. We seemed to have stopped. Heated words. In Turkish. "But we don't want a horse," Nahim said, half to us, half to the rider, in English. On to the coffee house. We unwrapped our limbs from the confines of the small car and went inside.

As time passed in Cyprus, we learned that the interior of a bar or coffee house was representative of the interior of any and all coffee houses in Cypriot villages. Cement floor, dirt floor on the outside part, undecorated, largely unpainted walls except for an old newspaper photograph of an admired personage, or a magazine event, tacked on a wall here and there, years out of date. A newer portrait of Archbishop Makarios as President of the Republic of Cyprus. Small square tables, very few of them, either bare or covered with green oilcloth, tacked underneath. Chairs were standard: simple wooden frames crudely whittled, rush seat of bamboo which grew wherever there was water, many of the seats in various stages of unraveling, serving both as chairs and as tables. They were lightweight, always unstained and unpainted. The wear and the coffee made their own stains. There would be, always, a large amphora filled with water on a tripod, with a communal cup for drinking. The water was always fresh and cold, chilled from evaporation through the porous clay. A simple bar, a simple gas stove with innumerable one-cup, long-handled aluminum or enamel coffee pots for the individually-made Turkish coffee. Boil up once to have *kimach* or foam. Boil up twice for no kimach. Sugar boiled in it, never added later. And sugar was necessary. Sugar for the sun, for the stamina to survive it, for a brief pick-up of energy.

Another prominent café feature was its lack of women. Except for the few Western ones, now and then. We ordered coffee. Lemonade for the girls. Bottled and artificial tasting, in a land of lemons. Lemons everywhere—left on trees, fallen on the ground, omnipresent in restaurants. But never fresh lemonade in cafés.

This café was nearly empty. But people filed in, seemingly on schedule. The *Mukhtar*, the head man, the mayor, came in. Because he was Turkish we knew the village to be predominately Turkish. Nahim, a Turk, told us that. The Mukhtar: rugged, handsome, white hair mixed with black, tanned skin, wearing *vlachas,* the traditional black trousers consisting of yards and yards of black cotton material, wrapped and folded, fitted at the knees. He was brought a coffee without ordering. Standard order for the Mukhtar. He spoke to Nahim: weather, time of day... Even I could understand, not because of the words themselves but because of gestures, inflections and the business at hand: "Someone in the village has a fine horse he may sell. If you know someone who might be interested."

Nahim answered by silence. The Mukhtar continued: "I've seen it myself."

"How good?" More a comment than a question.

"You should see."

"But I don't know anyone who is interested."

"Too bad."

"Yes, too bad."

More silence.

"Well, the horse is outside. In case you want to see."

"Don't want to."

Frank and I were confused but entertained. The girls were perplexed, disappointed. But having been in enough shops to buy some pots and pans, general things always needed after a move of household goods, I understood that the way to do business was not to do business in American terms, that is, to indicate one's intentions and then get to the point. Rather, it was to indicate the opposite. Not true for minor, essential items, but when it was important for buying drapery material and carpets, the gamesmanship required to buy a horse must be illimitable. I wasn't certain whether we would be prepared to see it through.

The door opened. Another player entered. We soon learned he was the Middleman, the village representative who conducted exchanges between buyers and sellers. Nothing was sold without his negotiations, his sanction. Even though he often seemed a mere onlooker, he orchestrated everything by a faint lift of the chin, an eye raised ever so slightly, a subtle shift in his position. Every part of his body's movements was an entire language to the Cypriots, but the meanings we could only guess. He was proud, white-haired, had a heavy but neat mustache, eyes quick and black, missing nothing. He took us all in, fair-skinned children from a northland heritage, hair like yellow straw.

"Kyrios Jorgos!" He was addressed politely. Turkish Mukhtar and Greek middleman. The ethnic problems didn't seem to exist in villages.

He spoke first to Nahim Bey. In Greek. Nice Day. Pauses. Good Weather (when wasn't it, I was wondering). Pauses. Then: "A cousin of Janni here (a man in the corner I had not noted to be a part of the game being played) has a fine horse. So fine he hardly ever rides it. He just likes to keep it because it is beautiful." Pause. "You might like to see such a beautiful horse, even though it is not for sale."

Nahim had of course seen the first horse outside and had disapproved. Everyone knew that, and knew that we had been more than dismayed. They had to bring out something better. Maybe this one would be it. But if not, how many more villages were there? Scores and scores, and this process could go on each Sunday in village after village. It could take years to find a pony. We were becoming apprehensive about the potential length of the day and were beginning to understand that we were not going to be consulted about very much on this expedition. Hopefully, if it came to buying this horse, we would be allowed to approve, or disapprove.

Nahim sat like a toad in the sun. "I don't want to see it. Don't know anyone who does." Faces remained very correct, very dead-pan. He paused a moment, and then, as though he were talking about the next rainfall, which everyone knew was not worth talking about (it would arrive according to a schedule varying in the plains, on the sea, and in the mountains), he said, "What kind of horse?"

Attention picked up in the coffee house. "Fine young mare. Spirited. Half thoroughbred."

"Where is she?"

"A few miles from here." Pause. "You can't see her, though."

Confusion again. To us, but not to the players. We were clearly unversed in undirectness. We wanted to say what we wanted. Hadn't Janni, or whoever it was in the corner that seemed to be planted there like a table, hadn't he just said there was a fine horse? Didn't that mean for sale? Nahim responded, on cue, "Who wants to?"

"Just in case someone did," from Kyrios Jorgos. "Wouldn't want to disappoint them."

"Well, shall we go?" Nahim said, turning to us. Go where, we wondered—home, or to see the mare? We said nothing with words but with exchanged looks said, "But we want to see her. We do." We might as well have shouted it.

Nahim led the way out of the café, followed by all of us. Who knew where we were going, what was going to happen? "But Mommy, aren't there any ponies? Are we just going home? We didn't know we were just going to sit around in cafés," from Jeannie. Our collective education in subtlety was just beginning.

"Ssh!" said Nahim Bey. "We get in the car and then see what happens."

"We can ride with you?" asked the Muktar of Nahim, but it was more of a statement than a question.

"One," Frank said. Three wanted to go, and we didn't even know where we were going.

"Two, said Nahim, immovably, as Janni squeezed in the back with me and Yashar and Kyrios Jorgos as well, past the large figure of Nahim and the Mukhtar squeezed in beside Nahim in the front. Their respective sizes were not as big as their *vlachas* seemed to indicate.

"Where?" and once more Frank was headed somewhere with no real indication of where it might be.

"Now left here, now right." Soon we had left the village of Karakoumi and were in the middle of a field, no road at all, driving on the baked ground of September, ground without rainfall since March, or maybe February, baking under the everyday sun. Up to a ledge of rock, potentially damaging to the car to drive over, loaded as it was.

"We walk from here." And Kyrios Largos, the middleman, disappeared over a hill. Then we saw the speck of him motioning for us to come. On the top was a shepherd with his large flock of sheep, one of the largest we had seen so far in Cyprus.

Nahim Bey explained the rapid conversation. The shepherd is the farmer who owns the horse. Says he can't show the horse because he can't get anyone to watch his sheep and the horse is not here.

"Where is the horse?" we asked together.

"Staked in a field not far from here."

"What if we watch the sheep?" Frank asked.

"No," the farmer-shepherd said. "You don't know how." We turn to go.

"Yes," he said. We watch the sheep. They are not like sheep we have known, with docked tails. Their tails are a kind of sack. A camel's hump equivalent, for storage of fat and water in desert climate. Skinny sheep with flat high legs and drooping ears. They look like goats. We studied them. Robin tried to pat one but it ran away, looking at her. Then the distant sound of hoof beats on a hard ground, and a galloping horse rode in, charging in front of our eyes, and the farmer-shepherd drew up this mare on her hind legs for a finishing flourish. Obviously, he thought, if we were Americans we would want a Wild West entrance, wouldn't we? We were startled, but we looked with admiration at a beautiful small horse. About fourteen and one-half hands, burnished mahogany with liquid, amber-colored eyes, full black mane and tail. Perfect! But was she gentle?

"Of course she is gentle," Nahim insisted, not to be argued with. "Now you let me do the talking," he continued, shutting us from saying words we hadn't said. Frank and I looked at each other in amazement. Had we said anything all all? Were we going to be allowed to speak, to express our opinions about a wild horse for our small daughters? We laughed together at the absurdity.

"Twenty-five pounds!" pronounced the owner, through the middleman.

"That is ridiculous," Nahim shouts. "You can't sell this pony anyway because she eats too much. Doesn't work. Can't pull a plow, carry burdens, can't eat donkey food."

"Who cares? She is beautiful." Spoken by a man of means, obviously, who with so many sheep could afford to have a thing of beauty, requiring grain and precious grass.

"But she isn't gentle," Nahim continued. "Look at these little girls. Do you think they can handle a crazy horse?"

There. He had said it. He knew she wasn't gentle. He knew. So what was he doing? Couldn't he just say it, and let us walk away?

"Gentle as a baby, as a lamb," said the farmer-shepherd and reached for Kristin to put her on the pony, but Frank grabbed for her. The pony shied.

"Nahim Bey," Frank protested. "We haven't seen many ponies today. Maybe we should wait."

"Now you let me do the talking. If you want this pony we have to finish the deal today. Now! You don't understand how we do business in Cyprus."

"But Nahim," Frank insisted, "the pony is too wild for..." Nahim proceeded, mindless of us.

Back and forth. Back and forth, with the middleman, Nahim the Mukhtar, saying nothing, Yashar rubbing his hands, Janni watching the sheep. Who was on whose side, we all wondered, knowing our fate by now.

Nahim: "Fifteen pounds." And the owner walked away,

back to his sheep, still holding on to the burnished pony wearing a donkey saddle made of slabs of wood.

"Twenty," he said, turning back, "with the saddle."

"They don't want a saddle like that. How do you think they could ride with a saddle like that? That's a chair." It was two pieces of crossed curved sticks, some boards across them, and a sheepskin on top.

"Eighteen, without." The middleman pronounced this, watched the owner hesitate, and Nahim saw his thrust.

"With delivery!" They all paused for thought. Jorgos looked at the shepherd-farmer, they all looked at the Mukhtar, the three of them in consultation with eyes only. Then their lids closed ever so slightly and their chins thrust slightly forwards as they approached Nahim to shake hands. You would have thought we weren't even there, we who must have bought a pony. Only after they had shaken hands every possible way, the Mukhtar with the owner, with Nahim, and around the group, probably following strict protocol, did Nahim turn to shake hands with us. We extended our hands (protocol or not) to the others, now insecure owners of a pony. Nahim was radiant, probably because he had just concluded a deal with someone else's money. The contract was duly recorded in Jorgos' head, witnessed by all, and binding. Back to the coffee shop for payment.

The café was the court house, the recording office of deeds, the town meeting. Yashar and the cousin were left to watch the sheep. This time Jeannie, Robin and Kristin had coca cola. Why worry about their teeth and what kind of dentistry we would find on Cyprus when we might have to worry more about orthopedists?

Over coffee Frank counted out eighteen pounds sterling. How much, we wondered, did Nahim get, and Jorgos? How much was left for the farmer-shepherd owner? And then, out of what remained, he would have to pay someone to ride the pony to Kyrenia, twenty miles.

By the time we reached the sea house that afternoon, each of us had ridden the pony to the ends of the earth, won races, and counted dreams. And bestowed the name, *Karakoumi*, the name of the village, upon a pony none of us had ridden.

While Frank was learning the problems and the players in the Cyprus game, I was free to explore possible houses for rent, to explore Kyrenia and the countryside around it. I was free to learn about the long and memorable history of Cyprus, to discover that, in antiquity, it was known as the Green Island. The forests were thick with trees, and Cyprus exported wood, becoming an important center for shipbuilding. Alexander the Great kept part of his fleet in Cyprus. The Apostle Paul, when he first came to preach the Gospel in 45 AD, noted the thick forests he had to make his way through.

The great forest succumbed over the many years of changing rulers, becoming treeless plains. The Mesaoria Plain, a blanket of wheat in the springtime, had been a great forest. Peasants cut down their trees rather than pay tax, extracting the trees' riches, pitch, and even firewood. Farmers with grievances against their neighbors could burn down trees to obtain more land for farming, or to curtail a neighbor's grazing. Enter the goat, who will eat anything, though perhaps not tin cans. The goat eats the early spring shoots of anything, pulling up roots and eating those. The goat is responsible for many deserts—it can survive where no other animal can. The goat has caused deserts in the Middle East. The poorer a farmer or nomadic tribe, the more the goat is needed, and the more he is needed, the less there is for him to eat. Hence the Cyprus which I had first observed from the airplane had seemed a barren rock.

Much of Cyprus has now been reforested, and orange groves proliferate. Olive groves as well, with their silvery leaves twisting in the slightest breeze—dark and light, dark and light.

# TOMBS

Robin has found a limestone leg...of a dog? a horse? a donkey? a lamb? a lion? We do not know. We do not know if it is ancient, nor even where *ancient* begins. We are not up to the dates of 7,000 years back. Whether or not the leg is ancient, it is primitive. It has no toes. Or hooves. It is just a leg. Or maybe is part of a tree. Or is something simple of a child's making. Why do my children think that children didn't mold clay and mud, or chisel soft stone...make things that long ago?

"Mother, it is a dog. I know it is a dog." Robin is studying animals in Animal Science.

"Mother, I think it is a giraffe. It is a child's version of a giraffe." Jeannie was teasing?

"Mommy, you know what I think?" Kristin said. "I think it's the middle part of a snake."

"Which part?" I asked.

"The part before it gets to be the smallest."

"You mean," I said, "the part either after the head, or before the tail?"

"Yup."

"Kristin, that's stupid. Too easy. Anything could be that. I say it is a dog's leg." Robin would stick with her theory.

"Listen, Robin," said Jeannie, who was to get a dog for her birthday in January, "it isn't a dog's leg, because it would have a curve, just there," and she pointed to the middle of the perfectly straight piece of limestone, or was it molded clay?

Our eyes are adjusting to the sun's initial blind dazzle and are seeing colors; our ears are listening now, hearing the lamb's bleat echo down from the mountains, the indignant donkey's bray; they are hearing names, words and names swallowed by the sea centuries ago, washed up on other shores, then carried back here again—the very names of streets we read and hear, lilting and meaningful: a parade of conquering and ruling kings, Evagoras I and II, descended from Teucer, House of Troy, who delivered the descendents of Aphrodite from the yoke of Persia.

Names of flowers: *triantafyllides,* which means thirty petals—a name and a rose, curling in perfect graduated convolutions of color in a tissue so delicate one would not believe it could survive the touch of the Cyprus Sun. But the rose grows in profusion. And the Western Christmas flower, poinsettia, is the burning bush everywhere, and well it burns. It is called "the tongue of the mother-in-law." Geraniums stand like miniature trees, rosy blurs of orange in a circle of furry green.

Every rock we once thought so dead now burns with hidden life, from mountains to the smallest stone, which could always be the missing shard, but missing from what?

Pentedactylos, a bigger stone, a mountain horizon, Homerically named, of five fingers standing unsheathed against the sky—the hand of God, of Zeus, of Prometheus throwing mountains as though they were pebbles, to form a land, a sea. A sea called *Thalassi,* meaning blue, the sea caressing the rock from which Aphrodite sprang, even though the sea around that rock is foaming with black sands. And Azul: a blue painted by Georghiu, who lives in Famagusta and gave each daughter a copy of his painting of a blue, kerchief-bound village maiden painted against a white sky which makes the Sun seem cool and the blueness bluer.

The blue, the sea, the stones, the sky...the sun shining and shining, perpetrator of life, witness to history documented by every stone carved in the likeness of gods, of goddesses, of kings, of men, or shaped from the earth itself. Clay, forming ribs, heads, limbs, made by hands 5,000 and more years ago: red-glazed clay, white, painted geometric shapes. The golden artifacts of kings and queens: snakes climbing arms, bulls' heads curving around an arm to face each other, yet forever held apart by the once-whiteness of an arm that is now a withered bone; golden breastplates, pectorals, hugging breasts and pelvises of dust. Red earth, golden earth, white pearly marble of the earth—goddesses of earth. Red Goddess of the slab plaque—square-headed, pinhole-eared flat top: eyes, mouth, hands are only punched holes in the flatness, her jewelry traced upon her neck in geometrics, with a stick.

"But that's a doll, Mommy," Kristin says.

Was it a doll? Or did she become...the Aphrodite of Soli, with pure white marble flesh? A woman, a virgin (was she?) who breathed and smiled down upon men, who made beautiful women rage with jealousy and ugly women bleed with anguish? Was there a Pygmalion, King of Citium, now called Larnaca? Did he father Paphos by caressing an ivory goddess of his own creation?

"What we have seen!" the stones of Cyprus say: this tiny kingdom given to Cleopatra by Anthony, though she never once came to see it, her gift of Cyprus.

"Mom, how can you give a whole country away?" Robin wants to know.

Jeannie is indignant because Cleopatra never came to Cyprus, never knew what the gift was. Unappreciative and rude, Jeannie says. The girls find the buried bits of pots, and they think that underneath the curve of a handle from an amphora, a simple jug, the entire piece will be found. They think they will find Pygmalion's Ivory Goddess, and that if they find a lion's toenail, one claw, they will find the foot, the leg, the head, the body. And that if they wish enough, all their treasures—toes, antlers, acanthus leaves, ram's heads, will come to life! They know that there are more things under this soil than earth. They know from the museum filled with figures: griffons, sphinxes, antlered jugs, animals domestic, wild, mythic, and the bull: the bull, who seems to smell or eat a lotus flower forever. So many animals. And villages of clay—votive figures giving birth, making bread, grinding wheat, squeezing olives, laying their decorated dead in tombs.

They have found tombs below Nahim Bey's house, our sea house, cut into the limestone cliffs, straight back into the chalky stone, about a yard square and two yards deep.

"What do you suppose these cut-caves were, Mother?" Jeannie asks.

"Tombs. But probably found long ago, and robbed. They were not very hidden. Yet who knows how much the sea may have worn away? Maybe some yards of earth, opening and emptying the tombs," I answer, feeling *my* way in the dark.

"Mother," Robin worries, "will we need...our things... when we die?"

Jeannie says, "I wonder if *our* things, which household things of *ours* would...last. I wonder which would be stolen." She is not asking a question; she is wondering.

But Kristin goes much further, not certain *where* she is going: "Mommy, what do we need?" She is all ready to pack a bag and go somewhere. She doesn't know what Robin is saying.

After seeing the empty tombs by the sea, we saw the recently discovered royal tombs of an unknown king. Evidence was there that horses hitched to the king's chariot were sacrificed and buried outside the door to the tomb. The girls were visibly upset.

"I don't believe it, Mother," Jeannie said with pure hope that it didn't happen, and that if it did, the deed could be erased, or not believed. But if it did happen, the girls knew they would have to believe it. That that's what believing was, knowing a thing to be true, whether you liked it or not.

Robin put her hand in front of her mouth, as though she could protect herself from the knowledge. Kristin looked at me as though she were going to be scolded by Miss Clark for missing a sum.

About the horses, how could they avoid knowing? Why should they, or why should Frank and I let them know? It happened: the horses were harnessed together, and to their chariot, and buried in front of their king's tomb when the king was killed. The gouging of earth by the tomb indicated a struggle and death by asphyxiation.

"But why?" Robin's voice was an anguished cry. Was she thinking of Karakoumi, buried deliberately by us under tons of that earth she'd found her "dog's leg" in?

"Mother," Jeannie said in a low voice, trying to be calm. "How do they know that is true? How can they be sure?"

"Jeannie, they couldn't very easily hitch a pair of dead horses to a chariot, could they?" Frank liked to give it straight. "The space around the horses indicates struggle. It is easy for archaeologists to tell...And this tomb shows, in the photos here, how this poor donkey escaped from his harness, but couldn't get out of the tomb."

"Frank!"—I pinched his hand and whispered—"Stop it. You'll have me in tears too. It seems so cruel."

"It was probably considered an honor," Frank said to the girls, still shrinking in their vivid contemplation of the act.

"Daddy, a horse can't know that," Jeannie said.

"But maybe the people didn't know the horse couldn't know that," I said. I had to say something. "Maybe no one else was allowed to drive, or ride the horse, but the king."

"I don't see what difference that makes," Jeannie said.

Actually, I didn't either.

"It's just that it was believed that the king needed his horses, where he was going...and all the other things in the tombs...You know—the pots and jewelry, vases and jugs," I said.

"Jeannie, do you remember seeing white cows carved on marble, or limestone—I don't know what kind of stone—

with flowers around their necks, being led in pairs? You see them quite often in mosaics, sometimes on painted vases. Their horns were painted gold, and they were paraded through the streets, to be sacrificed to Aphrodite. They didn't consider it cruel," Frank continued. He was going to carry on.

Clearly our moods had been changed by the knowledge of the horses. The girls didn't want to hear any more. We all looked across a horizon of broken stones, pavements that were once floors of palaces, squares, Roman columns, and looked down into excavations in Salamis, seeing Assyrians, Egyptians, Persians, King Evagoras and Alexander the Great, all, swooping up from the sea in bronze chariots, the horses in gilded harnesses, tasseled and proud. And every one we saw, paired or single, was galloping, galloping on, unaware of his destination.

# BEFORE THE RAINS BEGIN

"But Mother! Nahim Bey promised, this weekend. He promised."

It had been three weeks since we bought and paid for a pony. And she hadn't yet appeared. Why? Nahim Bey was impossible to reach. Yashar always shook his head and said, "It's coming. But the man, he has much work to do."

"What man?" I asked.

"The man who mends roofs."

"Is he supposed to ride the pony here?"

"Yes, but now is his busy time."

"Why now?" I asked.

"Before the rains start."

"But the rains don't start for a long time. Until December, anyway. Isn't that right?"

"Oh yes. That's right." Yashar didn't seem to understand.

"Then why can't he deliver the pony now? I want that pony this weekend."

Yashar shrugged his shoulders. I was beginning to shrug mine, looking at the small amount of brush he had cleared around the sea house. Cleared for Nahim Bey, really. At our expense. I couldn't see that Yashar had done anything during the twelve hours of labor on his lined school-paper bill.

"It depends," Yashar said. Yashar was beginning to irritate me. He could see that.

"Madam, Mustapha only has one donkey," he said, as though that might be an explanation."

"But what does having one donkey and rains and roofs have to do with delivering our pony here?" Yashar seemed to talk nonsense. At least, to me.

"Because only one donkey carries the clay. It's very

heavy." As though I understood.

"Yashar, I don't understand what you are talking about. Mustapha is fixing roofs before the rains come. He is carrying clay on a donkey. This is early October and the rains may not come until January. Now where is our pony?"

"Madam, the clay...it goes on top the roof. It's very heavy. It takes a long time to carry it, from where it comes from, to the houses. Every year, Mustapha does it...our roof needs it too." At least Nahim Bey's. He gesticulated in the direction of the roof.

I would have him out this time. "Yashar, show me. I want to see what you are talking about."

Nimbly, he produced a homemade ladder, crudely made and not very sturdy. But the roof wasn't very high. He placed it in the courtyard against the wall of the main room area, and climbed up, motioning me to follow.

"Now you come, Madam. You see."

I climbed up. On top of the flat roof was nothing but what looked like small hard lumps of gray earth. Clay, I guess it was. Yashar was pointing to several places where the brush showed through, brush which was laid on top of woven bamboo.

"You see?" he said.

"See what?" I asked.

"See the brushwood?" He said, as though it was the most obvious thing in the world for me to understand how to build roofs on farmhouses in Cyprus. "When the rains come, there will be a hole there. The rain will come in the house, by pails."

I was angry. Yashar was our caretaker. He was supposed to look after things like this. Why wasn't he doing it?

I told him my thoughts. "You haven't asked me to do it," he said.

"Well, do it!" I said. "Before the rains come!"

"That is what Mustapha does. And he only has one donkey." He smiled, as though I must have understood all along.

"Tell him this," I said sternly. "Tell him to *bring the clay on his donkey and to lead the horse.*"

Yashar shook his head. "Oh no. He can't do that."

"Why not?" I snapped.

"*Because he wants to ride the horse.* He is looking forward to it. He only gets to ride donkeys."

I gave up. I couldn't telephone Mustapha because there were no telephones. Not even one, I thought, in Kasaphani. Even Nahim Bey didn't have a phone in Nicosia. We would just have to wait. Wait for clay, wait for the brambles to be cut, wait for the pony.

"Find a saddle, then, while you're waiting," Frank said.

I went to ask Fikri, a large, jovial Turk who was one of the Embassy drivers, all of whom doubled as bartenders and waiters at the many diplomatic functions. Although Turkish, Fikri addressed me, and probably all non-Turkish women, with the Greek *Kyria*—as did the Greek drivers—or *Madam*.

"Ask at the race track, Kyria. Ask Yashar." But the race track had only worn-out racing saddles, flat and small as a pancake. And Yashar, I continued to learn, could not find anything, even tools to cut the brambles which had grown up around our house by the sea. Yes, he found a saddle, a donkey saddle, designed to carry stacks of hay, sticks, or the pails of gray clay he had just told me were necessary each autumn for the roof.

Sabri! Why had I not thought of him? I did not know Sabri, but if Durrell was true to his written word, why then, Sabri was my man. He lived in the harbor of Kyrenia where he owned and operated a milk bar. A milk bar in a land of wines which were named Othello, Arsinoe, Aphrodite, Cleopatra. But Sabri was Turkish, hence Moslem, and alcohol was against his faith. I telephoned him.

"Sabri, my name is Arlene Jones. I live in..."

"In Nahim Bey's house," he finished my sentence. "And

you have just bought a pony. You want a saddle, right?" I was stunned.

"But, but how do you know? We haven't met...I was just coming to Kyrenia to speak with you."

"Ah, Madam," he continued, "we know many things in Cyprus. Word travels. It is a small country. But as for the saddle, a bridle, too, perhaps?"

"Why yes, of course."

"A pony about fourteen hands, maybe?"

Sabri was probably born in Kasaphani, I thought. We probably bought that pony from his cousin, his brother! "Yes, about fourteen hands." And I wanted to ask him what color it was, but I didn't. "I will come to Kyrenia this afternoon," I told him. "I will come to the Milk Bar."

I was beginning to be quite happy with my no-house arrangement. I was free to explore, buy ponies and saddles in between car pools and dreaming. I nosed the car towards the Kyrenia mountain range where every turn, every coffee house, even the donkeys were becoming familiar to my eyes. Nosed the car downwards from the crest to Kyrenia, then right for a mile to our sea house, just to check on the pony's stable, to see if it would be ready. The telephone rang as I fumbled with the padlock, but it waited for me.

"Arlene, Frank here," as though he needed to tell me. "Before you reach Sabri, if you haven't already, an embassy driver has found a saddle and a bridle. I think they are fine; I've seen them."

"Oh dear, I told Sabri..."

"Well, I'm sure he'll understand. Don't worry about it. When are you coming home?

A needless question. Frank knew how I loved it by the sea, and that my school car pool was at 4:00 pm. Had I ever *not* been on time that he could remember?

I drove back to Kyrenia down to the harbor, found the Milk Bar and entered, asking for Sabri. Need I have asked?

There was a heavy-set man, black hair, thick black mustache, black eyes, quick smile. He wasn't fat, just a solid presence. He was "there."

"Madam Jones?" We both laughed because our eyes said hello to each other without words. But would he really be Durrell's Sabri? His clothes were Western. I wished that he wore vlachas.

"You have a saddle." Just like that.

"And a bridle?" I asked.

"Certainly."

"Where did you find it?" I thought he had another. Maybe I would have to buy two.

"I didn't."

"Then how, I mean, who did? Where are they?"

"An embassy driver found one for you through a retired English Major. It is in Nicosia."

"But, but, how did you know?" I was astounded.

"Madam, would you like a milkshake, a coffee? You are my guest. I am pleased to meet you." And Sabri bowed ever so slightly, extended his hand, his courtesies. I hoped that some-day I could ask him about Durrell, talk about him. I wondered if Sabri ever read books, if he had ever read Durrell's books. I knew that I liked him immediately, rogue that Durrell said he was. Or maybe it was that Durrell was told he was.

"I hope I didn't cause you any inconvenience," I said, truly concerned and truly perplexed about this grapevine.

"It is a pleasure," Sabri, inscrutable, replied.

"And now, I wish to tell you something else, Madam. Something which will please you, your little girls, very much." He smiled. His eyes were the color of walnuts.

"But what?" I was beginning to feel his magic.

Sabri made a suggestion of a bow, and said, "Your little horse will arrive on Saturday!"

So he was magic. Whose arm did he twist, Mustafa's, or the former owner of the horse? the Muktar? The list was infinite.

"Whoopteedo! Whee! Wowie, Mommy, is Karakoumi really coming tomorrow? Really truly, cross-your-heart?" Robin and Kristin said, nearly together.

How could we be certain of anything? But I said, "Sabri promised. A *Sabri* promise, I am sure, is a real one!"

"A promise is a promise, Mommy," said Robin. "Lippee," she always said, mimicking her earlier years when she transposed her y's and l's. "Lippee, I yuv it!"

The stable room was ready, grain bought, straw bought—not for bedding, but for food, which was worse than the worst of what I would call chaff—the chopped-up husks of wheat without the stalks. Yashar was primed to buy the green *trafili* daily in the Kyrenia market, so essential to the diet of a pony, because there was no grazing and no good hay. Cyprus was a parched island much of the year. Only sheep and goats grazed, and they could eat thistles, thorns, anything which grew, and what grew in summer were things which could survive the burning sun without rain. Bedding was sawdust, and I was charmed to know that right under Frank's and my bedroom, we would be able to hear the domestic and soothing sounds of Karakoumi.

Jeannie had carried jodhpurs with her from Poland. All summer in her hot-weather-wardrobe she often wore a pair of jodhpurs. Out they came and were put on. Robin and Kristin found too-small long pants. Last year's. This weekend, in addition to Kyrenia and the sea, there would be the monumental event: a pony's arrival.

"After lunch," Nahim Bey said. Lunch was early, had to be, so that the pony would arrive early. But early lunch only made the wait longer. Running back and forth to the beginning of the road to the sea house, each daughter, taking turns. "I don't see anything. They're not coming."

Three o'clock, and we heard no clatter of hoofbeats, but a tired donkey-walk. A tired pony, a sweaty pony, head down, nothing like the fiery mare we first saw, galloping in where we were watching sheep, rearing on her hind legs. Maybe she would be manageable after all.

"Oh, let us feed her!"

"Let her sleep!"

"Let us wash her!"

"Let her drink!"

Jeannie was the boss, the oldest. "Mother, Karakoumi has to rest. She is tired. We will feed her." And before the rider had discharged himself of a pony delivery, little hands were around her, touching, reaching, hoping. A halter, Jeannie leading. The access to the pony's stable was not so easy: down a short but steep hill with narrow footage, a narrow threshold to the room under the master bedroom, the only light from the open door and what little filtered through from the cracks in the bedroom floor above. The pony entered her room, and we all followed, put the chain across the door. "We'll feed her later." Jeannie hushed us out. "She must rest," she said.

That night the comfort of the Joneses was that of tired travelers given succor on a stormy night. The so-long homeless had found home together, had found pleasure, peace. An animal was sheltered for the first time in its life and it was the munching of grain by a pony whose presence made the world seem suddenly so safe, so good, so rich, so secure. Thunder might roll, and armies might march tomorrow, but nothing would take from any one of us the happiness of that night.

Until our noses began working in the morning. The sweet scent of horse, the sense of movement, was replaced by stable odors which strangely had not occurred to any of us. One night was all it took to alter the garage for the pony's use. But none of us, even Frank, would have traded that one night... we had had our star in the sky—not too far from Bethlehem— and the peace of it.

# THE THIRD HOUSE

"Arlene, what do you mean, the Cypriot army? There is no so-called Cypriot army. There is no Cypriot, for that matter. There are only Greek Cypriots, or Turkish Cypriots, period."

"But Frank, doesn't the country have any military?"

"This little island is an arsenal, Arlene. But all those persons acquiring weapons and ammunitions are private."

"But I don't understand that. If this is a country—well, any country, unfortunately, seems to have to have an army. And so...

"Yes, you are right in that. But these are peculiar circumstances."

"Well, go on."

"Why, Makarios himself, Archbishop and President, has his own arsenal. The presidential palace is a munitions dump, as are several monasteries."

"What is going to happen, Frank?"

"Probably just what you think will happen."

"You mean that someday, maybe even when we are here, that..."

"That this island will be bloody? Yes, I do. It will happen sometime. It is just a question of when."

"Frank, I don't know why I ever asked you."

"Yes, you do. Because you want to know. Because you have to know. You wouldn't want it otherwise."

"Frank, did you know this before we came?"

"Why do you think I wanted to come?"

"Damn it, Frank, don't you think I have a right to know in advance? Don't you think I have a right to be asked if I want to expose our children to civil war, to have our lives disrupted in the way they could be? For myself I would feel as you do. But it's not fair—you get all the action, the *in* stuff. I get car

pools and dinner parties to give and, I suppose, when I get that
far, the men have their port and cigars and women have coffee
upstairs in the boudoir and talk about maids. Shit."

"Arlene, don't use that word; it could get to be a habit.
What would the children think?"

"Well, *Merde*, then."

"Arlene, what if you hadn't come? What would I do?"
Frank was half-smiling in a way I knew. But here I was, we
were, sitting in a dump of a house, a bachelor's house, while I
had been looking and looking at dozens of houses. None was
right. Frank read my mind: "Speaking of houses..."

"Yes, I know. What am I doing about it, right?" I was
dragging my feet as I always did in a new post. I didn't want to
admit that we had really moved, that I had to get on with it.

"Well, I guess when you go to the Embassy to learn
more about the intrigue in this place, I go to learn more about
paint and plumbing and drink my twenty cups of Turkish coffee a day, finding out. Frank, if I see one more turquoise wall
and one more place where a bathroom is *going to be*..."

"Bye, Arlene." We smiled at each other, but I had swimming eyes in spite of my resolution. Damn.

I looked at four houses that morning, each with the
standard enormous entrance hall which took up a third of the
house. Chances are that it would have a marble floor. Chances
are that the portico, an extension of the house, really, but open
except for the roof, would be painted in three different colors. Even the entrance hall might be in three or four colors:
mauves, turquoises, hot pinks, apricots. Miniscule kitchens
and bedrooms. Metal gratings in front of downstairs windows
with painted half moons and balls. Looking out the window
would be like looking at Christmas decorations from some

small town's chamber of commerce. Discouragement each time. I was getting closer and closer to leasing the house which the Archbishop was building for his niece as her dowry house. It was a house with balconies under scalloped concrete canopies, but the Kyrenia range of mountains was visible from one side of it, and the Troodos range from the other. Compared to the other houses I had seen, it was a palace. But it wouldn't be finished until December!

"Well, of course you could choose colors, but I guarantee that you will be very happy with the colors selected. The Archbishop's niece wants to choose the colors for the walls. We (the royal we?) do not have the taste found in other houses. I assure you that..."

What could I do? Show it to the girls again just to stall, to pass the time, to help me decide. Maybe someone else would see something great I hadn't seen. Or something really bad. I could see if they approved of my waiting so long for a house.

The floors were not yet finished, nor all of the walls built. But the lay of the house was clear enough: enormous entrance hall, which took the heart of the house on two levels. Marble steps, wrought iron staircase, balcony upstairs in the center of the house with wide marble floors from which bedrooms exited. Three bedrooms only, but large. Two second-floor terraces. One bathroom upstairs. But I was certain that I saw the outline of another downstairs, at least a powder room. I seemed to be more interested in the bathrooms than in the living rooms (probably just what the architect would expect from Americans). But it *was* spacious. Two living rooms, one with a fireplace—wonderful!—and a dining room and study downstairs. A large kitchen.

"Mommy, this is wonderful. Can I have this room?"

"Well, two of you will have to share. But you always have, haven't you?

Who would be alone this time? It was always considered a privilege. "What color do you want your walls, Kristin?"

"Blue, Mommy."

But I knew that...

"Good Morning, Mr. Aristos. I am pleased to see the house coming along so nicely. May I have a tour?"

"But of course, that is why you are here, no?"

I headed straightway for the skeletal powder room. It was taking shape, as a cloak closet only. Rods for coats, that was all.

"Mr. Aristos, I thought that here," as I gestured helplessly, "there would be a powder room, water closet, toilet... But am I wrong?"

"But you have *everything* upstairs. Everything. Why do you need additional facilities here?"

"Why, for guests!" I was imagining life without a downstairs *facility*—children's things, my things all over the bathroom where the one toilet of the house was. Imagine important Cypriot guests using a bathroom with children's things all over. The Mickey Mouse toothbrush with green goo all over it. Girls' dirty panties strewn. A box of tampax lying forgotten on the floor. It would be quite impossible.

"Mr. Aristos, I am certain that you may find it, well, extraordinarily fussy, you might say. But you have probably heard about the number of bathrooms which Americans have in their houses. Well, it is true. It is, of course, an extravagance, it is luxury, but I fear that I must insist upon it. It is not too late, surely, to divide the closet and add a...a *facility*?" It was as though "bathroom" was a dirty word.

"Well, I certainly must ask my client." *Client* was pronounced in a threatening way, such as, "How dare you insult the President, the Archbishop, His Beatitude?"

"The house is lovely," I said, fearful of what other sur-

prises I might have. We entered the living room with the fireplace, where a workman was cutting blue formica on a saw-
horse table. "What a lovely color blue," I lied. "Where is that
going to go?" I feared the worst, assuming the kitchen, but the
kitchen was a long ways away.

"On the chimney, covered with this scalloped edge
of wood, and the bookshelves—you may use them for knick-
knacks, of course—will be covered with it. Very nice, very elegant, don't you think?"

Formica it seemed, had probably only just been brought
to Cyprus, worth its weight in gold, better than brick, marble,
tile, or just plain wood. What I was learning about my future
house was that expensive meant good, new meant better, supe-
rior was expensive *and* new. Now for colors.

"Mr. Aristos, please, could you now show me the colors. You know I am a very subdued person, and I like subdued
colors." I could lie, but I was becoming subdued, I think.

"Kyria, you may not like the sound of these colors, but I
assure you, this house is not like other houses built here."

As though colors had sounds and could speak. I was
beginning to be afraid that they would speak to me very loudly, deafeningly...

"This house is, well, different. After all, how could you
believe that a house built by His Beatitude would not be beautiful? You will be thrilled with the colors which have been
chosen. Chosen with painstaking care."

"Yes," I said. "Of course...May I ask...who...who will
choose them?"

"Kyria, you have little faith. This is, perhaps your first
time away from America, your first time...in Cyprus? Have you
been to..." but he did not finish. The distinguished architect
was not enchanted with the way things were going with his
tenant-to-be. "You will see," he continued, "that this will be
the finest house you have ever lived in...and the finest house in

Cyprus."

Different anyway. I thought. What a monster it is, architecturally speaking. A Marble Oasis. The shape of the house with its scalloped canopies of concrete on both first and second floors could have been designed for a gas station. Wouldn't the distinguished architect be distressed to read my mind? At least I had progressed to the stage of being addressed in Greek: *Kyria*.

Perhaps we had made a mistake in agreeing to lease this super house before it was finished. But maybe they needed a client in order to finish it. The contract was signed and sealed. We were supposed to move in the first of December. Did that mean one December? Or the first week? Or the first half? Did I care? I had no possessions to worry about, no place to put things which were still in storage in a local warehouse. I couldn't even remember what they were, which meant that they were all unimportant after all. But the girls were waiting for their books and toys, their remembrances of a favorite trip, a favorite shell from a beach, the charm bracelets with a charm from every place they had been. There were many. Too many.

"Kyria. I do not have the samples here. As a matter of fact, they have not been chosen yet. But they will be, by the owner of the house. Wouldn't you want to choose the colors of your own house, your new house?"

"Not if I were going to lease it. It is customary in our country to allow the lessees to choose colors, especially if the property has not already been decorated."

"We have quite different customs here," Mr. Aristos said, rather severely. I was treading on thin ground. I wondered if it would be any different if Frank were speaking. It was not a woman's world. So much for that. I demurred, hoping, but without confidence. If I got a toilet out of it, I would have made great progress. But it was not going to be a great day, I thought.

Two weeks later the painting was finished. Tangerine living room to go with the blue formica chimney. Bedrooms hot pink, mauve, robin's egg blue. Halls and dining room dark green, second living room...on and on. Mr. Aristos was very proud of the chosen colors. I was desperate. When a country was so full of natural beauty, exquisite artifacts, folk art, even, in colors tawny and golden and muted, why...? Here I was, in a tiny country about to explode, quarreling about colors in a house.

"Mr. Aristos, I must confess that your colors are like the sunset, like the dawns. Beautiful. But I have a terrible problem. You see, I travel around the world, live in various countries, have basic furniture. I cannot afford to re-upholster it, change colors in paintings, reframe them, even, so I am doomed to live with white walls, like a monk, like a nun, doomed to be color-less," envying the Archbishop his purple cloaks, I thought.

I was beginning to soften Mr. Aristos, who, I thought, pitied me. So I continued, "It is most unfortunate, you see, for me not to be able to enjoy your excellent, but for me, some-what extravagant taste. Extravagant only because, you see, it would cost me so much."

"Madam," he changed his address to me—it was more formal to call me *Madam*—"you have no sense of taste whatso-ever. You are plain and old-fashioned, lacking in a...a zest." He was holding his hand up, fingers pinched together, extended and turning clockwise, a familiar Greek gesture for pizzazz or the Greek equivalent.

"We cannot help what we are, can we?" I thrust home my point.

"But you will have to pay for the work, the paint." I expected that, and decided to forget the bedrooms. Let the raucous colors awaken us in the mornings so we wouldn't tarry in bed.

"Well, just the downstairs—halls, living rooms, dining

room, off-white. Will that be all right? Then we can enjoy the colors of the bedrooms..." At least Kristin would be happy. I was later told by a Greek Cypriot friend, "Well, you know that the Archbishop was born a peasant. When one of them builds a house, he includes a bathroom, about which he says, 'We hope we will never have to use it,' because it would be reserved for times of illness or death."

The move came in mid-December—an event which had never happened to us, moving into an absolutely new house which no one had ever occupied before, no corners filled with a left-over memory of a former inhabitant. No children's lost toys, no sounds, no Mustapha even, who had gone to live with his former master's friend, Dick Welch. We would have to fill the house with our presence, make it hear us, listen to our breathings at night, our breakfast words coming to us, make it wait for the children to come home from school, make it lonely with our absences.

Now I work at it alone—moving in, after the movers have been there and unpacked crates and boxes. I think the clutter will never find a place.

It does: remembered paintings find their proper space upon the walls, the silver wedding tray makes its way into the dining room, known bedspreads identify whose bedroom it is. Sue waits for Jeannie on her bed, Baby Bunting on Robin's. Raspberry Black waits for Kristin. All their once so-loved possessions will be in place after school today.

"Mommy, I didn't think we'd brought Baby Bunting. Anyway, I'm too big for her... But Skunky is here, and Tigger, and Lion." And on and on, all their toys, remembrances, out of storage, at home in a new house. Away into the closets went Kristin's pink summer dress, Jeannie's *dirndl,* the dress with blue velvet trim which Robin loved. "Mommy, maybe we'll never wear these again," Robin said with as much anguish as anticipation. The gray school uniforms took care of that.

Finally we ate accustomed food on remembered plates. Home again!

The cold we hadn't counted on. "But Kyria," I could hear the insistent voice of Mr. Aristos state, "it is never cold in Cyprus. No one has heated houses."

The cold came under the doors in rivulets of rain, wind-driven. The marble floors were icy. One electric heater in the one bathroom filled with little girls trying to dress for school, Frank trying to shower and shave, and I, waiting until they were finished, dreading to step out of the warm bed into a frigid bedroom.

One morning Kristin looked unusually fat. "Kristin, what do you have on? What are you wearing?" I went to feel her clothes. She was layered with pullovers and two cardigans under her gray regulation blazer.

"But Mommy, we have to take off one layer at school, and if I take off my blazer I am freezing. Robin's knees were as blue as Jeannie's nose when they came home from school.

We sniffed the kerosene fumes of the small space heaters, in the kitchen and the dining room, when we were eating. Except for the fireplace, there was no built-in heat. To stop the rain from flowing under doors, I had to make small sand bags the length of doors (everybody uses them but nobody sells them). The marble floors were continuous from the interior to the canopied verandahs, and did not have thresholds.

By now I was well-versed in grain for ponies and where to find it; the contents of Pourgouris Grocer, which were unlimited; pots and pans and all necessary kitchen items in Cyprus, different from any other country I'd lived in; the measures of weight and lengths—an *oke* was about two and one quarter pounds. And I was acquainted with what to wear in cold houses and what kinds of menus were suitable for Greek Cypriot guests. That was easy: get a cook.

Savvas was his name. He was small and quick, with distinguished graying hair, a neat moustache, and he was an excellent chef, butler, firebuilder, gardener. Savvas could do everything. He could cook anything, read recipes in English as well as Greek, and prepare the food of any nation: stuffed squab, suckling pig, soufflés, roasted whole lambs, pastas, English roast beef, Yorkshire pudding, plum puddings, and *sheftalia*. The last was a Greek dish of ground lamb mixed with aromatic spices, formed in sausage-shapes and wrapped with a part of the lamb I later learned was the *mesentery,* which, on the lamb-sausages, provided both shape, containment, and fat, to keep the contents juicy. Savvas could make everything, and what he hadn't made was a challenge to him to try. He served with elegance, and a little disdain, sometimes, for those who did not pass his scrutiny—those guests who did not adequately appreciate his offerings. And he loved children. He loved Kristin, the smallest, especially. *Kristina Mou*, he called her: Kristina Mine. But it didn't sound the same in English.

Christmas was nearly here. "Mommy, I think our Christmas presents are Karakoumi. And to be in a house. With all our things," Jeannie said.

"And Savvas," added Kristin.

Kristin came home from school the next day, the last school day before Christmas vacation, heaving unstoppable dry sobs. She was clutching her still-wrapped and apparently not-given Christmas gift for her teacher.

"Jeannie, what happened?" Instinctively, I asked the oldest sister.

"Mother, Kristin is a cry baby." Jeannie's embarrassment spoke. She didn't know why Kristin was crying. Robin didn't either.

It was the not-given gift that seemed to tell the story: Kristin was clutching it fiercely. "Mom...Mommy...she...she she said...sh-she said she...was glad-d-d she wasn't t-t-teaching u-us anymore. She she didn't l-l-like fir-fir-first grade."

Kristin's hands were locked on the prettily wrapped package. She had made cut-outs of colored paper to decorate it, cut-outs she had learned from that art so well advanced in Poland. The gift was frozen inseparably to her hand.

Savvas bundled Kristin in his arms to help him make tea. "But you are going to help me cut out cookies this afternoon. You have to decorate them," he laughed.

After her cambric tea, served by Savvas in a manner usually reserved for guests, and served in the living room where he built a fire, Kristin's hand thawed, and she held out the present to me. "Here, Mommy. You can have it. You are better than Miss Clark anyway."

Jeannie decorated the pungent pine tree we had for Christmas, Kristin and Robin helped with the turkey, and I learned a new recipe from Savvas via Kristin: "Mommy, Savvas washed the turkey and said he was bathing the baby. And then he let me help stuff it and said we were feeding the baby. And then Robin oiled it and Savvas said that is what you do to babies, and, and then, he put a carrot under its back and said it was a pillow, and then he put it in the oven for a nap...Mommy, did you oil us like that?"

Jeannie was more interested in getting the Archbishop's signature on Christmas Day, when he always visited the orphanage a few yards on our/his house's right. It was not so much his signature that the girls wanted as it was to know if he really signed in red ink. And did he carry his own red pen? What name did he sign? His given name, his President's name, his Church's name?

"Mommy, tell us again about Barnabas," they all asked, which, of course, would lead to the red pen.

"Barnabas, you know," I began, "was born in Cyprus, and was stoned to death near where he grew up, for preaching the gospel of Christianity."

"They killed him in his own town, Mother?" Jeannie always asked that question.

"Yes, in his own town. Where he grew up."

"Did they hate him?" she continued.

"Jeannie, anyone who preached a different religion, different from what the town, or country believed in, was not very well treated," Frank added.

"Even today," I said. I paused, and thought deeply about where we were, and what was inevitably going to happen, because of religion.

"Then he, the Apostle Barnabas, revealed in a vision to Anthemios, a Greek Cypriot, the place where his bones were buried. Barnabas' own bones."

"But, Mommy, who was Anthemios? I don't remember."

"He was the Archbishop of Cyprus. "

"When?"

"Well, a long time ago. "

"How long, Mommy?"

"More than 1500 years ago, Robin."

"How long ago is that?" Robin said.

"You can count, can't you?" I asked.

"Not that far."

"Oh, everybody can. But Kristin," Jeannie added.

"That' s silly," Kristin said, "to have so many years you can't count 'em."

"Just you can't count them, stupid."

"When she's your age, she will, Jeannie. Don't be mean," Frank said. Anyway, this is Christmas Day. What were you saying anyway, Arlene?"

"About the vision, Mommy."

"Oh yes, Barnabas came in a vision to the Archbishop and told him where he, or what was left of him, was buried."

"Where who was buried?" Kristin asked.

"Barnabas, Kristin. Aren't you listening?"

"Mommy, how could Barnabas tell someone where he was buried when he was dead?" Robin wanted to know.

"Because he was a saint, and saints are supposed to know everything."

"Robin, shut up. It's some kind of magic, it's a vision, sort of a dream. Now let Mom go on," Jeannie reprimanded.

"So, to get to the end of it," I continued, "Anthemios, the Archbishop, remember, went to look where the dead Barnabas, now Saint Barnabas, told him to look. Remember, it was a vision, or a dream. And Anthemios found Barnabas' bones under this carob tree, and with it, I mean them, he found a chest which had in it the Gospel of Saint Barnabas, written in Barnabas' handwriting."

"How did they know it was his? If he'd been dead for 1500 years?" Robin always challenged.

"I don't know, Robin. Somebody said so, I guess. Anyway, did I say when Barnabas died?" I was beginning to wonder why I was telling this, this miracle. I was only trying to tell about the red ink which, they hoped, they were going to experience today in the Archbishop's pen. Even though I'd told the story many times, there were always the same questions.

"You said he'd been dead 1500 years," Robin answered.

"Yes, I did, sometime or other. It is true: he has been dead around 1500 years. But anyway, later, Barnabas' bones and the copy of the Gospel were given to Emperor Zeno, carried to Constantinople by Anthemios...And because Zeno was so pleased to have these, these things..."

"But who would want old bones, Mother?" Robin always asked, not understanding religious relics. Could I explain?

"And then what happened, Mommy?" Kristin never quite understood.

I would explain again. "The Emperor liked the bones

and the gospel, and because he did, liked them, I mean, he let the Cyprus church be separate from all the other Christian churches, under his rule, that is..I was floundering. I never could explain religious visions—and he gave the title of Archbishop of Cyprus to the head of the Cypriot church, *and* let the Archbishop wear purple robes, *and* carry a scepter with a golden head, instead of a staff like Mehmet's, *and* (this was what they were waiting for) "sign his name with imperial red ink." So this is why the present Archbishop, who just happens to be President of Cyprus as well, will sign his name in red!"

"But why?" Kristin always asked.

"Because all those things, the purple robes and the fancy staff, were what emperors had. That was Zeno's way of thanking Cyprus for the bones and the gospel. And by the way, he also gave lots of money to build a church on the spot where the bones were found."

I was exhausted.

"Did they have to dig up the carob tree?" Kristin asked.

"I'm sure they did. But there are more, were more carob trees."

"Daddy, where is Cons...coos-tople? Is that a bygone place too?" Robin asked.

"Constantinople, Robin. No, it isn't a bygone place. It is now in Turkey. It's called Istanbul," Frank explained.

"But why?"

"But why what?"

"But why isn't it still Cons...Cons...stant...ople."

"Because it is Turkish, and it's name is changed."

"But why would it change?" Robin insisted.

"Robin, things change all the time. Even names of countries change. Sometimes," Frank added.

"Will ours?" she asked.

"Never, Robin. Never." Frank was emphatic, at least to

his children. Looking at the endless history of the Middle East and the brevity of ours, I wasn't sure.

It rained on Christmas Day, just a little. The sun kept trying to come out, as three little girls kept going outside, standing under the canopy of concrete, waiting for the known black Cadillac with the give-away initials on the front license plate: AK. For Archipiskopos Kypros, Archbishop of Cyprus.

"What are you going to have him write on? I asked. Kristin had a fat notebook.

"What should I have?" Jeannie asked, but she had plans already. Her school notebook, so that she could show her classmates. Robin couldn't make up her mind. She sensed that she was dealing with history, and she wanted whatever she had for him to sign on to be worthy of the occasion. She chose a not-often-used diary with a leather cover.

"He's here, he's here, he's here!" Kristin cried and jumped up and down. The girls gathered themselves together, trying to compose the manner in which they should approach him. Each stood up straight, and they kept down the level of their excited words, waiting for the right moment to approach.

"Daddy, Daddy, should we go now, or after he comes out?"

"I think I'd wait until he comes out, and then he will be facing you. He will see you leave this, his house," Frank advised.

More waiting, each child standing still and very straight. Then, the moment. Without looking back at Frank or me, Jeannie lead the descent from our stairs, then Robin, then Kristin. Age had rank. Very solemn, very deliberate, they walked slowly to the orphanage. The Archbishop and President of Cyprus did see them. He smiled. He waited. They stopped in front of him. Jeannie spoke the lines she had rehearsed:

"Your Beatitude, could we have your autograph, sir?"

He smiled. He touched their golden heads. He reached for his own pen inside his purple robes, an aide holding his golden scepter. He signed three times. By Jeannie's pleasure, I knew the signature was red.

Did I ever doubt it?

I saw Kristin say something, but I couldn't hear her. Jeannie looked annoyed, but tried not to show it. They walked slowly home, in procession. The Archbishop watched them for a moment, and nodded.

"Mother, do you know what Kristin said, stupid girl? She said "Mr. Beet-a-tub, we like your house.""

"Mommy, I just thought...he'd like to know. I'm sorry," and her lip quivered.

I hugged her to me. "Kristin, I know he was delighted to hear it, from you." I was secretly laughing, thinking about the second bathroom episode, and wondered if Frank had caught it.

"But let us see the signatures," Frank asked, as eager as I was. "Kristin, you show us first."

She opened her book to the right page, and there, in red ink, was *To Kypros Makarios*. Makarios of Cyprus.

# SPRING

It was spring of 1963. Cyprus was everything we had hoped it would be, that is, for me and the girls. Frank's world was different. He was pleased for the joy that we had in the sea, the sun, Nature's beauty of a kind we had never experienced before, being New Englanders, Mid-Westerners, Northern Europeans. The landscape, which I had initially seen as so barren, so bereft of anything green, had been a mirage. Life, past and present, teemed out from under every clod of earth. Traditions of centuries, customs, habits appeared in the superstitions gained by my children from Savvas and Irini, an illiterate and ignorant, good-natured woman who muttered to herself continually. Both loved the girls and had an easy relationship with them, as opposed to the more formal one which Frank and I had. We were "I Kyria" and "O Kyrios." Kristin to Savvas was Kristina-Mou. We had lucked out, as many said, to get the best chef on the Island.

I lived two lives. The most important one was in Kyrenia where I went at least once a week in the daytime, to ride the pony through the countryside, to sit on the terrace and listen to the waves pounding, an endless song that had been rushing and receding on this very shore for centuries. It had been heard on Lionheart's ship in 1191 and on the ships bringing the crusaders as they built their castles, Hilarion, Kantara and Buffavento on the highest mountains overlooking this Northern coast of Cyprus. Of them, only piles of stones remain.

Was it here the Turks invaded in 1570, only one of many dramatic changes to this small island's history? Assyrian king Sargon II had ruled in 700 BC, then Egyptians and Persians, and Cypriot kings helped Alexander defeat the Persians. In 294 B.C. Cyprus became an Egyptian province, then Roman. The Pax Romana meant years of peace and in 313 A.D. Christianity became the religion of the Roman Empire, and of Cyprus.

In 45 A.D. Apostles Paul and Barnabas arrived, the first Christian missionaries ever. Many centuries of rule by the Byzantine Empire followed a century of Venetian rule. And then, in 1570, the Ottoman Turks. It all makes me dizzy, when we Americans think about our short history, our country inhabited by Indian tribes, but not for centuries B.C. What accounts for the vast difference—that we were practically cave dwellers when other civilizations were making articles of impeccable craftsmanship: sculpture, jewelry, ships, armor?

The most important part of my life in Cyprus was meant to be in the inland capitol, Nicosia, which had an octagonal fortification surrounding the city, built by the Venetians. There, I was a diplomatic hostess, although all Embassy officers and their wives knew I was CIA hostess. In addition to entertaining, I drove car pools to the English School, taught American History to American students there, freezing in the unheated school building after two hours. I understood why Kristin put on layers of clothes, since pupils had to take off one, the grey blazer.

Nicosia also meant that the Country Team Wives' Meetings were to be attended by wives of the heads of all sections in the American Embassy: USA AID, Military Attachés, Public Affairs, Political Section, Economic Section, Consular Services. The endless missions attached to the US Embassy. At one such meeting, the Ambassador's wife, who took her duties very seriously, exploded, out of her frustration at not knowing what to do: "All of you women must understand that you are here to *work work work* and nothing more. That is your mission here."

I made the mistake, I know, of feeling sorry for her. We had ridden together in her embassy car, and I rode back with her, trying to comfort her. I knew she was serious about her position. She simply didn't know what to do.

That afternoon I went to Kyrenia. I rode Karakoumi by the sea. All traces of civilizations disappeared from me, and I was alone in the world, on a horse, by the sea. I was totally cleansed.

For the first time in its long history, Cyprus gained independence in 1960 and the Cypriots, the Greek Cypriots, are trying to destroy it. What do they want, I ask myself. I ask Frank. He says, "We want (and who are we to intervene in such a long history?) to uphold NATO! And Cyprus is a thorn in the armor of NATO, because it involves Greece, Turkey, and Great Britain, powerful members of NATO. And President Makarios, also Archbishop of an autocephalous church, is dancing on the world's stage, intoxicated by power."

And so that is what Frank is trying to deal with. Our Ambassador is called Mr. Three Button because his blazer is always buttoned up. His desk is clean. No clutter there, nothing like the clutter that is Cyprus. He has no idea. Only the CIA knows what is going on: I believe that because Frank's staff is tops: two fluent Greek speakers, one who also speaks Turkish, the other a Harvard classics scholar, informed, intelligent, and funny. Humor is essential in Cyprus. Especially at this time, in the spring of 1963.

Spring was coming. Signs were everywhere: the Mesaoria Plain was becoming ever so faintly green. It was a large canvas of a single color, and yet, looking closely, there were subtle shades of variance. Buds were enlarging on the acacia whose leaves in their downward thrust seemed to be perpetually weeping (there were three large acacia outside the sea house); the rains were diminishing; and, although the wind could still be cold, the sun was warmer. In Nicosia I could open the doors to the verandah and feel the sun. Leaves were pushing out of the dry stems of what I thought were dead rose bushes, planted by Savvas in January.

April saw the canvas turn pale green swept with yellow. Wind waved the changing wheat stems, shifting colors to gold, as wind in the sea stirred the blue into white, white into blue. Pink cyclamen peeked out from between their mottled greens of leaves all around our sea house, and primroses burst out of soil long dampened by the winter and spring rains. The acacia tree turned into a cloud of brilliant yellow—stalwart clusters thrust upright, away from the earthward directed leaves, but on close examination were thousands of tiny yellow pollen clusters, miniature pom-pom chrysanthemums. Spring was artichokes sprung out of stone—all around the sea house they had grown, bushy plants three feet tall, full of artichokes with their spiky needles on the fruit. Spring saw the Century Cactus with an asparagus-like center grow twenty feet tall before it opened into blossoms. We were promised blossoms from its thickened hide pointing its needles at us and making us walk in a wide arc around it. The bougainvillea, a dry stick planted by Savvas in January, turned into the Beanstalk planted by Jack.

Mehmet was now in the vicinity of his home because his flock had lambs. As spring advanced, he would retreat higher into the mountains and, as summer came, yet higher in his constant struggle to find grazing. Karakoumi was shedding: great patches of felt-like fur curried out of her. The Junior School was going to change from gray flannel skirts and long pants into gingham dresses for girls and gray flannel shorts for boys on the first of April, rain or not, as regular as my grandfather shifting into winter and summer underwear on Thanksgiving and Easter. But the sea was colder than ever, cooling as it did from October until possibly April. Local inhabitants didn't think it warm enough to bathe in (they didn't swim) until August, and then it was too cool for them in September.

Kyrenia was again the lollipop at the end of the week,

even though really warm weather was still far away. The girls spent hours with Mehmet, the Turkish shepherd, embracing lambs, talking with him, sitting on a sun-warmed stone with Mehmet, his crooked shepherd's staff, and his dog.

"Mommy!" they came screaming with excitement one day. "Mehmet says that there are vipers now, in spring—says to be careful," and Kristin held up a glass jar containing a small black snake.

"Where did you get that, Jeannie?" Frank, speaking to his eldest.

"Mehmet killed it, outside of the Ledbetters' house. Johnny somehow knew what it was and ran for Mehmet."

"Is it really a viper?"

"Mehmet says it is, and I'll bet he knows. He said they come out in spring and like to go into damp places, dark places. Like under sinks, he said."

"Let me have it, let me have it. Johnny wants it back," said Kristin, reaching for the jar in Frank's hand.

"That little bit of a snake is *the viper*?" Frank remarked, incredulously.

"It is a baby one, I think," Jeannie answered. "But it's real all right. I mean it's poisonous. Wow, right there in that jar is a poisonous snake." Robin didn't want to touch even the jar. I didn't either, somehow.

Karakoumi was left for me to ride. As Frank and I had thought, she was really too much horse for little girls. She was not gentle, not easy to manage. But they did ride her after I had tired her, though rarely away from the area in front of the house.

"Arlene, I think we ought to get rid of that pony. What is the point?"

I had my points. I explored the seaside, the small villages in the area. I rode her often in moonlight down by the sea. I was alone in a world of silver shadows, my own and the head and flashing legs of Karakoumi, reflected back by the moon's gold on the sea, past the white-washed lone cottages and tiny villages brilliant in moonlight, and as still as an empty world. No one was by the sea at night but me. Even worn paths shone silvery clear, occasionally spotted in darkness by the great hands of leaves that were the fig tree's, and silver-striped when a post or smaller tree interrupted the steadiness of the moon. On these silvery paths near whitewashed villages, I would pass the tiny chapels that I knew, left alone on hills even the villagers had forgotten, along with whoever had built them. But I later learned that it was bad luck to speak of a chapel so abandoned, or the relatives who had fashioned it out of grief. Should someone say, "It was built by Kyrios Efthyvoulou, for his dead child..." another would answer, "No, it was built by Papas Charalambous, for meditation."

But they would allow me to pass, unmolested by tangles of brambles—I didn't know what they were—almost with arms around the tiny crumbling walls, protecting them from invasion by intruders.

In the day, evening or midday, I meet friendly, warm and generous villagers. They invite me in. *Kopiaste*, they say, which I know means, "Sit down with us and share." They ask if I have sons. I say daughters, and they bless me and wish me a son.

"Frank, we will keep her," I said, keeping my thoughts. "The girls have to feed her and ride her, with me. She is, after all, a member of the family now."

Coming back alone from a ride one day, I was drawing water at the faucet in the courtyard. Someone was waiting for me—a brown and white carriage-type dog, who asked me for a drink. "Well, Charlie Boy," I said, as he wagged his tail, "do you want some water, then?"

He was healthy-looking, trim, with an intelligent face and, though homeless, still friendly to the world. The villagers fed healthy dogs, but when the strays were old, or mangy, they went quickly downhill, kicked around and stoned as they were. The countryside was full of homeless dogs. Few females were spayed, and no one put homeless, unwanted puppies to sleep. In summer dogs could eat lizards, hedgehogs even, although I have never seen a hedgehog.

I went inside for some of Pippa's dog food. Pippa was Jeannie's beloved poodle, who seemed stubborn and unteachable. Charlie Boy waited, looking at me, wagging his tail. I rubbed his ears, proceeded to caress his head. Silky, male, young. I secretly wished we didn't have Jeannie's poodle. It was a bull-headed dog. I didn't think he would ever be *someone.*

Charlie Boy stayed on. He seemed to be at home, even when the girls came back from their rambles with Pippa.

Robin saw him first and ran to him, before I could say stop. But Charlie greeted her and licked her hand. Robin thrust arms around his neck and Charlie smiled at me, over her shoulder. Her dog, she thinks, feeling left out because of Pippa. Pippa ignores him. I give Pippa credit for knowing superiority according to Pippa. Charlie ignores Pippa. Charlie is kind, and knows he is a guest.

He spent the night in the girls' room, as though he'd always been there. And the next morning he made another wish come true—he found a hedgehog. He was probably used to eating them, but this time anyway, he carried it gently in his mouth and brought it inside when we were having breakfast. He placed it carefully at Robin's feet. "Daddy! What is it?" Robin didn't take kindly to unknown creatures.

But Jeannie ran to it, saying, "Why, that is a Mrs.Tiggy-winkle! That is a hedgehog. Lippee! Alex told me about them, said they were all over Cyprus. I didn't believe her anymore because I never saw one.

"She said you could pick them up, they won't hurt you,

and their prickers are not at all like a porcupine."

Jeannie was right. Though clearly prickery, the hedgehog was gentle, its prickers no worse than a three-day beard. She looked at us hopefully, thinking we would spare her, protect her from Charlie. But why were we saying *she*? Because all hedgehogs were Mrs. Tiggywinkles? The hedgehog walked around on top of the table where Jeannie placed her, and then she announced, "Now you keep Charlie inside, and I'll go find a place to put her," and into the brambles went Mrs. Tiggywinkle. Charlie didn't try to find her.

Then the weekend ended, Robin's dreaded moment to leave Charlie Boy. "Robin, he will come next weekend, I'm sure," Frank said, as Robin clung to Charlie, crying.

"But why can't he come home with us? Why can't he be *my* dog?"

"What makes you think he wants to? What makes you think he'd like Nicosia, compared to here? I don't," Frank said. It was true, none of us did.

The next weekend in Kyrenia, we drove across the Mesaoria Plain at dusk. The fields were glowing in a butter-soft light. Rising towards the pass, the hills were wearing their rich spring garments of green shadows. At the pass we could see Pentedactylos looking like a brown dinosaur, with purple flames rising around his middle, up and up to the rosy ridges of his back. And then Kyrenia—its lights winking away at us, the castle and coastline outlined by a magenta bougainvillea-colored sea, shimmering away in its sunset peace. The winds always died down at night, or so it seemed. Night was too brilliant to keep the sea churned up because night too had to admire the sea, and admire itself.

The girls were anxious to get there before dark, not to look at skies and seas, but to find Mehmet, to feed the pony, and to see if, oh hopefully, Charlie returned. As our car lights now turned down the last road and reflected back against the whitewashed cottage and its spring cloak of yellow acacia, they flashed into a pair of animal eyes, and the white half of a dog. There, in front our house, was Charlie Boy! He had kept his rendezvous!

"Mommy, I wished and wished all week. I wished on my dog's leg, I burned an olive leaf with Savvas, and it jumped, and Savvas said that was good luck, and Ireni gave me a ring of red and blue threads to wear! And found me a pomegranate blossom and I put in under my pillow. Mommy it worked!" Robin was telling us things we didn't know.

Frank and I looked at each other quizzically. We knew that the villagers were filled with superstitions and ancient practices, but didn't know they taught them to our children. We laughed, stuck our thumbs in the air and said, "Here's to continued good luck!"

The girls scurried off, two dogs with them, towards the Turkish farmhouses in the direction of Kyrenia. And returned in a half-hour. No Mehmet. They started off in the other direction, down a little bank, skirted around the brambles. Charlie began sniffing around, barked excitedly. Jeannie jumped back, hearing something, thinking of vipers, but hoping for a hedgehog. Something moving, rustling, struggling, under the brambles. She peered underneath, Robin and Kristin waiting behind, saying, "Don't look, don't look. It's a viper, it's poisonous," as though a viper would thrash around in brambles.

"Vipers slide, sillies," said Jeannie as she raised a bit of the brambles to look underneath.

"It's a lamb! It's one of Mehmet's lambs! Tangled up in the brambles! We've got to save it."

Frank and I went out, and saw that the lamb was wound round and round, in the thorny brambles. The more it struggled, the more firmly was it a prisoner of the thorns. The very thorns that Yashar was supposed to have dispatched last fall. For which we'd paid him.

"Get Johnny," Kristin said, believing that boys were

cleverer than girls, probably because fathers, or men, were supposed to be. Or perhaps because he saw the viper first.

"Get the scissors, Kristin. No, the clippers. What do we have around here, anyway, to cut brambles like that? Do we have pruning shears?" No. We had scissors. Scissors would not cut the brambles.

"Try cutting the wool off."

"The wool is too short. Somebody find Mehmet."

"Daddy, we looked all over. We can't find him."

"Well, do you know where he lives?" They knew.

"Then let's go there."

But he wasn't there. His wife didn't speak English.

"But Daddy, she must wonder what is going on. Maybe she'll find Mehmet and say we came."

Frank and I were not at all certain about what to do, except wait until morning, by which time the lamb might be dead.

Kristin began to cry: "We can't leave him there like that. We've got to save him!" A lamb was a lamb, wasn't it? Even a dirty old sheep would make them feel the same. But a lamb! And why hadn't Mehmet missed it?

The girls went to bed wailing, and the next morning, Mehmet was there nearly at sunrise. He got out his shepherd's knife—he must have encountered situations like this hundreds of time—and went to work. Within minutes the nearly dead lamb was freed. He carried it off in his arms, followed by three little blonde girls who wanted to feed it, hold it, nurse it back to health. But Mehmet only said, "I lose several every year, somehow. This year I've been lucky. First one, so far."

"Mommy, he doesn't even care."

"He is a shepherd, and one lamb is not the world to him," Frank said. "But twenty lambs are."

"But that's one in twenty, Daddy. And then there could be one more, and one more...And then?"

That afternoon the girls came back from Mehmet's,

skipping and smiling. The lamb would live—the mother took it back, which they don't always do, and now it would live.

"Mommy, why wouldn't the mother take it back?" Kristin asked, puzzled.

"But it did," Jeannie answered.

"But maybe she wouldn't have," Mehmet said.

"Why?"

"Because, maybe, the lamb had somebody else's smell. But I don't know, really. Sometimes the mothers won't take them right after they are born, especially one of triplets," I said.

"But why?" Robin asked.

"A ewe has only two teats," I said. "Maybe that's why."

"Then why would there *be* triplets, if the mother can't feed them. That's not fair," Jeannie reasoned.

Kristin looked at me with startled eyes and her mouth open in disbelief.

"Is it really true?" asked Robin, not believing that any mother would abandon her child.

"It is true, Robin," Frank said. He was ever the realist.

# EASTER MONDAY

I knew about Easter and the Greeks' stringent fasting because of my wanderings on Karakoumi, around the countryside, down to the sea, back through villages and houses, where, with the warming of the weather, families were eating outside. They would gesture that I come to join them, calling *Kopiaste*. I would dismount, and sit at their tables, eating what they offered—raw artichokes, boiled potatoes, olives, bread and wine. Nothing at all which came from an animal. Normally their diets were heavy with cheese, yoghurt and meat, almost entirely lamb—from the lamb, they ate everything but the trachea and bones. Karakoumi would stand passively and wait while we ate and drank dark red wine. We spoke with our hands, and the Greek which I knew, that which I had absorbed and that which I'd studied with a classics professor. However, *katharevousa*, which I had learned—the language of the newspapers—was no help here in the villages and countryside. I had studied it and hadn't even known. When I found out, it was with amusement and some embarrassment.

"*Kali Spera,*" I said to Richard Welch at a cocktail party, daring to try out my newly acquired Greek language, feeling sufficiently confident to venture a word to the Embassy's Harvard classics scholar who had lived for years in Greece.

*Kali Spera, Kyria. Pos iste?*

*Poli Kala, efharisto.* Past the preliminaries, I launched into my last lesson, about bread. It didn't have much to do with the cocktail party, or my life in Cyprus, but Bread was my most recent lesson. I could even spell it, but then realized that I couldn't at all—I was seeing it in English transliterated letters: *Psoumi.*

Dick's face turned slightly to one side so that he could hear me better beyond the din of cocktail voices. "Say, who is your teacher, anyway?"

"What do you mean by *anyway?* I said, thinking how lucky we five women were to have as our teacher a retired professor of classics.

"Well, what I mean is that...that you are learning *Katharevousa*."

*Katharevousa* was neo-classical Greek, not spoken Greek. It was the language of the newspapers, of every school child's grammar book, of every published paper. We might as well have been speaking Chinese in the villages. We were not learning vernacular, and we didn't even know it! Dick howled with laughter. Finally, after I was over the shock of six weeks wasted, I laughed too, remembering how carefully we had insisted on learning to speak Greek in vernacular, how we wanted to converse in shops and villages.

"Well, Arlene, if your teacher is a retired classics professor, he wouldn't condescend to teach the language of the villages, and he knew you wouldn't know the difference."

Suddenly my nice old retired professor with the expressive talking hands and the mass of white hair on the back of his head had become disreputable. The spots on his one brown suit became clearly visible through the smoke of the cocktail party, and his once-friendly face became genuinely insinuating, conniving. I might have known. Trojan horse and gifts and all that.

So, on my village rides, at country tables, we spoke largely with our eyes. I must have been a curiosity: blonde woman, astride a pony with an English saddle, a pony which didn't *work*. They all had donkeys which they rode, often with a load so huge that one could hardly see the donkey that seemed a veritable haystack with legs. When such a load was required, the driver had to walk. Donkeys went to market and carried the goods; they were constantly in motion. Riding on a donkey was not a pleasure, but a necessity. For me to be riding for pleasure must have been, for them, anathema. I wondered if the English women who had lived here for years, before what the English so matter-of-factly called "the troubled times," sat down to their peasant tables to drink with them.

The wine was heavy and dark, the home-cured olives small and green and excellent. The raw artichokes were bitter to me. As for the fava beans, the women laughed about my eating them and indicated that I might not feed them to my son. They didn't know I had no son, only daughters. Fava beans, they believed, threatened the potency and the fertility of males, but the women could eat them. And old men.

They would sing for me, Greek songs that I didn't know: mournful songs, and then very lively songs. And I would sing for them, songs I thought they would like, even though they wouldn't understand the words. "Danny Boy," "Auld Lange Syne", "Chattanooga Choo Choo." We exchanged songs, one for one.

After two or three stops and two or three tumblers of wine, I let the pony take me home. If the villagers ate nothing from animals for their nearly fifty days of Lent, nothing which had come from flesh and blood, I could imagine how they feasted on Easter when they broke the fast.

But for now, they were to atone for Christ's blood shed for them. Each year they enacted *Epitaphios,* the funeral and burial of Christ's body on Good Friday night. It was a long procession, in each village, each city, each parish church, as everyone, including spectators, carried brown candles and sang a mournful dirge in a slow-paced, solemn procession. Then they returned to homes where their fires would be out, and could not be lighted until the next day.

Easter was the most important celebration of the year, augmented by the seriousness of the Lenten diet and the somberness of Christ's funeral followed by Saturday's food preparations. On Saturday night, all persons met in their darkened churches just before midnight, bathed, combed, dressed in their best, each one carrying an unlighted white candle. It was like waiting for New Year's Eve when one was a child, when the very atmosphere of one minute was supposed to change forever. And believing in the change so fervently made it happen.

We could watch, we could be there, but we were not of them—we were strangers to their customs. We could not feel as they did, we could not believe as they did, that at midnight, Christ arose, each year. *Christos Anesti* was shouted by all, as Christ himself sent down fire to the priest who seemed to become the flame itself, as he spread his holy flame to the entire congregation. *Alithos Anesti,* He is Risen Indeed! It was like Fourth of July used to be—when fireworks were allowed—combined with New Year's Eve, with one and all participants having firecrackers or horns and drums, pouring out into the streets full of bonfires, and all of them feeling purged and cleansed with light and with the great joy that such newness brought. Redeemed, again!

We Americans felt poor indeed. None of us had ever felt or participated in such profound sorrow and profound joy, all prompted by a festival.

Sunday was the breaking of the fast: eating and dancing and drinking and eating lamb grilled on open fires that had been kept alive all night, after *Christo Anesti* and Christ's fire. It was purely Dionysian. The lambs were slaughtered on the spot, skewered, and placed on a spit, sometimes with eyes still staring. There were *flaouna*, cakes made with cheese and eggs and almonds, sprinkled with sesame seeds, all things they had been denied for so long, making them all the more celebratory. Then games, and cracking red-dyed eggs, end to end. Was it the skill of the holder or the hardness of the shell which made one egg crack and another hold? To the Greek Cypriots, it was merely win or lose. All day, and for several days, the common greeting was *Christos Anesti* instead of the usual *Kali Mera*.

On Monday the celebration continued. These were the most important celebrations of the year for the Greeks, and we could only watch, and wonder at their age-old rituals in which all participated—the elderly down to the babies—all.

Easter Monday was only, to the Americans, a bonus holiday. As was Boxing Day, December 26th. Both holidays were acknowledged by Cyprus, and because there were no official Cypriots or other Embassies to do business with, the American Embassy was forced to recognize both days. What American holiday guaranteed four days in a row? Why, the government would fall apart, commerce would be slowed to zero. No American business would allow that! We were nothing but work work work! As Elizabeth had once said to Foreign Service wives. She knew what she was talking about.

As for Easter Monday, I was looking for something to do with my children, to take part in the celebrations denied to Americans by their own choice and inability to participate. Petey, the wife of the Peace Corps director in Cyprus, knew more about the countryside than I did because the Peace Corps crew worked in villages, with agriculture and crafts. We met often but not too publicly, because her friendship with me contaminated her husband's position as Peace Corps Director. I, too, was contaminated by the CIA, although I didn't know much about its operations in Cyprus

She knew about festivals.

"Arlene, you have to go to a fair being held in Karavas, just a few kilometers beyond Kyrenia. Take the girls and go. It is part of Easter celebration."

"What do you know about it? Have you been to it?"

"Well, no, I haven't. But Easter is a long celebration and in Kyrenia you aren't far from Karavas.

"Petey, can't you come?" No, she couldn't.

"Arlene, I can't go. I have so much to do; it's grand just to have a day when it isn't business as usual and I can catch up.

It was always the same with Petey and I knew I shouldn't ask her. She probably had instruction from her husband not to associate too much with the CIA, to prevent the Peace Corps from being accused of gun-running or intelligence-gathering. Guilt by association.

Did the girls want to go?"

"Yes! Will there be lambs? And shepherds?"

"Most certainly, at least I think. And maybe donkeys."

"Have you ever seen a baby donkey?" I asked, knowing that she hadn't. I had told her about the one I saw in a marketplace in Tunisia, no bigger than a large teddy bear. He was a Steiff toy except that he moved. He had a mat of hair upon his head, like a teddy bear, at least in its coloring. I would love to have bought it for its offered price of fifty cents, but how would it have liked the cold northern climate where we were living at the time?

"What shall we wear?" all three children asked as one.

It was a good question. I was thinking of the Easter dresses I had worn as a child. I always had one, a new one. Now that I thought about it, this was about as pagan as squirting water—both symbolizing a new beginning. I had always gone to church, and to sunrise breakfast in the church basement, had eaten sliced oranges that looked like the orange globe of the sun itself at six o'clock in the morning. And my mother always had an Easter lily growing in a pot, from the florist. But here, in Cyprus, after the rain of winter, long-stemmed, pearly white calla lilies nearly catapulted up from the rock-like earth.

What did my daughters know of Easter? A few native customs in foreign lands. But at least, I thought, I am happy that they don't know American Easters: colored plastic chickens and ducks, and even live ones, sold to parents for adoring children, abandoned in days to die, uncared for. Hordes of multi-colored candy eggs and artificially colored plush stuff made into rows of bunnies with cocked plastic eyes, winking.

Enormous chocolate bunnies in cardboard carrying cases, nesting in green and neon-colored paper grass. Easter bonnets and little girls with white gloves strutting and comparing theirs with other children's Easter Baskets. All my children knew was to color eggs with food dyes. There are only four colors, so they mixed them all, usually ending up with smoke-colored eggs smudged with little fingers. They never asked why they colored eggs. Anyway, I didn't think I could answer something which was really so hugely complicated. The Renaissance of Spring? Dionysian rites? Or just because the Greeks color eggs, only red?

I insisted on one thing: that they should wear dresses, even though they preferred shorts, or pants, something no Cypriot girl child, Greek or Turkish, would wear. They all hated the green-checked dresses, which did make the schoolgirls look a bit like waifs from an orphanage, but uniforms solved the what-shall-we-wear problem, and reminded me that I hadn't answered.

"Dresses."

"Oh Mother, can't we wear pants?"

"All the children there will be dressed up. You know they won' t wear pants."

"But we're American. We're not like them."

"Mother, what do you want us to wear?" Robin asked, impatient with the discussion.

They could never blend into the crowd of Greek Cypriot children with their white-blonde hair and blue eyes. But still, they would not look so strikingly out of place in dresses. "But not dressy dresses," I encouraged. "Come, I'll help you choose."

Robin wore a blue smocked dress, handed down from Jeannie (wasn't everything?); Jeannie, a brown and blue stripe, and Kristin, a pink dress with bands of ribbon across the front, handed down from Robin from Jeannie. Not fancy, just nice little girl dresses.

"But Mom, why can't Daddy come?" Kristin asked. "He never comes anywhere with us."

"He has too much work at the Embassy."

"But it's a holiday! Even Savvas is off, and Ireni."

Today will be quiet at the Embassy and Daddy can catch up. Maybe he'll be home earlier next week, who knows?" I always seemed to be saying that, I thought: "Daddy is working, he can't come."

"Mom, what will we see?" Jeannie asked.

"Well, I think lambs. Do you remember the lambs you once held in the village of the Tatras, in Małe Ciche?" They had patted the early strong spring lambs, and marched with the peasant and village families, carrying pussy willow branches to the new church, its new pine redness alive in the thin Polish Easter sun, the roof sloping steeply to the ground. "I remember. I remember!" Jeannie and Robin said.

"Kristin, do you?"

"Yes, I remember," she said, because she wanted to, but she had been too small to remember.

The drive to the fair was forty minutes, starting from Nicosia instead of the sea house, through the Mesaoria Plain, now thickly green and golden over the ridge of the Kyrenia mountains. The girls pronounced *Pentedactylos* and counted them, the five fingers of the mountain, with their own five. And then the sea, the great blueness coming up to meet us, hovering as we were between ascent and descent.

"Mom, why is the sea called *Thala* sea? What is a "thala"? What kind of sea is a thala sea?" Robin asked.

"It is one word meaning 'sea' but also 'blue,' like the color of the sea."

"No, it isn't one word. You don't understand Greek. We talked to Savvas and he said it was a *thala* sea."

But Savvas had also told them that the about-to-be

roasted turkey was a baby covered with baby oil, a carrot for
a pillow, and that it was about to have a nap in the oven. I did
have to laugh: I couldn't compete with Savvas as an authority on seas, or the efficacy of a burned olive leaf, or anything
else on Cyprus.

Two or three miles beyond Kyrenia, Petey had said,
somewhere in Karavas. Surely there would be people enough
to determine where the fair was?

There were. I parked where cars and the passage of
many feet had turned the earth to powdery dust. We walked
into the pure sunshine to find the baby animals, but saw only
people. Crowds of people in groups, and if there were so
many cars they wouldn't be country people, who only had
donkeys. Village people, city people? We saw crowds of people
in groups, with small charcoal fires in their midst, and smelled
roasting meat. A picnic with a charcoal fire. What could be
more normal? But instead of hot dogs they had kebabs. *Souv-
lakia* the Greeks called them, or simply *souvla*.

We turned towards the games, foot races, jumping over
the fires with no singeing of the *vlachas,* a feat which must be
difficult, considering the amount of fabric in one pair. There
was weight-lifting of a heavy stone, the *docimi*—the winner
would keep the title until next near. What I really wanted to
see was the men's dancing, which required controlled hesitation, delicate movements of the entire body, endurance. The
body was as paint—the shadow and light—to the canvas of the
painter. They would dance all night, so there would be time to
see some of it.

But my children were impatient. Where were the
lambs? They wanted to know. Kristin spotted them, Kristin
with the sharp eyes who always saw everything first: the fox in
the far field, the nest in the tree, the fish in the brook, speckled
as the sand, the shard buried in the earth. "There they are!" and
there, indeed, were several young lambs with their shepherd

bearing his shepherd's staff. Not baby lambs, but lambs. White and wooly with drooping ears and sweet, sad faces. Kristin ran to them and caressed a lamb as the shepherd smiled. And soon Robin and Jeannie were offered a lamb to fondle.

"Do you suppose one of them is the one we saved?" Robin asked.

"Probably not, if you don't see Mehmet. But maybe."

The sun was hot now, and the shepherd in his vlachas and cape and the lambs in their woolly coats were more insulated from it than the bare arms of the girls, who had shed their sweaters. They retreated for sodas, coca colas, as omnipresent as Turkish coffee, and found them under the nearby carob tree in its thick shade, sold by a boy. We were comfortable under the carob tree, and close to the shepherd and his lambs. We would see more of the games after we cooled off.

And then, caught with a mouthful of cake, four pairs of frozen blue eyes were fixed on the events in front of us. A knife emerged from the folds of a pair of vlachas, and with no visible motion at all, a lamb fell to the ground, blood gushing from its throat. Jeannie's lamb.

Four open mouths gaped in mid-air as that lamb was inflated by the shepherd's blowing into a deft cut in a hind leg, and as quickly hung from the tree we were under. In an eternity, which was seconds to the shepherd, the woolly coat lay beside the steaming entrails on the blood-soaked earth, the lamb Jeannie had just caressed.

Instinct took the girls and me as one body to the safety of the car, unconscious of getting there, wordless, unanimously and instinctively fearful. I should have known. How naïve could I have been! Eating lamb meant killing lambs!

I found myself with a dimly perceived knowledge that blood had everything to do with life and that here, death held no fear and no mystery. Unwittingly I had led my children to witness a slaughter that I would never be able to explain. We were strangers in a strange land: it was I and my children who were the island, afloat in an unfamiliar sea.

# WEDDING IN KASAPHANI

We were living in the Old Testament. We had experienced the sacrifice of the lamb. Now we were going to see the wedding of Solomon's Bride. All the experienced Greek hands, like Dick Welch, said that one of the musts on Cyprus was to see a village wedding, and all the Greek hands were extraordinarily enthusiastic about life in the Greek-speaking world, with emphasis upon village customs. The *hands* were more or less fluent in spoken Greek, could read *Katharevousa* as well, could dance the Greek dances, and could eat grilled sheep's testicles—in a dish called *Kourkoritsa,* consisting of the entrails of the sheep: lungs, liver, heart, kidneys, testicles, all skewered and wrapped with the cleaned small intestines and then grilled. The intestines kept these normally dry-when-cooked innards from drying too much, and they actually become crispy in the manner of fried onion rings.

The hands could also eat *Beccafico,* pickled migrant warblers. The tiny birds, primarily blackcap warblers, are caught by their adhering to bird lime placed on tree branches. The idea of eating warblers, in itself, offended one's love of birds, of the warblers' celebrated singing abilities. But what also offended, once the singing miracles were reduced to edibles, was the fact that, other than being plucked, they were not *dressed*. They were pickled and eaten whole. With interiors and heads, Songs and all. Whether you were lucky or not, sooner or later, in a village coffee house or restaurant, there, in a large jar, something your eyes couldn't avoid if you were alert would be *Beccafico,* dozens of them. This would be the moment your stomach feared. And then, as honored guest, you would be presented a Beccafico, the delicacy, the highest offering. Refusal would not be taken lightly by the host. It could not happen.

But of all of the events to experience in Cyprus, a village wedding combined most of the customs of the villagers, customs engrained for centuries. So when Yashar told us of a village wedding in Kasaphani, just a few kilometers from our sea house on the road winding through silvery olive graves towards Bellapais, it was too close to miss.

"Frank, this one we can't miss. It is so close. It is Yashar's village. People have driven miles to go to village weddings, and this one...well, we even know some of the villagers." It would be a Greek wedding, although the village had a large number of Turks. Yashar was one.

"Let's tell Dick and the Kelleys." And I mentioned a number of the Greek hands.

"I've been to one. No, two in Cyprus, but uncountable numbers in Greece," Dick said.

"But wouldn't you like to go again?"

"No thanks. But you should go."

"Dick, are you sure that we will be welcome? I mean, isn't it presumptuous of us—wouldn't we be butting in, crashing the party?"

"Everybody is welcome at a village wedding. If a busload of tourists arrived, they would be welcome. The bride and groom would be honored, will be honored."

"Why?"

"Well, in the village itself, everyone, I repeat, *everyone* is not only welcome, but expected. It is a village responsibility."

"Turks too, at a Greek wedding? Or Greeks at a Turkish wedding?

"If they are villagers, yes."

"What time does it start?"

Dick was waiting to see my reaction, looking at me with his good eye and his teasing. "It depends...how much time have you got? All week?"

"What time did you go when you went to a village

wedding?"

"Too early."

"But what time was it? And remember, I have three little girls going along. And Frank, of course."

"Well, Patty went, and my three children."

"Did they enjoy it?"

"Why don't you ask them?" Dick was teasing me.

"Look Dick, everyone says a village wedding is an absolute must. But you won't tell me anything about it. Not even when to go."

"It is true that everything is an event and something is happening all the time, but it all takes time. Let's say that the actual church wedding is approximately noon. But you have to get there before, or you'll miss half of it."

"Which half?"

"The preparation half," Dick replied.

"What is the other half, then?"

"You'll see. But you said that Frank is going?"

"Why shouldn't he?"

"Well, he mentioned something about a brief meeting on Sunday." Dick was looking at me sideways again. Checking out my reaction.

"Well, he told me that he *wasn't* having a meeting with you, that he was going to a village wedding." I was going to have the last say.

He smiled his Mona Lisa man's smile and said, "Have a good time. You will."

At the wedding, I learned what Dick meant. Preparations for the wedding taking place today had begun long before. Had begun at the bargaining table of the parents of the bride and groom, when the bride's parents determine if they can pay the price asked by the groom's parents, and if she can provide a house for them to live in. If she doesn't have a house already, her parents must build one before the wedding takes place. I thought of Savvas saving all his money to build his daughter a house so she would not be dowryless. Then furniture is decided upon by the parents. A big engagement party follows, the priest blessing exchanged rings. Some time later, the wedding.

The wedding begins a week before the designated Sunday. Always Sunday. Begins with women gathering at the bride's house, baking cakes, preparing for the long weekend of eating. Saturday night the villagers gather to *spread the mattress*: the priest blesses the many washed strands of wool brought by the married village women, who dance with it. No virgins take part in the preparing of the mattress. The wool is stretched to the length of the mattress, then moved in four directions, to form the sign of the cross. Songs are sung, sad folk songs. Men dance their light and shadow—hesitation and leaps. Aromatic pine and cedar needles are placed on top of the wool, and then the women sew the mattress together: the strands of wool are fixed firmly in place, and a covering is sewed upon it. The completed mattress remains in the center of the room, and gifts of linen are laid upon it by villagers.

We arrived in Kasaphani at 10:30 A.M. The streets of the village were nearly empty, but we followed the thin, squeaky violin sounds to the house they came from. Around it some of the village children were playing, and they hurried to us to invite us into the house of the bride, her dowry house. Paths were opened to us, and we were escorted inside—I, with my female children, to the room where the bride was with the village women; Frank to a separate room where the men were, and the groom. Three musicians sat in a corner of the room: two violinists, and one who played a large mandolin-type instrument, a *laouto*, very ancient, very homemade. There was the mattress, covered with various linens. Bed linens, lace-trimmed—Cyprus is famous for lace-making. Table cloths lay there too, I thought. Everything on the mattress was linen, not cotton. It all lay as linen does, weighted down with itself.

"Mother," Kristin whispered, "why do they have a mattress in the middle of the room with no furniture?"

"I don't know," I said, but I had an idea, which Kristin didn't. I was thinking of my conversation with Dick: evasive.

The women in the room smiled at us, patted the heads of the girls, and pointed to the mattress, with broad smiles. I think I got the idea. I couldn't see Frank from where we were. The attention was on the bride, who was seated in the middle of the women's room near a pan of water on a stool and a tray laden with a bridal dress. With hand towels, white linen ones. women were taking turns washing the bride, over and over, mostly her face and arms.

Women after women came, and went through the same ceremony: washing the bride's arms and face, and drying them. The same thing, over and over. More guests came, and added linens to the mattress.

"Mother, what are they doing?" Robin whispered. She needn't have whispered, because I doubt much English was spoken here, and the noise was enough, anyway, to drown her voice: the music and the singing, which was more like story-telling than a chant. A Greek chorus, that's what they were, I thought. Probably telling the story of the bride, how she grew up. Maybe *the breasts shall be as clusters of vine...* I had to supply words for what they were say-singing.

"They are washing the bride. It must be a custom."

"But why?"

"Because she isn't allowed to do it herself," I said, making it up, because I didn't know. Preparing her for her bridal bed, blessing her union with a hands-on routine, everyone touching her body, which would thus be fruitful.

I could see the groom in the far room, but I couldn't see Frank. The groom was seated on a chair with a towel around his shoulders, in trousers and a sleeveless white undershirt.

Someone was shaving him with a straight-edge razor. Then another messed up his hair with his hand, and combed it. Another guest did the same. Over and over the procedure was re-enacted by every guest.

Then I saw Frank, who had edged himself to the door of the room where he stood, almost in the room with the mattress. More guests, more linens piling up. Frank saw the mattress, caught my eye and winked. Then he looked at his watch. I knew what that meant.

"Mom, Dad's getting bored," Jeannie said. Not boredom, I knew. Just restlessness. Did he have an appointment today with Dick?

"Are you bored?" I asked Jeannie.

"No. But when are they going to have the wedding?"

"At noon, I think."

"Mommy, look! She's putting on her dress!" But not until after many women had danced around the room with the dress on a tray. The same was happening to the groom's clothes, held aloft by the *cumbari,* the groom's friends, who, I was told, paid for the wedding. Did every villager have to dance with the bride's or the groom's clothes, I wondered. Now, quickly, many hands dressed both bride and groom, the mattress was rolled up, and the men who had shaved and combed the groom danced with the mattress on their shoulders. Then it was placed on the floor, and women seized a boy child, bouncing him up and down upon the mattress by his hands and feet. Up! Down!

"Mother," which was my name when things were serious, "what are they doing to that boy? Are they going to kill him?" Kristin wailed.

Kill him? My God, what was she thinking of? The lamb. That was it.

"No, Kristin. They want the bride to have a baby boy," I added, wondering if she would note that I said boy.

"But why a boy? Can't she have a girl?"

And then one of the women pointed to me and then to Frank, and then to the mattress, looking at me. I decided that I spoke Greek, neo-village. It was a language of the hands, the eyes and the chin. I could have answered her by shutting my eyes, and raising my chin ever so slightly. And that would have been an emphatic no. And that would have separated her from me, definitively. Smile with the eyes and nod, meaning "Yes, I hope to have a son." Did I?

I could not tell if the bride blushed, or if it was the high coloring of excitement on her wedding day—the most special day of her life. Next week she would be ordinary, but in a different way: she would take her place among the village women, no longer as a maiden, but as a married woman. Love had no mysterious meaning and virginity no charm, except as a requirement for marriage. Virginity belonged to a child, someone under the care of her mother. Tomorrow she would be mistress—Kyria. And of course she would have children and, hopefully, a son.

The bride and groom rose, and were joined hand in hand, led by the musicians, by the *cumbari* or best men, followed by the *coumera*—bridesmaids— and by the mothers, fathers, and families of the couple. We were led into the procession, swept along the road to the church, the aged remembering, the children anticipating, secure, belonging, their parents proud to show them off—the fruits of their marriages.

In the church the air was smoky with darkness filtering through the dim windows, the sun left behind in the streets. And all the swirling duskiness of color settled in one spectrum on the white bride, her groom undistinguished in his black suit.

Two *Papas* presided, dressed in blue and gold robes. They chanted the ritual over an enormous silver-backed Bible. The voice of the senior priest in his golden garments, his white,

knotted hair showing at the back of his headpiece, was haunting, resonant and church-filling. The guests talk and chat and
add to the chanting and the noise. Every villager talks and
chants his own thoughts. The rings are tied to red ribbons,
brought forth by the *coumeri* and the *cumbari*, blessed by the
priests; then each ring is placed on top of the couple's heads.
Large white crowns are placed on each head, as well, consisting
of white streamers wound round and round to form a crown.

There are gasps from the crowd—the priest has dropped
the ring from the head of the groom. Everybody talks. Some
shake heads. Others nod. What is it, we wonder? Now the
priest leads the couple three times around the table with the
Bible. Children who have been across the table from the bride
and groom now throw flowers—I detect jasmine, maybe orange blossoms, and their perfumy odors mix with the incense
and the age-old mustiness of the church. Even the pages of the
Bible have an odor of age, of moldy, mildewed paper.

The bride's headdress of white, rolled-up ribbons is now
undone, unwound, meters and meters which each guest signs.
Some attach coins which are deftly sewed into the ribbon, and
wound up. The bride's head must be reeling with the weight of
the ribbon wound with coins and signatures.

The long ceremony nears its end, and the bride and
groom both tense, waiting for the moment in the ceremony
when the priest says "To have and obey," when the groom attempts to stamp on the toes of his bride and she to avoid his
step. A shuffling of feet, and cheers for the groom, who suc-
ceeds. Doesn't he always, I am thinking. I squeeze Frank's hand,
and he finds my toes in the dimness, pressing them gently
with his shoe. I press his back with mine, and we smile. The
girls are bored.

When it is over, the exit is explosive, tumultuous. The
couple is showered with more coins, cascaded with the bud of
the pussy willow, and the children rush to pick up the coins for

her. The musicians again lead the way.

When-can-we-go looks come to me from all my family, but I am determined to see the food, at least, which is mutton ground into wheat and steamed. Whole kids are roasting, steaming, I should say, in mud ovens in the sun, filled early in the morning with a burning fire, then sealed with mud, the young lamb or kid taken out in six to eight hours, well-done and steamy. Cakes with almonds, nuts—everything a kind of seed, fertile. Wine, Wine, Wine! The bride drinks only ceremoniously.

We are all handed glasses of wine, even the girls. "Mommy, what shall I do?"

"Taste it," Frank whispered. "Speak to the bride."

"You are welcome," someone says, approaching us. "You are welcome."

"How long does this last?" Frank says. We hope our generous welcomer understands English.

"It lasts all night. You will see much dancing, much wine, much food.

"When did it begin?" I ask.

"When the bride was born," he says. I know what he means. He is speaking symbolically, but it is very real to him. The girls' lives begin when they marry. I think of the German language, which gives neuter gender to a maiden. "But come and see very fine dancing." The men have begun already, twisting the white handkerchiefs in their hands to hold a partner by the handkerchief, not by the hand. Hesitation, leaps. It is beautiful.

"Frank, why can't you dance like that?"

"Why can't you roast kid like that? And make lace like these women make? And have a son?"

We parted, feeling that we had witnessed a play that was rather long, and in a foreign language. I understood what Dick meant, and why he didn't want to go again. The villagers had *time*. And we didn't. We were always impatient. Always in a hurry! But for what?

"What were they singing all the time?" I asked Dick later that afternoon at the Slab.

"Words they make up."

"But what are they about?" I was thinking of Solomon's Song again, and hoped it was something like that. I said so.

He laughed. "Well, there is some of that, certainly. But much of it is pretty earthy."

"You mean like old-fashioned bachelor parties the night before weddings in America? Dirty jokes, and all?

"Well, they don't call them 'dirty.' Just down to earth. But they also pass the time of day, weather, usual stuff people talk about when they meet and see each other every day of the week."

Damn my Greek teacher who taught only the language of the newspapers.

On and on into the night from our sea house we could hear the voices, the squeaky violin and mandolin. It made me somehow sad. It made me feel rootless and adrift, when each of these villagers was secure in a way we would never know, always wandering as we were. It made me teary, a little: where and how might I give my daughters weddings? Who would be their friends, their bridegrooms? Where would they have homes?

Frank *did* have a meeting with Dick.

My sadness turned to wonder. Later that afternoon a jeep I didn't know drove up in front of our sea house. Out came someone I thought I had seen working in Sabri's milk bar, and in his arms was a mass of white calla lilies. I had never seen so many lilies, and I wondered if they were for sale. "Kyria Jones?" he asked.

"Yes I am Kyria Jones."

He smiled broadly. "These are for you. Do you have a

container, something to put them in?"

"But surely, not all of them for me?" He must have made a mistake. There were too many to hold.

"For you, Madam. From Sabri. He sends his compliments. He remembers that you said you had not seen lilies grow like this, *out of soil dry as rocks* he said you said. They grow in his garden. He wants you to have them."

"Surely not all of them?" I was incredulous.

"All of them, Kyria. Sabri's compliments."

"But," I insisted, "he must not have any left."

"Oh yes, there are many left. Thank you."

I had to get a pail from the pony's stall to put them in, and yet another jug.

"Tell him I said he has a good memory. Tell him I said he is a fine neighbor, generous to strangers in the land."

"Oh yes," he said, pleased. "I will tell him. Oh, they are for your daughters, too, he said."

"Well, daughters," I said to them as Sabri's man departed, "how do you like receiving more than one hundred lilies, at one time? You know, I had five in my wedding bouquet. They are my favorite lily, more than the trumpet kind. You know the trumpet kind—do you know what I mean?"

"What will you do with so many?"

"We'll take them back to Nicosia and fill every room in the house. Each of you will have some in your rooms. And we will all write to Sabri. OK?"

"And I know what else. We'll remember the wedding because that's when we got the lilies," Kristin said.

"You mean you wouldn't remember it otherwise?" I asked.

"Well, Mommy, it was long. Wasn't it?"

"Yes, it was long. But you know, we didn't see much of it, the things that happened earlier yesterday, the dowry arrangements."

"What's the dowry?" Robin asked.

"Well, the house we live in, in Nicosia, is a dowry house. It belongs to the Archbishop's niece, and becomes part of the property of her husband. It's an old system, having dowries. You know, don't you, that Savvas is working and saving money to build a house for his daughter?"

"Why?"

"Because if his daughter doesn't have a house, she can only marry a very poor man who doesn't have many opportunities for a job, for anything but daywork, I guess."

"You mean men marry girls because they have money, or a house?" Jeannie wondered.

"The customs are just different," I said. "It does seem as though a bride has to buy a husband, doesn't it? But I don't think it is thought of in that way. Still, if the girls are too poor, they don't marry well. St. Nicholas, our Santa Claus, became Saint Nicholas because he gave gold to three sisters who didn't have dowries. Their father was poor. But Nicholas gave them balls of gold, and then they could get married." I admitted that it was beginning to sound like buying a husband.

"We are three sisters," Jeannie said, half-teasing me.

"Would you like to have a wedding like that?" I asked them.

"Mommy, we don't know that many people. We don't have a village, do we?" It was Robin who worried about things like that.

"No, but we have a hundred lilies with golden throats."

"Stamens, Mother." Jeannie was studying biology.

# SUMMER

In early summer of 1963 we saw the first blossom of our giant climbing cactus. It was the size of the moon coming up on the sea, a moon-colored, many-petaled, bell-shaped flower, luminous, pearly, with long yellow stamens. It opened after dusk, imperceptibly. One could watch it and nothing would happen, but by ten o'clock it would be in full bloom. It seemed to *be* the moon, hovering for a moment in our own little courtyard of the sea house. Above us the dark leviathan of Pentedactylos waited its turn to speak. We gathered around the flower, our faces glowing, Pippa disappearing in his black fur, Charlie seen as half of a white dog.

The bloom seemed to be going somewhere. It was. When the blossom felt the full force of the sun, it wilted like a crushed lily, never to open again. The heavy stamen hung down below its drooped and weighty blossom, alive with bees.

I felt the grief of this short bloom, the aloneness of its life, how so few of us were there to admire it, when the world would have knelt down in awe at so much and so brief a beauty. Maybe our own lives could be so unnoticed, yet full of beauty.

"But look. Here are more blossoms coming. Here, and here," and Kristin's arms were pointing up to the top of the house, to blossoms tucked under the leathery and prickly cactus. Kristin has "sharp eyes." We could now see one, maybe two, three, six, ten moon cactus flowers. If only we could be here when they bloomed. And if we weren't... Was it for its fleetingness that it was so desirable, so beautiful?

"Mother, just think how terrible it is during the week, if they bloom and we aren't here to see them!" Robin said. She truly grieved at the loss. "And Fikret wouldn't care one bit, I'll bet." Fikret had replaced our faithless Yashar a few weeks before. Mehmet had found him for us.

"Mother, I think it should be called the Moon Cactus,

don't you?" Jeannie remarked.

"Well, let's call it that. Or Aphrodite."

Why, Mother? That's the name of a Goddess." I had my own reasons, but I wouldn't insist.

We didn't know all the nicknames in Greek, as we did the poor poinsettia's. So Moon Cactus it was. The next weekend we had five blossoms in one night, and forgave the plant its spines, the flowers their brevity.

It was water which turned the stones into anemones as cheerful as puppies, or cyclamen—shy doe faces looking downward. But the whole effect of these wild flowers together reminded me of Cyprus lace. Did the springtime parade of wild flowers above Bellapais, or any Cyprus mountain, provide the patterns for the age-old, famed lace of Cyprus? Ask the village women. But they won't know who first copied the flowers or made the patterns that have been theirs for centuries, much less be aware that their lace is a spring flower garden.

The rains stopped and the ground turned away from green, except in watered gardens and irrigated crop gardens or orchards. Only water made the earth go riotous and lavish with richness to look at and richness to eat.

Summer was tawny, bronzed, the color of old stones worn by the years they had lived with wind and sun and rain. Nothing seemed to need water: olive roots went deep into the earth searching for their sparse sustenance—the bitter olive didn't need rain. Nor the succulent fig. Nor the carob. They bronzed a bit, and the leaves yellowed slightly, here and there. But the fat juicy fig was profligate, sweet as honey. Why, then, was the great fig tree avoided, planted away from houses so it did not have to be looked upon each day? And why was the olive good, and its burned leaves which curled, good luck, its branches carried into the church for Easter and for weddings?

The colors of the plain turned from bleak to the colors of putty, of dark purple mottled with gold-leaf, the color of New England oaks in the fall after they have lost their brilliance. The plain had what was left to it after the rich quick flush of spring. Dust was its color in the harshness of the midday summer sun. That sun we avoided.

Life in Kyrenia in summer was to be on and in the sea. Kadir's "Slab," built for the three houses he owned and rented to diplomats, was the gathering place for the diplomatic community. It was a broad, flat cement patio of sorts, built between and on the rocks. We could swim to it from our rocky beach—good swimmers could—or we could walk the few hundred yards. But walking was a trick. There were no sandy beaches in this area, and the beach below our house was covered with round, smooth stones, difficult to walk on. It was impossible to enter the sea from them when there were waves of any size.

Four or five American Embassy families had summer rentals nearby, the English and the Israelis as well. The Cypriots may have liked to look at the sea, but to be *in* it was another dimension. They *bathed* instead of swimming. Nor did they want to have the sun on their skins. So it was unusual to have Kadir around much of the time. The Americans and English were sun-tanned, sun-burned, leathering away their skins as though the sun would never shine again, enjoying the hospitality of Kadir, who owned Tatli Sue and his small beach house, and had built the Slab.

It was the custom of the country that when a man was wealthy enough he could buy land on the sea, even though it was the also custom of his countrymen, Greek and Turk alike, not to like the sea, except to look at it—all but the fishermen who lived on it and the sponge divers who lived in it. The sea was salty and unhealthy, and the sun on these shores was burning to white skins, made them ugly and leathery like a lizard, red like a crab. The English, the Cypriots had always thought, were eccentric enough to not only bathe, but to swim. Women, children, all. But what Turk or Greek would ever want his wife to look like an Englishwoman with pink-red face, moles emphasized, freckles and large pores intensified, exposed with traced, white squint lines in the corners of their eyes? They were foolish people who suffered sun damage of all sorts, but Kadir accepted them with all their eccentricities. Was he surprised to discover that when the embassies arrived after Cyprus' independence, most of the Western diplomats were as eccentric as the English about the sun? But now he, Kadir, had the most unique and accessible beach at the closest distance from the capital of Nicosia! He was in an advantageous position. He knew it was of great value to know diplomats. True, he was out of favor with the English, but he didn't need the English anymore: they no longer ruled Cyprus.

There were rumors about how Kadir had come to own so much valuable property on the sea. Newcomers asked. The locals knew. Mrs. Worthington Pembroke had inherited from her uncle, a Governor General of Cyprus under British rule, thirty hectares of coastland, along with a stone and stately house called *Tatli Sue* perched high over and looking down into the multicolored sea below. In the semi-competence of old age, she returned to her homeland and entrusted to Kadir the disposal of her Cyprus estate. Kadir, knowing the habits of the Greeks and Turks about living on the sea, could find no prospective buyer but himself, and no one bid against his small offer. So he became the owner with no trouble at all, renting Tatli Sue, eventually, to foreign diplomats.

Squat on the sea's stone shoulders, he built a cottage, which became a repository for cold drinks and a changing place for swimmers and sunbathers. He also built the large cement "beach" called the Slab, which became the center for the summer diplomatic community, for those diplomats who mattered—for those, that is, invited by Kadir. One invitation meant more or less a standing invitation and solved the summer beach problems for the receiver.

Kadir was small, cat-like, and raced a roaring motor launch up and down the otherwise quiet, sea-lapped coast. Had anyone ever see Kadir's wife? No one remembered. I asked others. "Well, of course, I have seen her," Estelle said, who lived in Tatli Sue. "She is small and round and quiet."

"But she doesn't like the sun," said another, as though that was anything new in Cyprus.

"Her children are too small for her to leave them," someone else added to the general conversation about the general host, not too kindly.

I would ask Dick Welch about Kadir, I thought. "Where did he study law?" I asked. "Who was his father?"

"Standard WASP questions," Dick replied, with the kind of banter he always used, half-serious, our Embassy Harvard classics scholar. "Well, his father was a merchant," Dick began.

"And?"

"Well, his father believed, so I have heard, that it was best to understand the law to know if it *needed* be broken, if it *could* be broken, if it *should* be broken. So Kadir studied law, as his father hadn't, at Grey's Inn, of course. His father, I am told, came to an understanding of the law by dealing with it."

"Dick, you are talking in circles," I complained. But he always implied more than he said.

"Do you want me to go on?" I nodded. "Kadir studied law, urged by his father. And so, eventually, his shingle went up in the narrow streets of Nicosia, and Kadir flourished. And now, you can see him flourishing."

"Is that the end of the story?" I asked.

"Well, the end is that you and I and our kids are here, enjoying ourselves, at Kadir's invitation. Right? What is one man's meat is another man's meat? Right?"

I laughed because it was true. Why should we judge Kadir?

"Ask him, sometime, how his family came to Cyprus."

"Why should I?" I said.

"Because it is a great story."

"True? Or false?"

"Does it matter?" Dick asked.

I thought about it. No, it really didn't. Myth and fact were getting more and more fused. So I asked Kadir, that very day. He was seated by himself, in front of his cottage. I approached it; he motioned me to climb up the pathway.

I sat down in a chair. "It is nice of you to allow us to use your beach," I said.

"Oh, you mean the Slab?" he responded. "You know, I didn't name it that."

"Who did?"

"Oh, it looks like that, I suppose, and the name just stuck. That's all right. It isn't exactly a beach."

"No, but it makes the beach accessible from the rocks, without destroying the rocks around it. It's nice."

"How do you like Cyprus by now?" Kadir inquired of me, and again, I had the feeling that he knew everything about me, and about Frank. He reminded me of my conversation with Dick.

"Well, it wouldn't be nearly as nice without the Slab. So I came to thank you." A good comeback, I thought, without saying anything. At times like this I was always on guard, fearing that I might say something about something I knew I wasn't supposed to know, that I might start to question in a way I shouldn't. So it was easy to come back to Kadir.

"Has your family been here for ages, since the 1570's," I asked, and then caught myself, not meaning to imply that perhaps one of his ancestors had killed Bragadino so treacher-

ously, after guaranteeing him safe passage in exchange for surrender. But I soon felt that Kadir would have been proud to
say that his ancestors killed him, flayed him, stuffed his skin
with straw and dragged him in derision around the ramparts
of Nicosia.

"One of the earliest..."

But Kadir was interrupted by a sudden dogfight down
on the Slab. It was Charlie Boy and Mustapha, now Dick's
dog. Mustapha was twice Charlie's size. Robin screamed, I fled
to the scene. Everyone was getting out of the way. The dogs
circled each other, snarling, waiting for the moment to slash
or hold, however they fought. This was territorial for these ad-
opted dogs, and they were serious. Everyone was in bare feet,
and the only potential weapons were bath towels. The dogs
slashed and circled, and the next thing we knew, Charlie was in
the sea. A guest had seized a moment, when Charlie was near
the end of the Slab, to scoop him up and drop him into the
sea. We hauled him out and took him home. So I never heard
Kadir's story that day.

In August the sun was a red-hot burning ball turning
Cyprus into a furnace. We spent it in the sea. Hours in the sea.
Children snorkeling around the rocks, adults swimming and
water-skiing occasionally when Kadir came with his motorboat. As much gin disappeared at the Slab as to make the sea
swell. Everyone, it seemed, was in high spirits. It was almost as
though a great celebration was required before what was sure
be a dark winter. That almost certain knowledge made all of us
in the foreign community nervous and a bit wild.

*Yah Sas!* Why not? *Yah Sas* everything. Grilled *Padakia,* or tiny lamb chops. Nearly six to eight per person they
were from such young lambs. Melons. Tomatoes with the sting
of the sun's taste. Plums, peaches, zucchini, strong-scented *cilantro* (so redolent in the market places), garlic, greens I'd

never known, and peppers of all kinds, sizes, colors.

Summer brought a few minor mishaps. The ageless, gigantic fig tree between our house and the beach, as venerable as Adam to us, became Kristin's tree house. The branches spread graciously at right angles, inviting children into its leafy enclosure. Kristin found each limb of the grandfather fig tree to be a room in a house of leaves, the leaves enclosing the space like walls. But, for Kristin, there was a serpent in the fig tree. He bit her foot, and on the spot grew a large blister. A blister so big that she couldn't wear shoes, which she didn't wear anyway in the summer, but she couldn't wear her flip-flops either, which we all wore. The blister was the size of an almond in its outer shell, which is three times the size of a peeled almond. Nahim Bey, who called frequently to sit on our/his patio, looked at her foot suspiciously, looked at Kristin suspiciously, then at me, and at Frank. What village myth was dredged out of his memory, to make him wary of a girl child who had a blister from the venerable fig tree? "It happens sometimes," Nahim Bey pronounced slowly, and carefully.

"What do you mean, sometimes?" I pounced on this pronouncement. Which it was, flatly and directly, and it meant something else.

"Well, the fig tree is old. It is ancient. It has, therefore, wisdom."

"And?" I nearly shouted. "And, so what? What wisdom?"

"Wisdom," he said, like a motionless, pompous toad, blinking solemnly. "Wisdom," he said again. I could have choked him. These village superstitions, insinuations. Why, he was suggesting that...that there was something sinister about it, that a little girl, only six years old, was tainted, was bewitched. The old devil with his fat belly and his ill-treated wife with the sad face—what was he implying? The Wisdom of Cyprus was going too far.

I took Kristin to the medical officer in the American Embassy.

"Common," he said. "In the early summer the fig tree often has a substance, which, if in contact with an open wound—let's say a scratch, even, in which the underlying tissue of skin is exposed—often causes this sort of eruption of the skin. A blister, I mean."

"What do we do about it?"

"The only danger is infection from the blister. Keep her off the fig tree, out of the water, and here is some antibiotic ointment until it heals. It is no problem, except in summer when it is difficult to keep dry."

"You mean...dry?" I wondered how that would be possible in a Cyprus summer, the only time all children are barefoot or wear thongs.

"Yes. That is what I mean."

Damn Nahim Bey, I said to myself as we left. But how could I condemn the local people for their superstitions? I had already envied many of them their belonging, too much. I had envied them for their wisdom, but how very skewed it could be. It was their heritage, and they were comfortable with it and comfortable with ages of knowledge I'd never had and certainly my children wouldn't. That is what *home* means. That is probably why villagers planted fig trees far away from their houses, knowing customs and not knowing why. Customs are not challenged.

Summer brought a few sharks. No, not summer: an American naval vessel, anchored a half-mile off the coast of Kyrenia, brought sharks.

This is how I came to that knowledge. I walked down the path of stones from our sea house to our pebbly beach, under the fig tree I now loved no less, even though I had to accept that it did have a fault. On the pebbly beach, I put on my swim fins and backed over the hard, round stones into the sea, flipped over, and started swimming flat on the shallow water, out to where it was deeper. I could look left to see the Slab, and when I was in deep water, I could see the destroyer much farther out. I also noticed, under the water, a small black-and-white, pencil-shaped fish, worm, or—I didn't want to say—snake! It swam right towards me, wiggling as a snake wiggled. I turned over, splashed my fins hard in front of it, and looked under water again. There it was, swimming directly for me. I swam faster. It swam faster. It seemed to be going for my legs. I splashed my fins harder. It swam faster. I turned around and headed for shore. It turned around to follow me.

I have been dreaming too much, I said to myself. There is no such creature as this, and anyway it is too small to bother me. But it followed, figment of my mind or not, to where I stood up and backed out of the sea. I sat down on the stones to think about it. I was alone, but Frank was on his way down for a swim. The girls were off with Mehmet, along with Johnny and Susie and Kathy.

"Hi!" Frank called, descending the path to the sea. "How is it?" As though the sea could ever be anything but fine. He meant to ask if it was too wavy to get in easily.

"It's...it's usual," I said. "Makes you a new person every time." I lied about the serpent, as I now called it. Maybe it had gone. I would watch Frank.

He walked out with his thongs, and then threw them back to shore. I waited. He too eased himself out of shallow water and started swimming. So far, so good. And then he too did a frenzied splashing, and turned around, face under water. He turned and swam faster, stopped, looked under water. He changed directions, splashed his feet, two, three times, then turned towards shore. I was laughing at my ghost, pleased that it was not that, but feeling a bit unfair.

"What's the matter?" I shouted. But Frank couldn't

hear me. "What's the matter?" I called louder, into the lapping of the waves, as he started out of the water, walking faster on the hard pebbles than I had ever seen him.

"There's a snake-like creature following me. It's no bigger than a pencil. Longer, maybe. Black and white, sort of black with white spots, I'd say."

I burst out laughing. "You mean *you* knew it was there, all the time? And *you* didn't tell me!"

"I thought I may have imagined it. I thought it may have gone. I wondered if *you* would see it too." Frank was squeamish about what creatures might be in the sea.

"Just wait until there is a shark in the waters. We'll see if I tell you!"

"Frank, *you* are my truth seeker, my verifier. You tell me things are real. I tell *you* they aren't. What would we do without each other?" Frank smiled, because he knew that it really was true.

"Whoopee! We get to go on a ship!" Kristin shouted.

"What ship?" asked Robin.

"A boat, a gray boat. That one," she answered, pointing to the naval ship.

"It's true. There is a naval ship which is going to anchor outside of Kyrenia, and anyone from the Embassy who wants to go aboard, can."

"Lippee!" she cried. "When?"

"Tomorrow. Do you want to go?"

It was a destroyer from the Sixth Fleet, long, sleek, battle grey, its white numbers clearly visible from our sea house.

"But why doesn't it come closer? Why is it way out there?"

"Because Kyrenia is not a harbor, except for small boats. Such a boat needs a greater depth. But you will be taken on small boats, and you can see where the sailors eat, and sleep too, probably. Do you want to go?"

We all went, climbed into the tenders, which pulled alongside the destroyer, and up we climbed to the deck, taking the willing hands of sailors who steadied the children, determined, at that very moment, to be sailors. But summer sailors, I thought. How gray and cold and confined and dreary a boat could be in a winter sea, and in wartime.

But the ship's presence, and the fact that many like them were not so far away from Cyprus, was a thought comforting and disturbing at the same time. The good times had beguiled us, lulled us with the quiet lapping of the warm summer sea. Trouble was buried in the depths, in the dark shadows under the sea. Maybe not to emerge at all. Leviathan may sleep...I was being hopeful.

We returned from the harbor of Kyrenia, fully warned that the sailors had seen a few sharks follow their ship, and when asked, they knew about the shark parasites which had tried to attach themselves to Frank and me.

Returning to our house, we wound our way down past the house of leaves, the fig tree, and along the pebbly beach. Pebbles were baking-potato-size but smoothed, rounded by the years of water and difficult to walk on, although the girls by now could run on them. This time there were a number of men swimming and playing water polo. Who could they be? Cypriots didn't play like that. American sailors from the boat? Suddenly they all stopped playing and started staring at a cave-like rock overhang, into which the water rose and fell. Someone was there, screaming. But the sailors soon started laughing. We walked down farther and out into the water to see under the overhanging rack. And burst into laughter.

"Frank, it's Ireni! Caught in her bra and panties!" She was holding her arms over her breasts of white cabbages, trying to cover herself up and to keep the constant waves from flowing over her head in the cave. Her clothes lay further up the beach, telling us how she had been caught unawares, and hence had retreated to the cave in the sea. Ireni was illiterate in letters as well as in the sea: she couldn't swim a stroke. For her, the predicament was unbearable; for us, a bit of theatre at Ireni's expense. No one would be able to rescue her in her undressed state. Only the departure of all of us would help, but the sailors were having too good a time.

The summer is lazing by, lulling me, at least, into peace, into the pleasure of watching my children grow and strengthen in the sun and the sea, after years in a cold Northern *and* Communist climate. I concentrate upon daily life, and I see how their bones lengthen, their muscles form. I see the figs they eat, the melons, the grapes, the artichokes, the myriad vegetables turn into their flesh. The children are also becoming expert swimmers. I remember Jeannie in Warsaw, standing in a shivering line of eight-year-olds, grey-blue skin to match the water in the pool, the floor, the walls, knees knocking and teeth chattering with chill. Now she dives into the sea, her grey-blue color turned to golden skin, golden hair, haloed by health. I see that the children don't huddle around me: they are secure and free. In less than a year.

In late afternoon of most days by the sea, I lead a caravan of swimmers from the Slab to our own beach, a distance of approximately four hundred yards. The swimming caravan goes from the Slab to our beach in single file: I follow and watch everyone, towing a rubber raft, in case I need it. The sun lengthens in late afternoon: the rocks on our beach will not be too hot after our swim. We have adapted to the heat of midday, and the comfort of the sea. We know how to live.

We use swim fins, because with them we cover so much more distance; we move in and around caves of rocks where fish swarm, and watch them. We prowl the sea. The water is so warm we can stay in for hours without chilling. The air is so hot that the water is also a refuge, a preferred habitat. We belong to Nature, to the Sea. We have left the land for the summer and are creatures of the Deep.

I feel my own body stir as well, grow stronger, my muscles tightening from swimming, from the splash of salt water over my skin. I have become a physical being: I exist for the feel, the touch, the taste, the scent of sea, of fruit, of summer in a dry land and the perfume of cactus flowers, jasmine. I exist for the sight of me as well, for my beauty has blossomed like that of my children. I am as tawny and golden as they. I do not even chide myself for living in my flesh only. Frank, too, is tanned, younger. We make love. Frank enters my rooms of motherhood, the narrow chambers. I feel my power, my creation. And I do not care that at this time I think I will never create as much by a thought as I have done with my body. My body acts for me, outside of my thoughts. I do not need thoughts. My body is a harp and the strings are played by the wind, by the sunrise, by the waves in the sea, touching me as I pass through it. Guilt slips by me as easily as the sun rises. I want everything to stop at just this moment, and never change, and to preserve this time forever. I would turn us all into a canvas, a painting, and with it stop the growth and decay of which the world is made. I would turn us into four Mona Lisas and one David, for Frank will always be a warrior, but I will turn him into the watchful David, the pebble of death resting quietly in a relaxed hand.

But the next day my perfect children disobeyed the Rule: never swim alone to our beach from the Slab. Frank heard them yelling, and looked down to the sea from our patio. One was trying to push the other—it turned out to be Jeannie pushing Robin—under water. Robin was sputtering and fighting back. Frank ran down to the beach and threw himself in as fast as he could, swimming out to them, bringing them both in. I knew that Jeannie would be a sorry little girl when Frank was finished with her. *Someone's going to be crying!* is the family statement on such an occasion.

"You could have drowned her, you hear? And what

were you doing swimming there by yourself? Can't we trust you?"

"Robin started out, and I tried to stop her," Jeannie said.

"And you tried to stop her by drowning her? Is that it?" Frank was angry. His finger marks showed on Jeannie's arm, and I knew that, before he was finished, they would show red on her white buttocks.

We climbed the path to our sea house and Frank took Jeannie into her room. I didn't see her until dinner time when she emerged, eyes red with crying, sniffling. I did not know what had happened, except that my model children were probably behaving normally.

"Monsters," Frank said. "Robin could have drowned. I don't know what got into Jeannie. It's damned lucky we were here and heard them."

# BUFFAVENTO

It was the first of August. It was Kristin's birthday. This year she would have a party, because this year we were not traveling to or from home leave, or to another posting. The party had taken shape long before. We would climb to Buffavento, the highest of the three Crusader Castles. They were really fortifications, and Buffavento, from the Lusignans, meant "the Defier of Winds!" The castle was perched on the windy heights of one of the highest peaks of the Kyrenia Mountains, the mountain range of Pentedactylos. We would climb it on donkeys.

No one could have asked for a more beautiful day to have a seventh birthday. It was easy to forget that every day was beautiful, its quality depending upon the clarity of the sky. Whether or not we could see the Turkish coastline from Kyrenia, or if driving from Nicosia to Kyrenia, whether or not we could view the sea just over the crest of the mountains would determine what kind of swimming day it would be: if we would have to remain close to shore, if we could go swimming at all. There would be no swimming if the wind was blowing and therefore the waves might be too high.

Today was perfectly clear, the sea mirror-like. But perhaps the lack of wind was not so important because we were going into the mountains, closer to that hand of five fingers thrown in anger by a jilted lover, or a god, which we saw both from the sea house and from Nicosia.

"What should I wear, Mother? What should we take with us? How long will it be? Can we go all the way to the top? Will it be hot? What color are the donkeys? When will we be back and have the cake?" And presents, Kristin meant, but didn't want to ask.

Kristin's (only-a-bit, as she said) older sisters were equally excited and were quite confident that they would manage their donkeys much better than Kristin. They had already ridden Marulla's donkey. Marulla came to clean once a week and lived in another little whitewashed mud brick cottage with blue-painted shutters by the side of a Century Plant. What if the day they rode her donkey, it *had* put its head down and refused to move? And what if Marulla had been forced to catch the donkey running back to her home with Jeannie, Robin, and Kristin on her back? Jeannie, ten years old, was certain that she understood the ways of donkeys. Robin was less sure, but she was, at least, bigger than Kristin and knew that donkeys were guided by a stick tapping left or right on their necks.

The birthday party guests lived in Tatli Sue, a real house compared to our cottage, and they *lived* in it rather than coming only on weekends. But the girls liked *Pushkululu* better, as Nahim Bey called our house. Kristin always wanted us to get rid of our beds so the whole family could sleep on the platform just like it used to be, when the family was cozy and snug together. Johnny and Kathy and Alice all liked our house better too, and were very excited about Kristin's birthday party.

"Halo Kristin!" It was Johnny. He had his pen dagger in his blue jeans. And a rope.

"I'll probably have to lead my donkey, or tie him up, or something. You always need a rope, don't ya know. You could get one too; I have another one you could borrow."

Kristin had wanted to ask Dina Arazi, but she was home in Israel. She had asked Stella Polyviou and Tulay Acar, but their parents didn't let them do anything fun, such as wear pants and climb over rocks and down to the sea in Kyrenia. They always wore dresses and just stayed home and played with dolls, out of the sun. Why, she wondered. They couldn't swim and they didn't get in the *sun*. Julie and Tommy had gone on home leave. Birthdays were always like that, she thought, if you had one in the summer. But this year was different: she was having a whole-day birthday, going to the mountains on a donkey. Anyway, they could only get seven donkeys.

"Hats, everybody." A general groan.

"No, Mom. We like the sun. We are brown." They *were* brown. And the hair of my naturally blonde children was almost white from the sun. Alice was the same. But their noses never got over being slightly pink from always peeling, and those three noses were never in the morning sun, noonday sun, and afternoon sun, all on one day in Cyprus as they would be today, on the first of August.

John and Kathy, both dark-haired, and Alice, blonde, went home to get their hats. "I'll stop by for you. You needn't come back," I said. Making last-minute preparations, I packed sandwiches, peaches, grapes, raw vegetables, candy bars, cans of juice and anything with liquid.

The six children fit easily into the small Taunus station wagon, and we were off on the narrow winding road to Bellapais, where the donkeys had been ordered for 9:00 A.M. The road hair-pinned through the silvery grey-green of olive groves, and as we climbed, more and more of the outline of the island was visible. We could see a few slow white waves uniformly rising and descending upon the shore and an occasional donkey loaded with straw or sticks, its driver often a little boy, more often a black crow of a village woman with her gnarled hands and leathery face. The farmers and villagers could not avoid the sun.

The children had been singing a song for days, adding more and more verses to the tune of *Were you ever in Cardiff Bay*, so that I had forgotten the real words. I preferred the new ones:

> *Were you ever in Bellapais,*
> *Drinking sour lemonade,*
> *Under the Tree of Idleness*
> *Waiting for a donkey.*

*Hey! Ho! Away we go!*
*Donkey riding, donkey riding.*
*Hey! Ho! Away we go!*
*Riding on a donkey!*

The variations by this time were becoming endless, but the chorus was always the same. I secretly hoped the line about waiting for a donkey didn't have any significance, but it was probably a natural premonition. We drove into the village and parked near the spreading *Tree of Idleness*, which Durrell made famous. I entered the tourist office that had a black-penciled placard that read "Donkeys for the Day," but my heart sank when we saw no donkeys in the square.

"Oh yes, Kyria Jones. Did you say seven? Well, I thought it was for ten o'clock and we were having a little trouble finding so many. Would you like a coffee?"

Coffee was soothing, persuasive, friendly. Sometimes I was convinced that it had opium seeds in it because the impatience of Western attitudes was soon consumed by it, or with it, consumed in that cup of coffee brought in by the nearest handy boy from the nearest coffee house, carried on the much-used tray suspended by three wires. Coffee: thick, black, sweet if one wished, and a glass of cold water coming from the enormous clay amphora on a tripod. For the children, the inevitable coca cola, or unlemony lemonade in a land of lemons.

There we were, sitting under the *Tree of Idleness,* waiting for something to happen. But the waiting was soothed by the very name of the tree, and we were patient, but expectant too, knowing the donkeys would arrive. The courtyard was laid with rounded stones, patterned in continuous arches, the very stones which, on the beach were so difficult to walk on, unanchored and rolling as they were with each wave. The great spreading tree covered the sky, gathering all of us into its shade. The ruined Abbey of the Lusignans, a cut-out against the lapis lazuli sky, the honeysuckle scent, and lemon leaves from the Abbey's gardens contrasted with the pungent coffee. So what if there were no donkeys? I could have spent the day there. But the children?

They were devastated, silent, casting furtive looks at every little street which emptied into the square. And then, from somewhere, the sound, the unmistakable sound of shod hoofs on stones. A white, long-eared head appeared, and then a brown one with a tan muzzle. And six children ran for the donkeys. "I get the white one, I get the white one!" in unison.

"And because it is Kristin's birthday," I said, "maybe she should choose first?"

"Aw, Gee!" But Kristin smiled with secret pleasure. One had only to look at her to know that she was *having a birthday.*

"But that makes only two donkeys. Do you suppose..." I spoke to the donkey driver, Socrate, who was definitely the leader.

"Gregori is coming. But we didn't think you were coming. We didn't think you wanted *seven* donkeys," Socrate said. "We didn't hear anything more."

More than what, I wondered. "But I ordered them a week ago," I protested.

"But that was a week ago," Socrate said, as though a week wiped out the order. Maybe the day was too still. Or too hot, I wondered. Anything could be wrong with the day for the donkey drivers.

"Might be a wind coming," Socrate said, in a flat tone of voice, off hand.

"Is that bad?" I asked.

"Kyria, if there is wind, no go. Donkeys won't go. They know better. Drivers won't go."

I remembered what Marulla had told me about the first fifteen days of August, especially the first four days. But I didn't believe it, that those days were called *Wicked Days*. Rubbish, I thought. But Marulla wouldn't wash any of the sheets during them. She said the sheets would burn, or tear, and she might burn her hands as well. She said she couldn't wash her hair on those days, and that I shouldn't wash the hair of my daughters. Why? I asked. "Because their heads will be full of sores, or their hair will fall out. Or both," she said.

I wondered if Socrate was going to believe in the evil days, today being one of them.

"But Socrate, aren't the other donkeys coming? Look, I ordered them. I promised six children." I never knew, before I lived in Cyprus, that even if the sun shone every day in summer, there still might be a weather problem. Or was Socrate making excuses for the absence of the others? Or...?

"It is a bad time, Kyria. The other drivers maybe don't want to go. And with only two donkeys," he continued. "We can't go with two donkeys."

"But why wouldn't they come?" I asked. I wanted to know if he, too, shared Marulla's beliefs.

"Bad days, maybe, Kyria. No one wants anything bad on the first of August. Or tomorrow. Or the next day. For four days..." He paused. "But fifth day is OK. Maybe very good. If you see the sky open at night."

"The sky open at night? I don't understand, Socrate."

"Only if you're lucky," he responded, enigmatically. Socrate wasn't going to tell me very much.

"And if you are lucky, what happens? Couldn't it happen to...to me, to us?" Meaning, would we be lucky enough to have the other donkeys arrive.

"You have to believe, Kyria. And you have to look carefully, for the light that comes."

"That comes when?" I was perplexed.

"When the sky opens up. You have to stay up and watch carefully. Then you may have your wish. But you have to avoid the badness of these days," Socrate said.

Another sigh, another coffee. The two drivers have coffee; the second man is called Spyros. The children are looking into every alleyway that empties into the square. They know the donkeys will arrive—they are used to the ways of Cyprus: waiting. I am discouraged. I don't expect donkey drivers to subject themselves to the whims of foreigners, to risk bad luck for the rest of the year, for themselves and for their donkeys. The donkeys are extremely important to them: their transportation, their livelihood, their friends.

They do arrive. Five more! Wonderful! And now, the question of the wind.

No other driver mentions it. Subject closed.

Kristin gets the white donkey. The others, eager to be off, choose the one nearest them—all the others are brown.

"And Kyria, your baskets." Socrate takes everything out of my carefully packed baskets: sandwiches, fruit, napkins, cans of juice, chocolate, and squashes them into his saddlebags. Squish squash, I can hear my food collapse. What have the drivers brought to eat? Bread. A piece of hard cheese. Wine. No more, I am certain.

Each driver takes hold of his donkey and starts the ascent up a long, narrow cobblestone street, and all the children cry, "But I want to steer my own donkey!" They are taken by surprise.

"Kyria, we always drive our own donkeys. You cannot take them alone."

"Of course, Socrate." I knew of the potential temperament of donkeys and nothing at all about the potential temperament of the mountains, let alone the way to go. And no driver would let his valuable donkey out of his sight.

"You must have a driver, or you don't go," I announced. That was a grim choice, hence easily resolved.

"Hey! Ho! Away we go! Donkey riding, Donkey riding" was the next response as each child turned her or his attentions to the driver. How far was it? How many miles? How high?

"What will we see? Will we see an eagle's nest? I want an eagle's egg!"

I decided right there and then that life was very good, very good indeed, and very beautiful, and the donkeys and the children and Socrate and his men were very very real. I hadn't expected to get an individual attendant plus donkey for the price of one pound sterling each for an entire day. Plus the ancient wisdom of Socrate, free.

One driver was named Mehmet. Only his name distinguished him from the rest, and in that name was the difference of centuries, never to be forgotten. Did the drivers, so amicable, care very much about names? But because of names, they couldn't share the same feast days, the same religious celebrations. Did that fact make so much difference, really? Rarely did they intermarry, and then, certainly not in the villages. Was marriage the only taboo? Why, then, were they arming against each other?

Each driver probably, undoubtedly, belonged to some fighting organization with its cache of arms, and if they didn't belong, they would quickly enough when and where the difficulties, the fighting, I may as well say, began. Everyone said the fighting would begin, Greek and Turk alike, and so did Frank. They said it as though they said "I am going to buy a loaf of bread" or "The rains begin in December."

We left the uppermost reaches of Bellapais, the streets narrowing; we had already passed Durrell's house. Could one blame him for his heartbreak in leaving, despite the struggle of religions on Cyprus? But now, that struggle which the British named *the troubled times* (so very British for something which had been a war) had led to Cyprus' independence.

*Chittim* was the Biblical name for Cyprus, and it was

in Cyprus where Saul, reborn as Paul, first preached the Gospel with Barnabas, a native of Cyprus. Paul and Barnabas often traveled together in the Roman Empire, preaching Christianity. After many journeys writing and preaching, Paul of Tarsus, the Apostle Paul, and Saint Paul, as he was variously called, laid the foundations of early and subsequent Christianity. As legend has it, he was eventually beheaded in Rome, and Barnabas was later stoned to death in Paphos. Cyrpus' long history is a parade of kings, war and warlords—Persians, Crusaders, Byzantines, who sacked and burned and raped...on and on. Is any war ever over?

Surely Cyprus wouldn't throw away independence now that it had gained it for the first time in its three-to-four-thousand-year history? But the island's independence had a strike against it: British colonial policy was to divide and rule, thereby making each faction weaker than one whole. This policy had been used in strategically important Cyprus, where the British had made the Cypriot Turks their accomplices against the Greek Cypriots, giving them thirty percent representation when they were only eighteen percent of the population. The situation was inherently unstable.

Up through a pine forest, the earth soft with discarded needles, the air heavy with the scent of Aleppo Pine, of juniper, of cypress. There were dwarf oaks, with tiny leaves, and bigger oaks. These great forests of Cyprus had made it historically coveted, conquered and reconquered. They provided the lumber for the ships of foreign sea powers, the ships that made their power possible. The forests of Cyprus were important long before Alexander, even, who conquered Cyprus from the Persians.

"Hey! Ho!" continued the children's voices from their varying distances on a single path. We met a few old women carrying bundles of sticks, true faggot-gatherers. How queer they must have thought us, we who always rode in cars, riding donkeys when we didn't have to. Always a greeting: *Mera* or *Spera,* with the *Kali* (or *Good*) dropped off, preceding the day's greetings, and always *Kyria*. The *Mera* changed to *Spera* at noon.

On through a plateau covered with almond trees, the green furry nuts well formed. On through sparse grass, an open space but rising steeply, and beyond that, I could see only rocks. It was getting late in the morning. The children were quiet now. How long could they stand those saddles? How long could I? Not so bad, to begin with. But after a time, those wooden "U's" crossed in an X for the pommel and for the cantle, and the boards forming the seat were harder and harder, padded though they were with sheepskin. Stirrups didn't exist—the Cypriots usually sat sideways. So I tried it. Socrate smiled: "You learn, Kyria. But now we stop. You eat your lunch."

He had chosen a wide, open grassy plot surrounded by rocks. Several scraggly trees gave us enough shade. Pentedactylos rose steeply in front of us, that very hand, the fingers of which had been counted by the children so many times. It was far steeper than we could ever have imagined. It looked like a giant razorback wild boar, or the back of a prehistoric dragon with five fins, and was as inaccessible. The sea was a great emerald encircling the sun-bleached stone that was Cyprus. Looking closer, we could see dots, flecks of green and grey—the olive and the orange and the carob trees. The roads were mere pathways, the string of pebbles left by Hansel and Gretel, winding through trees to find their way home.

The floor of the stone mountain we were on was carpeted with anemones and cyclamen and wild hyacinth. Below, houses were startling white cubes, here and there, as randomly placed as children's blocks.

"Hey, which one is ours? Which one do you think? I think that one way down on the sea, the last one."

"No. That isn't it. Look, find the castle in Kyrenia and go along the coast from there." Johnny was right. That was the only way to find it. "There it is! Next to Orek's house with the red shutters." Kristin couldn't really see the red shutters, but she was probably right about the house. They stared and laughed, each child shouting a new recognition of this place and that place.

"Look where we swim! It's only an inch long, half an inch, if you shut one eye!"

"Wow! Did you ever think Pentedactylos was so big? Kristin, I'll bet you don't have another birthday in such a small house. You'll be too big." It did look like a doll's dollhouse.

"Mom, can we go to the top? How far do we go?" Clearly no one was tired.

The top loomed ahead of us, a great pile of rocks. None of the children had yet observed the steepness, the barrenness, intent as they were on spotting known places viewed from a great height. The castle of Buffavento was built on a rock ledge over three thousand feet high, not so very high in itself, but when it rose so steeply at such a short distance from the sea, it seemed twice as high.

"But aren't you a little bit sore where you sit?" I asked.

"You mean you are, Mom? Hey, Mom's got a sore..." They pealed laughter across the landscape, down to the sea, from which it came back to them like a rubber ball. So they shouted endless words and names, which seconds later sprang back to them. Only the donkeys were perturbed.

The drivers sat a polite distance from us, eating their bread, hard cheese, and drinking wine. Except Mehmet, who had brought water. Our lunches were a little squashed, but our hunger never noticed. I wished that I, too, had brought some wine. I felt denied. Mehmet didn't drink, but I noticed that he was offered.

Why did they offer him wine, I wondered. Out of

politeness? Did Mehmet, as a Moslem, sometimes drink wine? Or were they trying to make fun of him? The custom of the country was to offer, to share with friend and stranger alike. Just then Socrate noticed me, and came with his jug from which they all drank, offering to pour some into my paper cup. I accepted. The wine was dark and a little sour, but tasted better than my canned juice.

"Socrate, how much farther is it? I mean, how much farther do we go?"

"Kyria, the trip to the top is three hours, one way. You must walk the last hour. Do you want to do that? But you know you can't get to the very top. It is much too steep. Nobody climbs there."

"But we won't see any eagles, if we don't. I promised the children!"

"You wait. We go up one hour more, one more up, and then see. It is quicker going back but harder on the driver. And for you too."

"Why harder?"

"The donkey, he wants to go back home. Fast. We have to make sure they don't. And the bumps. You will see, Kyria."

Mounted again, off we went. Side-saddle for a little while at least. The children were doing the same, raising themselves with their hands, now and then, from the brutal hardness of the saddle. "Hey! Ho! Away we go! Donkey riding, donkey riding..." Full chorus again, and I joined in.

"New verses!" I cried, and began: "Were you ever in... Cyprus, Kypros." It didn't work. Needed three syllables. I tried again:

"Were you ever in...."

"Dactylos," Jeannie answered. "Riding on the jagged stones. Singing a song of happiness, Riding on a donkey."

"Again."

"Were you ever in...?"

"I know!" said Kathy, clutching her saddle sideways:

*Were you ever on a mountain pass*
*With a little birthday lass.*
*Where there isn't any grass*
*For my little donkey.*
*Hey! Ho!*

Then the donkeys stopped. "Kyria, if you want to go on, now you must walk. Gregori and the others stay here, with the donkeys. Mehmet and I lead the way...If you want."

"Well, Birthday Girl," I said to Kristin, "What do you want to do?" But I looked at the others as well.

"Go, Mommy. It's my birthday, isn't it?"

"Hooray for Kristin. I was afraid she wouldn't go, that she'd be scared to go up there." That was Johnny, the brave boy talking.

"If we are this far, and don't go all the way," I said, "we will always look up here, won't we, and say, 'Why didn't we do it?' So, let's go."

An hour's climb, and most of the time we saw the step in front of us, saw the three-point contact I insisted upon. Mehmet and Socrate had it too, two legs and a staff. The heat we felt was produced from our own sweat—the temperature was cold, not like the coast in August just after midday. Gradually we became aware of a whispering in our ears, becoming louder, and louder. We were too occupied to think of what it was. It hummed, droned, and then we all stopped, our hair blown in front of our eyes, our hats tugging at their elastic under our chins. It was the wind! It was Buffavento, Defier of Winds. We stopped, looked upwards through two holes in the ruined wall of the castle. There were only remnants of one wall. The rest, nothing but a pile of stones from where we looked. The Defier of Winds had lost. All gone but this crumbling wall, still attempting to defy the force of the wind. But the view through the gaps in the wall—all of Cyprus! Across the Mesaoria Plain to Troodos Mountains, echoing and echoing each other as they receded into the ever-unfolding distance. In the opposite view, down to the sea, all of the coastline curved in front of us—Kyrenia and its square fortress on the sea, the rounded harbor, Karavas rounding a slight curve of the island, the point of land encircling Morphou Bay, and the Turkish cemetery we passed every day we went to our sea house. Distantly, the southern coast of Turkey floated like a battleship upon the sea. The whole world below looked like a diorama filled with its miniature buildings, its trees made of tiny green-dyed sponges, its people like upright ants. We were the Eye of God, observing what He had made, past, and present.

The children were shouting into the wind, and the echoes bounced back and forth and back again, and disappeared into the infinite. The castle—former castle, I must call it now, was called "Castle of the Lion," because of Lionheart. As the children shouted endless calls into the buffeting winds, waiting for the returning echo, I watched Richard the Lionheart, Coeur de Lion, his fleet below, banners waving gently in the slight sea breeze, before he routed this castle in 1192. Having left Sicily enroute to the Third Crusade, Richard's squadron was splendid, with two hundred vessels and thirteen great warships carrying stores, tents, provisions, horses, ammunition, and military engines to rout such fortifications as Buffavento... Richard sailed at the head of his fleet in a wondrous galley, the Sea-Cutter, a huge lantern hoisted in the stern.

But Richard's fleet was shipwrecked, ships lost and others cast up upon the shores of Cyprus, only to be seized by Isaac Commenus, Emperor of Cyprus. Richard was enraged, and took the island.

From here, it was easy to imagine the troops of Emperor Commenus of Cyprus on the shore, wearing costly armor, many-colored garments, riding war-horses that champed the bit, beautiful mules, the troops with gilded swords and breast plates. The Emperor's tent was filled with booty—gold and silver vessels, brilliant arms and woven garments—waiting for Richard's men.

Suddenly, I was shaken out of my wonder by Jeannie's hand upon my arm, because the whisperings had turned to screams, carried piercingly through the force of the wind-song—two screaming sounds grappling with each other for dominance. The wind defied by Eagles!—still high above us, but not so high that each child could not see the talons and the beaks and hear those screams. Lonely and terrifying, the imperial eagles, like great black warplanes swooping in the lapis sky. Their talons were curved like grappling irons, their beaks sharper and stronger and bigger than anything we had ever seen. No mere birds, surely, looked like that. They must be dragons with feathers.

Each child silently decided that she and he, Johnny, didn't want an egg, didn't need an egg, wouldn't try to get an egg today, or tomorrow, or ever. The *eyrie* seemed to be held in the arms of the wind, but in reality, Socrate said, was weighted clown with a ton of branches and stones. The fortress of Buffavento must have been copied after the eagles' eyrie—perched high as they were, nearly impenetrable, except to Richard and the succeeding Lusignans to whom he had given it. And the wind.

Each child agreed that nobody had ever seen a real eagle's egg, not even by helicopter. The entire world was, at that moment, wind and the scream of the eagle, so mixed that we couldn't separate one from the other as they competed for dominance. Sounds that would have drowned our voices if we hadn't already been made speechless. Sounds sometimes discernible: wind pierced by screams of the competing eagles, yet plaintive, threatening, a beauty so alarming that one's senses were paralyzed by incredulity, while fear rose strangely in the earthbound heart.

We retreated. And started the descent, hating to leave a view we would probably never see again. Each downward step was much harder than the climb. Braking hurt the thigh muscles, jolted the spine. We couldn't wait to reach the donkeys, to let them bear the burden of us, do the braking. The children were strangely silent as we descended.

Silently we made it down to the donkeys, and as silently, and relieved, mounted them again, each happy to have a driver, each happy not to walk any more. We found that Socrate was right. The donkeys needed a strong brake, and the going was rough for the drivers. For the riders, each step was an injury. Two hours down, with a break in between. The riders gratefully walked across the plateau, seeing nothing but our toes in front of ourselves. Then we mounted again, reluctantly. Quicker to ride.

The landscape went by unnoticed except for the rise and bob of the donkey in front, and its lame passenger's twisting attempts to minimize the inevitable thrust as each front hoof took the weight. Sitting on the donkey with both legs on one side, hands on the wooden saddle, taking the weight off our bottoms, was the best way. Until the arms were tired.

Finally, to Bellapais and the last descent through the streets. Shutters were closed for the afternoon rest which the drivers had missed. Some faces peered out of windows, to see who would break the sacred time of day and shelter from the heat, and possibly the evil time as well, with the clatter of donkeys' metaled hoofs upon stone. Then we were there again, in the square, facing the Tree of Idleness. No driver accepted a coffee but Socrate. Six lemonades and two coffees: *metrio glyki,* double strong and sweet for me. *Glyki,* or sweet, for Socrate.

"Thank you, Socrate. That was a lovely day. You were good guides. You know the mountains well."

"Yes, Kyria. I know them well. They are my friends. I

lived in them and they protected me for many months. Some years," he added, quietly.

"Ah, you mean *before independence,*" as the Greek Cypriot always said.

"Yes, Kyria. I was hunted. I had escaped. I killed two British soldiers. For freedom. I hid in the mountains. They caught me once, but I escaped and killed a guard. The guard was Turkish. They brought me food." He motioned so that I understood that *they* meant his fellow drivers.

"Mehmet too?" I asked. I had to know.

"Mehmet too," he said, quietly.

"And now?" What would he do with his friend, Mehmet?

"We will fight again. If we need. We will fight to keep our freedom."

"But Mehmet too, you will fight Mehmet, after what...?" I could not phrase the words.

"We will fight anyone. It does not matter, friend or not, if he turns enemy." Socrate had finished speaking. "Addios, Kyria." He issued the same parting greeting to each child, and gave each a parting handshake.

"Addios! Efharysto! Addios! Addios!"

"Addios, Socrate," I added.

The birthday party was nearly over. Except for the cake, to be found in the sea house. And presents. And my sudden weariness.

A. Kristin in Kyrenia holding young goat   B. Robin by the Moon Cactus
C. Jeannie watering courtyard of Kyrenia cottage   D. Robin (left) and
Jeannie in courtyard of Kyrenia cottage.

*A. Jeannie, Robin, Kristin and friends at Kyrenia Castle   B. Arlene on Karakoumi C. Greek woman spinning yarn   D. Cypriot children on donkey carrying wooden plow*

A. Mehmet the Shepherd with flock    B. Charlie Boy    C. Cyprus coastline near Kyrenia    D. Pentedactylos (Buffavento on the left, halfway up)    E. Roman amphitheater with Ambassador Belcher, Charles McCaskill, and friend

# THE WALL

*Walls have ears, and fences eyes.* – Cyprus proverb

It was a relief to be at the Slab again. The trip to Buffavento made one feel as though autumn were on its way. At the Slab it was full summer, a full complement of diplomats, gin bottles and swimming and dogs, although we kept wary eyes on Mustapha if Charlie was with us. Conversations were mixed in with drinks and dunks in the sea to cool off, when sitting or lying on the Slab became too hot. It was a beautiful life, but haunting everyone's mind was the shadow of the future. *When* would it happen? *Where* would it happen? *How* would life change for us—officers, wives, children, Greek friends and Turkish friends. The Greek Cypriots had already given up bathing for the year: for them the summer was over. Kadir was still racing around in his motorboat, the only disturbance visible or audible from the Slab. In the great vastness of the sea and its endless endlessness, it was only a gnat. Through the August haze, the coast of Turkey was rarely visible, but some days would be crystal clear, and there *loomed* Turkey, we now said, instead of *appeared*. The very nearness seemed to be threatening. And Greece was only hours away. But for us, it was still summer; for the children, the specter of school loomed.

Dick Welch, the voice of us all, was also there. "Well," he said, picking up his towel and throwing it over his shoulder, "I guess I'll wrap up this day. Maybe this summer. Got to prepare for a hard winter." He spoke as though he lived in Maine, or Canada, or somewhere where a hard winter was soon to follow, instead of living on a Mediterranean island where September was still summer, and October and November were more like New England's September. But we all knew what he meant. We shifted uncomfortably.

I saw Kadir climb down to the Slab from his house. I

hadn't noticed the absence of the roaring motorboat. I didn't even know where he kept it. Now, I thought, is my chance to ask him about his ancestors. I moved higher up the rocks to where he sat, a kind of observation post looking down on the rest of us on the Slab.

"Hello, Kadir...How long do you keep your boat going? I mean, when do you stop using it for the year?"

"Greetings, Arlene...Oh, it depends upon my mood, or when all of you leave the Slab for the summer. I like being here among you, you know."

"Without your Slab, we'd be sitting on rocks, and we couldn't sit very long, so we wouldn't have this perpetual cocktail party. I don't even like them in Nicosia, but it's different here. I guess we don't have to be on our best behavior. Don't you think?" I wondered if he liked the round of cocktails in the capital. He was invited, of course, because of his hosting the Slab.

"I guess I don't put myself in your position," Kadir responded. "I like them. After all, we haven't been so *free* for many years." He knew I knew what he was talking about—the fight for Independence. But I was always wary of discussing it, knowing the British had used the Turks, and therefore insisted that they have thirty percent representation for an eighteen percent minority. That was the root of the problem, wasn't it?

I took another tack, changing what was foremost in my mind—*What do you think is going to happen*? Instead, I said, "Kadir, has your family been here...forever?" What I meant, of course, was since the Turks invaded Cyprus in the 1570's.

"It is a tale out of Arabian Nights, or out of a romantic and cruel past, maybe crueler than the past and the future may be for Cyprus. All based on how the powerful man wins, the powerful country. The majority..." He paused and I saw his eyes narrow and his chin thrust forward.

"It was treachery!" said Kadir. "My ancestor was Kattirdji Tarik, Robin Hood of the East. Long ago in Smyrna, he was employed by a gentleman, and had the misfortune to fall in love with the man's daughter. They planned to elope, but his love was discovered by a fellow servant who betrayed him, and he was thrown into prison by his master. He escaped—it was near the ruins of Ephesus. He organized a band of daring men and they lay in wait for rich travelers, to rob them, or to take them for ransom, if they didn't carry sufficient goods on their persons. This highwayman of Smyrna gave to the poor. He became a famous *equalizer* of the world's wealth. He gave one thousand dowries to undowried girls, who otherwise could not marry, except as drudges. Slaves, almost. Kattirdji Tarik knew what it was to live without the world's goods!

"So he lived with the poor, ate with them, slept outside their doorsteps, he and his band of highwaymen. The poor felt saved, protected, lucky even, if Kattirdji Tarik rode into their village, and not one of them, upon pain of death, would reveal his hiding place to the Grand Vizir's men.

"Only the rich feared him. But not his treachery. Kattirdji Tarik killed no one. Nor did any of his band." I hoped that fighting dogs or anything else would not interrupt us this time. Kadir was deeply engrossed in his story, and I was completely captivated.

"Now Kattirdji Tarik got tired of being an outlaw," continued Kadir, "of being hunted, even of being admired by his people, because he was not in any real sense free. 'I will give myself up,' he said, 'in exchange for exile in Cyprus. I can never wear chains. Dungeons are not for me.'"

I saw Frank get up, wave to me, and lower himself into the sea, "See you at home," he called, meaning he was going to swim home. Kadir saw him leave, paused for a moment, then continued.

"The Caimakam and the Grand Vizir both agreed to his exile because they secretly admired Kattirdji and didn't want to see him in prison, in a dungeon, which is what it would be. I think they wished that they were as free and as loved as he. For Kattirdji was loved. Yet it was love he couldn't have because he was not equal...Anyway, he decided to give himself up. He was tired of being hunted."

"'Kattirdji has given himself up! He will go to Cyprus!' And rich men were happy and poor men in despair.

"But there was a young French consul whom Kattirdji had robbed and who wanted justice. He persuaded his ambassador who persuaded the Grand Vizir that highway robbery of diplomats, as had happened to this consul, was barbaric to a Frenchman. The bandit must be severely punished, or certain 'unpleasantries' might occur in Turkey's relationship with France." I could only think of Turkey's relationship with Cyprus, with Greece, for Cyprus was the burr under the saddle, the one buzzing mosquito that wouldn't go away and that no one could catch.

"The great Kattirdji went to Cyprus, yes, but who knew, besides the Grand Vizir and the gloating Frenchman, that he arrived in chains, chains from wrist to ankle, links five inches long, three inches wide and one inch thick. Kattirdji was chained for seven years in darkness. After seven years of never seeing the sun, he was freed to walk within those thick walls of the citadel of Famagusta. And though his chains were made lighter, he was never freed from them.

"He suffered seven years in darkness. He had never committed such treachery. And then he was allowed to walk the eastern wall of the Famagusta citadel. He could see the sea! One day, some English ladies came with their consul husbands, official visitors, to see the Venetian tower that Shakespeare had made famous and that made Othello live forever. Kattirdji had never killed anyone as Othello did, for he was a gentleman, not a barbarian. So he plucked a flower from a cranny in the wall and reached down to the ladies, extending his chained arm as much as he could to hand the red flower to them. The ladies pitied Kattirdji, still in chains, so they appealed to Azziz Pasha, who appealed to Constantinople to have him released.

"For such were the ways," said Kadir, "such *are* the ways of the world—to grant favors to friends, to yield to persuasion of power or to crush a betrayal. But he did not redress his grievance!" cried Kadir. "*Kattirdji Tarik did not redress his wrong!*"

The sentence cried in my ears!

I looked around to find that everyone had left the Slab. Time to go home, time to prepare to return to Nicosia. School would begin on Wednesday...

Returning to Nicosia brought more uneasiness than usual—there was Charlie Boy, still faithful every weekend, and there was Karakoumi. I was beginning to feel each time that I was abandoning all of them. Socrate, Mehmet, now Kadir, and the strange story of his background. There was something sinister about it. I wrapped my towel around me, stopping to pick up Frank's. The girls were already off with Kathy and John, and would now be at the cottage, hugging Charlie, preparing their scenario about taking him to Nicosia. About that, Frank and I remained firm.

He never followed our car. He simply stood there by the locked blue door, and watched us leave. Karakoumi whinnied. It was becoming as bad as leaving children.

When I returned mid-week, I noticed that the leaves of the fig tree were yellowing. Strange, I hadn't noticed before. Some leaves were already brown at the edges, curling before their fall. Soon the tree would stand naked, its house of leaves gone. The olive stood unchanged throughout the seasons. Even before harvest, the bitter fruit did not greatly change the tree's appearance, so hidden among the leaves were the small, hard, green olives.

The sky was no longer cloudless, but the haze of summer heat was gone. The rains would not begin until December. Days were lazy with warmth; the mellowing sun felt good again, though the nights were getting colder—for them, the summer had passed.

Every mid-week I came to the sea house, to ride Karakoumi, to feed Charlie Boy. Each time I had a kind of premonition that it might be the last, but for the time I was there, I could forget. Charlie accompanied me on the rides, and each time I left, he stood there looking at me intently, his tail waiting to wag, hoping for me to stay, for him not to be left, though he feared the car because of car-sickness. We had tried him in the car many times, the girls taking turns in the back of the Taunus wagon, holding up a paper bag for Charlie's vomit. The girls hoped we would weaken, and take him to Nicosia.

On the narrow access road I met a large truck with building materials: bags of cement and what looked to me like scaffolding rods. Peculiar, I thought. The truck could only be going to Tatli Sue, to Rustem's, or to our house. I knew they weren't going to our house, and didn't think Kadir was reconstructing anything at Tatli Sue. Rustem? What could he add to his square box of a house? I stopped, as a curious villager would, to see where it went. To Rustem's. Odd, I thought, and continued back to Nicosia.

I forgot about the building materials, and I forgot about Charlie. We were unable to return for two weeks, with school commitments and some Duty Cocktails. When we went back to our sea house, Nahim Bey was there, sitting in his car at the edge of a field, and on their hands and knees under an olive tree were four village women, digging through the stony earth.

"What are you doing?" we asked, looking at what should have been obvious, but wasn't.

"Gathering the olives." Nahim didn't move, except for his eyes, which blinked in the sun.

The women stood, and shook the tree, then dropped to

their knees again, searching through stones the same size and color as the olives.

"But why don't you get a large sheet or a big tarp, and shake the olives on that?" we asked, unbelieving what we saw.

Nahim Bey smiled his smile of infinite wisdom, and responded, "Oh, it's never done that way in Cyprus." He looked like a frog that had just caught a fly, and was pleased with himself.

We continued on towards the house. There was Charlie: he knew our schedule. And there, by Rustem's house, were piles and piles of building materials, even though we could now see that they were outside Rustem's fence, and therefore on Kadir's land.

"Who do you suppose is building something, Kemal Rustem, or Kadir?" I asked Frank.

"I don't know. But I do know something."

"What?" My curiosity was whetted.

"I do know," Frank continued, "that Kemal and Kadir have a sort of feud going on."

"Why?"

"I don't know why."

"But you can find out! Surely your intelligence is that good!"

"Yes, I can find out. If I want to." Frank was holding back.

"A need-to-know-basis, you mean?" I asked. We always had this phrase between us, when I wanted to know what was going on.

"Well, I suppose we'll see for ourselves, soon enough." Frank wouldn't say anymore.

In the following weeks the countryside was buzzing with the question of what Kemal was building. Kemal wouldn't say.

Questions and answers buzzed like bees.

What is Kemal building? What can he add to his house he never uses?

"He will add a fence," observed Estelle in Tatli Sue.

But Kemal has a fence.

"He will bring water from the sea."

But he doesn't have a swimming pool.

"He will add a beach house."

But Kemal doesn't ever go to the beach, to the sea that is not a beach but a rocky coast, and Kadir owns the land in front of Kemal's house, on the sea side.

More and more materials were unloaded. But no one knew what was to be built. Not even the truck drivers, or the men who unloaded. Not Mehmet. Not Orek. Not Fikret. Not Nahim Bey. And when the workmen began whatever it was they were beginning, still no one knew and the men said only, "A fence."

"A wall," said another.

But what for? What kind of wall, where?

On they worked, digging big holes, pouring cement, and placing two-inch vertical pipes in the cement, each of which was twenty feet high. Every four yards. It took shape. It was a "U" of metal poles on three sides of Rustem's house. Only the side away from the sea was without them. But still no one knew what it was. Kemal would not say.

One Saturday another truck came. It unloaded sheet after sheet of corrugated metal. Two more trucks came, and then there was a stack, two stacks, each fifteen feet high, of corrugated metal sheets.

"But I don't believe it," the grocer said.

"Believe what?"

"What he is going to do."

"Who is 'he'?"

"Kadir."

"What is Kadir going to do?"

"He is building a fence. An opaque fence."

"But it is Rustem's house. Why is Rustem building an opaque fence?"

"It is not Rustem; it is Kadir who is building the fence. Kadir is building a no-see-through fence in front of Rustem's house."

"But why is Kadir building a no-see-through fence in front of Rustem's house?"

"Because it is on Kadir's land," they said, seeing but not seeing. And when we all saw the fence grow and when we saw the sea go away from Kemal's house, and the land go away, with nothing to see but corrugated metal from the house's big window-eyes, we did not see what we saw because we didn't believe it, and seeing something truly requires a belief in what one sees—that it is to be a certain way, and that because a tulip is appointed with one long thin stem, it is not a rose.

Rustem never came to the sea the entire time the wall was building, and Kadir was nowhere to be found.

When the wall, which could no longer be called a fence, but a wall, was completed, it was two sheets of metal high, each sheet big enough to shelter a car, and it was two hundred yards on three sides, and Kemal could just as well have stayed in Nicosia with his windows shut as come to Kyrenia to see the sea.

Now crowds of people came to look, and our quiet sea house was invaded every weekend by people, including the diplomatic community, and Greek and Turkish Cypriots alike from Nicosia—people not used to coming to the Slab, or even to Kyrenia. They came to stand and stare, and to say, "I don't believe it, that a man would spend that much money to spite his neighbor," meaning that there must have been cheaper ways. And some said it was because Kemal sent his bills too late, which was true, as everyone knew, but in this case, they said that Kadir had declared a Statute of Limitations on a two-year-late bill from Kemal for some law books, perhaps for the very books which told Kadir he didn't have to pay.

And the fence cost more than the entire bookstore, Dick Welch said. But some said it was because Kadir wanted to buy Kemal's land, and Kadir did, after all, own the land whereon the fence was built, and if Kemal's house had no sea view, why would Kemal want it? Maybe he *would* sell. To Kadir, of course.

The British Military Attaché said that there must be a law against a spite fence, but others said that Kadir knew the law, or maybe he knew that the Greeks would not resort to the courts in a case between Turks who usually settled disputes in their own ways. After all, there were enough problems on the island without inter-ethnic disputes.

I remembered the story that Kadir had nearly told me not so long ago, and now I was wondering why Dick had asked me to ask him. Kadir had told me the most improbable story, I thought. And now, maybe the story explained the fence. Maybe down deep inside Kadir, it was a way of getting even, *redressing Kattirdji's wrongs.*

Not so very many weeks later, the winds blew hard across the sea, a quick early season storm. No one saw the wind blow down the wall, but there were new sheep shelters throughout the countryside, new carports, new lean-tos for storage— all made from corrugated metal sheets.

Perhaps the wind itself had spoken. Judged.

"Kyria, the telephone, please, is for you." Savvas had returned from his afternoon off, so it must have been five o'clock. I took the telephone upstairs.

"Yes? Who? Oh, in Kyrenia. You mean it's Fikret?"

I didn't have a chance to wonder why Fikret would call, or even wonder how many occasions he had ever had to use a telephone. His news was alarming.

"You mean, very sick?"

"Yes, Kyria. Very bad, Kyria. Very bad."

"But, how do you know? I mean, what is happening?"

"On her back, Kyria, rolling all over the stable. Skin gone on her head. Very sick."

"All right, Fikret. I'll come. I'll be there."

So much for that dinner party. What a lovely excuse, and except for worry about the pony, I nearly giggled with pleasure at the thought of not being present at the party of the Armenian dentist who cultivated diplomats and was suffered by the Cypriots, Greek and Turk alike. But the island did need dentists, and he was one of the best.

Michalakis Petris, the island's chief veterinarian, loved horses. That I knew. He had studied veterinary medicine in Ireland, of all places, where he'd fallen in love with horses. Big, beautiful red Irish hunters. And now he had to take care of donkeys, and goats.

Yes, he said he could go. Would go. Could he follow in his car, so that if I had to spend the night, he could come back?

Yes, of course. But I couldn't imagine why I would have to stay the night. Not that I minded. I would much rather be in the old Turkish farmhouse under the solid eye of the mountains than be forever turning in the endless who's-who diplomatic stare, the pastime of Nicosia. I often thought that we really ought to live in Kyrenia, but the sea house was too simple, too small, too inconvenient to do the entertaining that Frank and I had to do.

"Frank," I said, ringing him at his office and trying not to sound excited, "I can't go to that dinner tonight. Fikret just called to say that the pony is terribly sick, and Mike Petris will go with me at seven. Says I may have to stay the night. He thinks it is colic..." I waited for Frank's response, but he said nothing. "Well, I have called to give my regrets, and to say why. I hope it's OK, but honestly, the way people treat animals around here, I'm not sure they'll understand." Then I remembered how long the island had been British and wondered if perhaps even the Cypriots had dog cemeteries by now. Still, it wasn't likely they'd understand.

"Well, if you have to. But I'll hope you'll be back in time. Call if you aren't."

"Back in time? I won't even get there until the time we are due for dinner. Don't count on me."

I drove the grey Taunus wagon around the outskirts of the Venetian walls, past two bastions. The state veterinary clinic was just outside the third bastion, a row of long stone buildings containing some stalls, delivery stables, all very primitive, and in winter and early spring—the busiest time, when the lambs arrived—mired in a bog of mud. But now it was October, the time of the most perfect Cyprus weather. Dry and green-gold, but not the color of a New England autumn: the gold in Cyprus is the color of the earth and stones, and the rosiness of the sun is no longer scorching and sticky.

"Kali Spera, Mike!" I would rather have called him "Michalakis," but he preferred "Mike." He could at least have been Michael.

"Spera, Kyria."

"Arlene!" I said, but he resisted calling me by my first name.

"Yes, now, about this horse?"

"It's a village pony. Lovely, thought to be out of a thoroughbred and a village mare. The man who looks after her says she is rolling all over the stable. On her back."

"Could be very bad. Acute colic. She must have had some bad greens."

Yes, I thought. Now I knew. The chopped straw diet of all Cypriot ruminants would have astounded my father. To think that a good horse ate such poor fare when even his straw for bedding was richer than what the best of the Cypriot horses ate. Chaff is what he would call it. So the greens bought at market—*Trafilli*, like clover but without flowers, tied in small bundles—are a necessary addition. The greens must be bought daily because in only one day they heat, in the process of beginning to decay, and the heat causes gas. Fikret knew better than to feed day-old greens. A farmer-shepherd himself.

"Well, let's go." Mike took a pail, a pump, horse-sized syringes, some assorted bottles of medication.

Following the narrow road out through the Turkish sector, a series of small Turkish villages and their cafés always full of men drinking coffee, playing backgammon, or just watching whoever passed by. They were very friendly. And didn't object to Western women in their coffee houses. Their own women were clustered here and there in front of doorsteps, chairs facing the road, spinning as they always did, with a single round weight which twisted the wool as it was dropped, endlessly and endlessly, leaving their eyes free to wander over the plateau of their known world, which was really the faces of the neighboring women and their men in coffee houses. Faces they had known every day of their lives.

Across the Mesaoria, the grain belt had returned to its moon crust appearance, after the green and gold flowering of early spring. As we rose towards the mountains, the plains looked more and more like an enormous crater, ridged around the north and south by mountains.

I thought of the division in my life in Cyprus, half sea-cottage, half Nicosia: a marble-floored house with a butler versus a mud-brick cottage, visible to two Crusader castles with encircling eagles and a rock hand with fingers I constantly reached out to touch. But I had been close once, and remembered that only by distance were they clearly visible, and distance kept me aware of my own inability to really see. Each time I descended from the mountains to the sea, I was just stepping into Eden with the full knowledge that I would never really know it.

Then we were in Kyrenia, passing through the village, turning right a half-mile beyond, and then left towards the sea, past the carob grove, and maybe past Mehmet with his flock. Then the acacias and the whitewashed house shuttered in blue. No whinnying greeted me as usual, and Fikret was not there.

Mike close behind me, we sprang from our cars to the garage-made-stable. I was not as prepared for what we saw as Mike was. The skin was gone from Karakoumi's hipbones, eye sockets, anywhere a bone protruded from her roundness, from her barrel of a body. Her breath came in agonies, her eyes were glazed.

"But, what on earth...?"

Mike knew my question. "It's the distention and the pain it causes. We've got to get her up at once...if we can." Pulse, heartbeat, breathing: all registered, and at once two pint-sized injections from the horse-sized syringes. "Here, now help," Mike said as he pulled on her legs to roll her over, like a barrel butter churn upside down. "Now you pull on her tail. Hard. Harder... Pull!"

Mike nearly lifted the pony. We got her up. "Now halter her. Now walk. Lead her," and he slapped her, pushed, poked her hind quarters with a hayfork. "Got to get her walking. Look, if she were a sheep I'd knife her, to relieve the air, right in the belly. But horses get infection too easily. She wants to be on her back because it relieves the pressure. At the same time it twists the intestines, and it can cause strangulation and acute infection. She has to be kept up, if at all possible. You'll have to stay here all night. Inject her every three hours with alternate medications: an antibiotic and an anti-colic. Here, I'll show you how."

Mike took the syringe and drew out the stopper. "Forty cc's of each. If you can't get the needle into her neck at least an inch," and he showed me the needle the size of a ten-penny nail, "take the needle out of the syringe and hit her with it. Hard. She won't object. She is too sick."

Mike looked intensely at me, searching for my assurance that I could do it. How could I not?

"Okay?" he asked. "Just remember this: her life depends upon it. Even then, good luck. I'll be back tomorrow morning. At seven."

He drove off into the mountains' purple dusk. It was only eight-thirty. But the darkness would come quickly. And no moon. How many nights, moonlighted nights, had I ridden Karakoumi across the stones by the sea, along the pathways to villages, and back down to the sea?

So far, the pony was still standing. Walking a little. Walk. Walk. Push. Pull. It was easy. To begin with. *If she must lie down, and she will, and if you can't get her up, KEEP HER OFF HER BACK.* I heard my instructions still. I heard the sea below as well, the flickering sound of its tidelessness. It was calm. Warm. I could get a blanket from the house later, if I needed it. But now, I wrapped the halter rope around my waist and leaned into it, back and forth, slowly. Stars became brilliant. The Milky Way thickened, intensified by the moon's absence. The noise of the world was only the breathing of the pony and the sea's insistence.

When Karakoumi collapsed, I did as I was told: kept

her on her side. Never on her back. Injections. Afraid of hurting, I pushed gently, at first, with a certain amount of courage, and found that it took more strength. Finally, it took a full sword-thrust with the naked needle, and then I fitted the syringe back into that sword. For a few moments I slept on a beach chair from the house, and finally covered myself with a blanket. More injections. Roll her over. All night. But finally out of weariness, I slept. And awakened in the dawn.

Despite my weariness and the mid-morning chill, I felt more useful than I had felt for most of my life... How long since I had been up at dawn? It had been a long time, and then only when the girls were sick, or we were arriving in Europe from a night flight, feeling rumpled and disagreeable, the children and I, cranky and sleep-dusted. I saw the sea turn to glass, reflecting a pink silhouette with five points on a pale canvas. I touched the air with my hands as I heard so faintly, I was certain, the *pipes*. He, Pan, had played for the lamb entangled in the rose brambles—that time I'd heard it too. Had he played for Karakoumi while I slept? I was getting a little *loco*, as my down-to-earth father would have said.

Groggily I looked around into the stillness. The breathing was still there, an enormous breathing machine, and so attuned were my ears that my total consciousness had been within a moving mass of breath: in and out. But how long had I been there? It was five A.M.

Coffee first. I opened the latch door of the house, and swung open the two panels. Through the corridor, past the climbing night-blooming cactus and into the kitchen, remembering vaguely the adder that had been under the sink. But now I had Charlie Boy as well, and it had been in the spring... Nescafé was all I had. No milk. Only now did I remember that I hadn't eaten dinner. In the refrigerator was a lonely pomegranate, and some butter.

Seven o'clock. Mike should be coming. I had given up

rousing the pony. Impossible, now. Then I heard the car on the gravel as I dozed in a circle of pomegranate seeds. Pithy. No wonder the girls had left that one. Mike had someone with him.

"How is she?"

"I don't know. Still breathing. But I can't get her up anymore. She is on her side, and I did inject her every three hours. Tough skin."

Mike laughed. "I told Kiki I'd left you here with a sick horse all night, and she was horrified. She can't imagine why American women, and English women," he quickly remembered, "do such things."

We turned our attention towards Karakoumi. The two men got her up and supported her for Mike's arm-length entrance into her intestines. "All twisted," he said. "Worse than I thought."

They pumped and worked and hosed. The pony collapsed, a knee-buckling fall. "Look, it's not your fault, Arlene. You did what you could. Stay with her this morning, same routine. Inject her at eleven. I'll be back at one o'clock."

I was bone-weary, but somehow the experience called up my reserves, as did the strangeness of being where I was, alone, wondering why I spent so much of my time at cocktail parties. However, I had met Mike and his wife, Kiki, at one of them. And the Armenian dentist. And Nikos Sampson, who had scanned me, as he did all women, from top to toe, appraising something he hoped was for sale because he believed that everything has a price.

I fell asleep in the beach chair and awakened in the hot sun, perspiring. Eleven o'clock. I prepared the needle, and the courage to drive it into the flesh of the neck. Jabbed. Karakoumi's eyelid fluttered as she raised her head ever so slightly, life signs slowly awakening, flickering. I helped, tugged, cheered, encouraged, yelled, a lump rising in my throat. I cried joyfully at these signs as Karakoumi struggled to get up. I cried as she made it, stood like a newborn on shaky legs, head drooping. I wanted to give her coffee, rolls, wanted to dance together, Charlie and Karakoumi and I. Charlie whined and wagged his tail.

Mike Petris arrived at noon, saw the pony standing: "She made it!" And his voice was husky: "Look, I'll show you what I brought."

He led me to his car, and out of the glove compartment he drew a pistol. "I was convinced that I would have to use it. Worried about what to do with you when I did. I've had to use it many times. When there is no chance. I gave that pony one in a thousand, really...You know how I love those creatures?" he asked, but it was not a question.

It was over. I remember only that in my joy and fatigue, I could say nothing. Nothing relevant.

"But why did you study in Ireland?" I asked in my daze. "Why not in Australia where they have more sheep? Or Scotland? There are no horses to speak of on Cyprus."

"I didn't choose it, Kyria. The British government sent me." He seemed relieved to have something to say other than what he too was feeling.

"Oh, you had a scholarship?" I queried. I had never understood why he who loved horses so much was tending sheep.

"I suppose you could say that."

"They just recognized what the best damned vet ever could do for the island, though they needed you in Britain, I know."

"Well, it was a sort of debt of honor."

"How do you mean?" I realized that we were getting close to something that mattered

"Well, I thought you probably knew," Mike continued. Everybody does...My father was chief veterinarian here, before independence, you know. We felt sort of British, I guess, and

certainly were, in terms of our education. My father was reading to his kids one night. Bedtime stories. Funny thing—it was
*Black Beauty.* I was on his lap. A shot shattered glass. My father
crumpled under me. Died immediately.

I was stupefied. "But who? Why?"

"The island was threatened with hoof and mouth dis-
ease. My father had ordered the killing of all newborn lambs
that season...One irate shepherd..."

"Was he...?" I interrupted.

"Greek." Mike answered my unasked question.

"Oh, I see." But I didn't see. "How old were you?"

"Six."

"My God. I'm, I'm sorry."

"Kyria, I must go. Take care of that pony now. And
speak to that shepherd about his greens. His fault, you know...
And you did a good job!" he called to me as he drove off. I
stood there very tired, and with a somehow tarnished victory.

# THE STATUE OF MARKOS DRACOS

"Morning, Frank," I said at breakfast, hoping that he would notice that I was wearing white tennis clothes. "Time to get back into the game, like Alicia. I've found my racket and she's found her ball."

"Morning, Arlene. Starting tennis again?" I hadn't played since Kennedy's death.

"It's about time, don't you think?"

"Good idea...By the way, how is your game these days?" Frank inquired.

"Well, Nikos promised we'd play one. A game, I mean. But my playing isn't great. I wish I could play tennis without having to serve. I just can't judge when to hit the ball after I've thrown it up. I keep thinking I ought to throw it higher and then I'd have more time to decide as it comes down...So how's *your* game?"

"Livelier and livelier." Frank paused, fingering his big breakfast tea cup, blue and white with quiet English pastoral scenes.

"Arlene, don't play tennis today."

"Why not?"

"Because an EOKA Hero's statue was bombed last night."

"But, why?"

"Something inevitable, because of the *Proposals*. The Turks had to make some gesture of protest."

"How could Makarios have announced those Proposals, just like that?" I asked, knowing perfectly well why, but in the useless gesture of wondering why, I would get the known answer.

"Can you stop the wind from blowing, Arlene? Makarios does it because he wants to equalize the vote of Greek vs. Turkish Cypriots to that of actual population. Who wouldn't?

But he can't. Unless he wants to invite trouble with Turkey. But he can try."

"Frank, do you think, do you think that this is the...the beginning of..."

Frank interrupted me: "Now don't get worried about this. Anything could be the beginning, and yet the beginning, so-called, could be far away."

"Frank, you've already told me you think it will be soon...that the Proposals will ignite..." will ignite this storm into a hurricane, call upon buried hatred, forgotten wounds. Nothing is so shallowly buried as hatred; nothing sprouts so easily, needing only a little scratching to make it grow to full bloom. To make Mikalakis hate Sabri and Mehmet, to make Mehmet fear Socrate. Fear and hate are Siamese twins, I thought, remembering the donkey ride to Buffavento.

Frank stood up to leave, and leaned over to put his hand on my arm and repeated, "Don't play tennis today."

"Why not?"

"It was the statue near the courts."

"You mean, the *Markos Drakos?*"

"That's the one," Frank answered.

"I'm playing anyway. I don't care. Look, I've got an appointment with Nikos."

"He will understand why you don't come."

"Now, look, Frank. This is the first time, since... Anyway, you can't order me not to."

"I could. But I won't. You know the situation here. Judge for yourself." Frank left the table, and I heard the front door close softly. His large teacup, which was always filled at breakfast, year after year, country after country, was never emptied. And there it was, again half full of tepid tea. Today it was left almost hot.

I went anyway. Nikos was waiting for me.

This time, living in Cyprus, I swore to learn tennis. I think it was the courts themselves that convinced me, located as they were in the former moat of the citadel built by the Venetians five hundred years ago to keep out the marauding Turks. Walls encircled the small town then, three miles in diameter, with three gates and eleven bastions wedged deeply into the circle. Around the entire wall was an empty moat, now used as playgrounds, promenades, and the tennis courts. Sometimes you could see laundry hanging in one of the bastions in the Turkish quarter.

The walls were thick and ominous: dark, threatening. Was it the knowledge of the 20,000 citizens put to the sword after the city fell to the Turks in 45 days? Or was it thinking of Marc Antonio Bragadino, the Venetian general who held out against General Mustapha in the citadel of Famagusta for a whole year, a feat known as one of the great acts of military leadership in the annals of European history? The walls always made me remember this event, how with his surrender, Bragadino and his small band were guaranteed safe passage to Crete. But the "guarantee" was treachery instead. His lieutenants slaughtered, some specialties were reserved for Bragadino: his ears and nose were cut off, he was beaten, then hung like a bell, for all to see. But that wasn't enough: still alive, noble Bragadino was dragged to the town center, tortured to the beat of drums, and flayed alive. His body was stuffed with straw, dressed in his uniform and medals, paraded in the streets of Famagusta, then hung aloft on a ship and transported as a gift to the ruling Sultan in Constantinople.

Such knowledge made the walls heavier, weighted down with grief.

Nikos himself was another incentive to learn tennis—he was a local fireman who knew about the layers of Cyprus. In addition, the lessons were free because Nikos wished to retain his amateur status. He enjoyed his position—winning from doctors, lawyers, diplomats, government officials, when he himself was a fireman. He was acceptable to all ranks because he excelled in something, whereas I was acceptable because I was the Wife of Somebody.

Nikos was somebody because of his skill. As were the government leaders of Cyprus. They had *become* by being heroes of the Resistance, which had won them their freedom from Great Britain. To the British who had served here, they had been nothing but assassins and terrorists. The dead ones had their statues erected; the living ones had government posts. There were no British heroes.

"Kali Mera, Nikos. Today's the day. My first game." It was, after all, my thirty-first lesson.

"Yah Sas, Kyria. I hope we finish it," Nikos replied.

"Well, it won't take you long to finish me. Probably six-love in six minutes."

But I knew what Nikos meant. I had read the *CYPRUS MAIL* after Frank left: *Georkadzis, Minister of Interior (a live EOKA hero called Houdini because of his numerous escapes from the British) arrived on the scene after the explosion and "condemned the barbarous and cowardly act" but called on people to remain calm in the face of the obvious provocation.*

The honored effigy of Markos Drakos almost peered over into the tennis courts—it was a realistic bronze representation of the young man, rifle in hand, in guerrilla outfit, perched on a marble base in the center of a nondescript square of cement, not even square-shaped, probably a leftover from the demolition of tasteless or even bombed buildings.

Markos Drakos had been a twenty-two-year-old clerk of a mining company when Grivas arrived in Cyprus, and began his push for *Enosis*—Union with Greece—by indoctrinating the youth in terrorist policies and tactics. Marcos Dracos became Grivas' best disciple—he carried out the most successful sabotage attacks, and became Grivas' bodyguard and leader of a group of guerillas based near the Kykko Monastery.

Upon his death by British ambush, schoolchildren went on strike to mourn him: *Markos Drakos, beloved of the gods... Troodos is in silence, the wind still, the birds mourn with their stilled song...*

In the shadow of his statue, I learned tennis with Nikos. Nikos had time and he had patience. And today, I thought of what I had learned from him about this island since I had been here—about the shards of scores of civilizations upon every pathway and road, under every turned-over stone. *A race advancing on the East must start with Cyprus. A race advancing on the west must start with Cyprus.* Ptolemies, Alexander, Darius, Sargon, Coeur de Lion. The Lusignans, Venetians, Turks. The English. Now, the Americans?

Was there even one great civilization of the past that had not had some contact with Cyprus? How many mixtures of races and blood must run in the veins of the Greek Cypriot. But they insist there is only one: Greek! They long for a Motherland most of them have never seen, and from which they were never torn because they had never belonged to Greece. Their *Greekness* was mythical.

"We have only until ten o'clock," Nikos announced.

"What happens at ten?"

"A demonstration."

Oh. So it was arranged. I might have known. A spontaneous demonstration. Scheduled. Well, I would have a good view.

I played well. Out of some fear, some anger, some frustration, all prodding my adrenalin.

"You're good today, Kyria." Even Nikos noticed it, but how couldn't he notice even the slightest improvement? I was not an instinctive tennis player. Thiry-love. Thirty-thirty.

Forty-thirty.

"Bravo! Kyria."

And then, *it* began.

Shouting in the distance, coming from every direction. A distant hive of honey bees, coming closer and closer. Nikos' face was still. "That's all, Kyria."

He shook hands. Was it an after-the-match handshake? Or good-bye? Was he off to join his gang? Well, I was a captive audience—I wouldn't be able to drive my car through the marchers if I tried. Nor would I dare, I thought, with a slight chill.

The marchers approached the maimed statue—only the marble base was cracked—from every direction. It was not really a mob scene at all. School children, in their smocks with the big white bow typical of them all, and flags, blue banners. Not Cypriot flags, which represented the present divided government. There were high-school-age boys, fourteen to eighteen led by schoolmasters, and some priests in their flowing black robes and stovepipe hats with knots of hair visible behind them. The girls came too, as participants, not spectators. The marchers came purposefully. Group by group, they kept coming, blue and white flags flying from their hands—blue and white stripes, with a white cross in a blue square in the left top corner. If their flags and banners had been changed to red, they would have looked Turkish. There would have been no difference. The difference was in what I remembered, what I had learned:

*Greek Cypriots regard Cyprus as an integral part of Greece, historically, linguistically, socially, culturally...Byzantium was Greek in Christian apparel...Dispute between Eastern and Western Churches, Christianity and Islam, kept the conquerors distinctly apart. Therefore blood remained undiluted.* I heard Grivas' words: *Cyprus commands, and not the family.* Just like the Communists in the Poland we had just left.

I stood, trying to put my tennis racket into my press, fumbling, climbing on top of the near bastion, where I would have a perfect view of the statue and the oncoming marchers. On they came, hundreds of them, still buzzing, but not roaring, as I had expected. Reasonably organized. And then the "business meeting" of the marchers began. Uniformed men, six of them, wreaths in hand, passed their way to the foot of the statue's cracked base. One of them raised his arm to silence the crowd.

"Greeks!" he began. "Our heroes have been cursed, shamed in the streets. Humiliated in front of God."

Absolute hush fell over the crowd.

"We are an honorable people, we descendents of Homer, the House of Teucer. We are the children of Aphrodite, who was born full-blown off Paphos on the sacred rock. Our nation sailed the seas, bringing light to the dark disbelievers, to the *barbari*."

Pause, while the implications of *barbari* raised the tempers of the crowd. God! I thought, he means those who don't speak Greek are the *Barbarians*. That included me. From ancient Greek beliefs, from Homer. Maybe I owed my Greek Professor more than I realized.

"How has our nation, Mother Greece, our Mother, taught her children?"

"She has taught her children honor!" the crowd echoed back, weakly at first, and then again, led in unison. And again, more loudly: "She has taught her children honor!"

The speaker raised his hands in the air for silence. "You have been suckled by the running waters of heroic acts and now you spring up active from a holocaust...Are we born to serve honor?" Grivas' words again, I knew.

*Timi!* they shouted. "Honor!" they cheered.

"Our hero here, Markos Drakos, his memory has been defiled! He served me, you, every one of you standing here. He gave you liberty. He gave you freedom"... Pause. The speaker kept his eye on his crowd. "Do you know what he did for you? Do you know he saved you from tyranny? His heart was shot out for it. He paid his price. For each of you! His blood should be on us; he should anoint us all with the price he paid, if we do not avenge this act."

His face grimaced, his teeth ground in anger, his eyes swept the crowd. Both fists thrust upwards to hit the sky. And school children stiffened their spines; their arms shot upwards with their Greek flags. The hum of bees became a swarm, then the deepening buzz of bumble bees. The speaker waited for the converging rumbles of locusts, the deafening shrill of cicadas. He had them.

The crowd had been shaped into a single roar. My God, here he was: Mark Anthony in the market place, turning a chipped piece of marble base into the open wounds of Caesar. Soon they would be dipping their fingers in it, anointing themselves.

"At the price of our blood? Will we serve honor at the price of our blood?" The speaker's voice had reached crescendo.

A roar went up. *Timi! Timi! Malista! Malista!* Honor! Honor! Yes! Yes! Honor bought with blood!

Honor. Yes, Honor, I repeated to myself.

"Greeks, liberty is won with blood." It was the slogan of Grivas' indoctrinated school children in the early Fifties. Here *were* Grivas' schoolchildren, still. They had never changed! The EOKA fighters were continuing Grivas' business, and here was the next wave of terrorists, with their PEKA schoolmasters and priests.

The slogan was picked up, chanted, spit into the air. It fed upon itself. The slogan dripped with age-old heroism: the spilling of blood, the cleansing power of blood, the ultimate sacrifice.

The crowd was on its own, the youthful minds inflamed

with the nobleness of youth serving honor. Glory of country, pure and clean. Did they understand that the speaker meant blood, their blood? "We are young. If we allow dishonor in our youth..." But the speaker didn't need to finish. The crowd was a hurricane of voices, locusts on their way to consume the earth: *Eleftherios! Freedom! Liberty! Enosis! Honor! All!* They would have it all.

They could not understand the price. Such boys and girls as these, only five years earlier, had accused Savvas Menacas of left-wing sympathies, tied him to a tree in the churchyard of his village, Lefkoniko, and beaten him to death, in front of his wife. Four years earlier, such children had seized Zacharias Karaphotias in his village of Ayios Amrosios, soaked him with gas, and lighted him. In front of his wife. His fault was not to support EOKA brutalities. I looked up at the once-peaceful bastion, now blurred by my own tears which rebuked my responding heart, and I knew that Grivas had returned to complete his unfinished business and the children were again on the march. And I remembered that four hundred years before, the very bastion I stood on had been built for war.

ALICIA STRONG

The siren over the city of Nicosia was not unusual. Today
for the second time the wailing sound, mournful and arresting,
was heard. People stared at the police van, wondering where
it would stop this time. It pulled up next to an abandoned lot
by Pourgouris Grocer, and the shoppers watched, wondering
what there was of interest in an abandoned lot.

The Greek Police were very excited, very nervous, their
conversation static in the air. Never was there such a big one,
they said. There must be fifty pounds of dynamite! They were
not able to cope with it. The British army must be called in.
They no longer ruled Cyprus, but they had been allowed two
sovereign bases during the Tri-Partite Agreements.

The British Military Attaché was informed and called
to the British military base of Akrotiri. The demolition squad
would arrive within one hour. The Cypriot police stood guard,
at a great distance. The street was cordoned off. Who knew
if the bomb might be timed? And what group of terrorists
was responsible for this one? One of the five Turkish Cypriot
militant groups or one of the five Greek Cypriot ones? No one
would ever know.

The squad arrived. Four men calmly carried a heavy
net of metal chain mail and threw it over the bomb. They set
to work to detonate it, working through the interstices of the
net, then suddenly stopped working, threw off the net, picked
up the bomb with bare hands, one man placing two fingers
and a thumb into three holes of the 'bomb,' and rolled it to
the Greek police. The police stood solidly, but nervously. And
then flushed. Who should laugh first to see the finger holes
staring at them like empty eyes, and the embossed initials, *AS* ?

Only the Americans had a bowling alley, so the *bomb*
was detonated there and the explosion rocked the island, but
*this* time only with laughter. Everyone at the American Embassy

knew that Alicia Strong's bowling ball, in its carrying case, had been stolen from her car.

"Now who in Cyprus would want my bowling ball when there is no Cypriot bowling alley?" was her indignant question.

Everyone on Cyprus knew Alicia Strong, sooner or later. The flamingo of the American Embassy, even of the entire diplomatic corps, twittered brilliantly in the great social whirl of service to her country. What service there was to perform she would find, or make. How many women, after all, wanted to chair the great fund-raising enterprises staged by American Embassy women abroad, staged out of their inner Puritan need for a pure conscience and an assuaged guilt?

American wives were collectively guilty for all sorts of reasons: for the fact that they could not *have* as graciously as their European counterparts could so well *have* and *hold*. Guilty because they imported grocery items not available locally and because they indulged their children with car pools, birthday parties, and schools founded whenever one was lacking. Guilty for having their own club and swimming pool and bowling alley, for being so many in number and having cars so large. Guilty for drinking whiskey more than wine and not caring. Guilty for having clothes more serviceable than chic and for having tastes so utilitarian.

But few wanted to chair the events that needed to be chaired in order for them to do the things which were necessary for them all, the dedicated enterprises to which each would contribute time, money, and with those contributions achieve a measured peace, an absolution.

Thus it was that Alicia was useful to them all, Alicia who was not representative of their approved standards, who wore her flowing dresses with a flair, who dressed every day as though she were going somewhere that mattered, rouged two little spots on her doll face, and painted her cupid mouth that would say more words that day than all the other Embassy wives put together. Alicia had no children to speak to or with. She combed out her thinning blonde hair and eked it out with scarves and turbans, swishes and swirls! And became known forever as "Mrs. Charity Ball," pronounced just the way Alicia said it, quick on the tongue with a twinkling eye, sounding like a Southern name for a Grand Dame.

Alicia created the Charity Ball as an avenue for her natural talents while her willing helpers helped for charity's sake. "It is going to be the greatest diplomatic ball that ever hit the island!" Twenty-five hundred tickets were going to be sold to the aspiring guests from the ranks of the diplomatic corps and the Cyprus government. Posters of glamorous evenings propagandized the community for weeks in advance. Her spirit was indomitable, her horizons illimitable, her persuasion engulfing. Her army of Embassy women combed every merchant in Nicosia, Kyrenia, Limassol, Famagusta and Larnaca for lottery gifts. The biggest persuasion was a car. She shamed, flattered, cajoled merchants, using one against the other to give, give, give! Give to the Charity Ball, come to the Charity Ball, biggest social event in the history of independent Cyprus. Give to the Charity Ball and the Charity Ball would give to charity, those charities named and approved by the Government of Cyprus, although no member of the committee had ever visited them or knew their needs. But one could assume that the needs for charity on an Eastern Mediterranean Isle would naturally be great. After all, it had been at war with the British for four years, up to its independence, and that had come only two years ago.

Finally, in the Ledra Palace Gardens the romantic music of the band drifted over the soft summer night, the scent of honeysuckle pungent in the air already pungent with the perfume of two hundred ladies. Alicia's red chiffon streamed after her, while she steered the evening as Mistress of Ceremony, to the perfection she had longed for, the prominence of the Charity Ball as a one-of-a-kind event. And afterwards, Alicia' s corps of women dropped into normal obscurity, but for Alicia, high time was always after the ball—or before the ball.

Other women lived on frontiers they had to learn to cope with. Alicia created her own, and carried each one in a new-made shadow box always on display, in miniature, and framed with silvery laughter. She managed to arrange good food without a cook. Her garden: she always had a garden and she would have a garden, even in Cyprus, where no watering was allowed in summer. She could always find a gardener, having found water, but gave the appearance of having done everything herself. One could see her, in her garden, trowel in hand, gardener invisible, immaculately groomed and ask, "Where is Alicia, really?" Did anyone know?

Hugh Strong. He must be the key. He was not. He had needed a wife to make him seem bigger than he was. He succeeded, as Chief of the U.S. Information Service in Cyprus, a position that enabled him to allow his subordinates to perform if the subordinates knew how to perform at all; and if they were good, the subordinates were grateful to Hugh for his not knowing how. As Alicia was perhaps grateful to Hugh for the freedom to realize her potential as perpetual emcee, self-employed. Her cocktail parties were not dull, and she had excellent food. Whatever one can say that a diplomatic cocktail should be, hers were—a little something for everyone: multiple ambassadors, a quorum of junior officers, locals of sufficient position to be interesting to the ambassadors present. Her position through her husband's rank was enough to enable her to invite persons of any rank. Hugh had little to say, but no one noticed. Many guests were grateful not to have to talk or to be allowed, for once, to talk to each other.

Alicia knew the art of seduction, knew that everybody

basically would like to be seduced. The senses seduced, the mind beguiled. Her catering was therefore to the senses: her colors both strong and subtle. The flowers she chose were mood flowers, perhaps of the season not quite arrived but awaited, anticipated. All the senses she accounted for, prodded, awakened, but with the awakening came a lulling of them all, a pause. The world, meaning Alicia's world, was, *is* a party. And Alicia's were a momentary stay from life's everyday failures, a bright spot in the somberness of the reality on Cyprus.

So everybody came to Alicia's parties. And wondered afterwards what they had said, to whom they had spoken; but each remembered with pleasure and could not say why. Life was far too serious and Alicia had a remedy for that.

For a November party, she had chosen large yellow and white chrysanthemums, the flower of November and her birthday flower with the motto "Fidelity." The yellow ones were to remind her American guests of the college football season, taking place perhaps at that very moment in the thousands of college campuses across their homeland, and to remind the American women of their Homecoming corsages of long ago. Perhaps one of them had carried a dozen of those giant yellow chrysanthemums as beauty queen. The white ones, those pure petalled globes of honor to the saints, were for Europeans, for All Saints Day. Well, for the dead too, but she didn't know any recently bereaved guests. And the occasion was also for the British Guy Fawkes Day. All in November. Nothing too sad, everything stirring memories. What chrysanthemum meant to Cyprus, Alicia didn't know. The mums were only a memory scent, she thought, having no scent of their own.

To eat, there were shrimp on toothpicks looking like miniature turkeys, red pimento for the cockscomb. And roasted turkey—imported American ones. And there was a native specialty for every nationality invited because Alicia wanted each guest to feel special, and to feel a general thanksgiving.

Alicia was feeling particularly cheerful, particularly happy, with not only the preparations but also the beginning of her party. It was going well. The guests were lively and re-laxed. All was well, wasn't it, more or less in the world? They, as American diplomats particularly, had at last a President not only loved in the world, touted by Europe, worshipped by Cypriots, but glamorous as well. Glamour in the White House! A beautiful, elegant First Lady—after all the dumpy first ladies they'd been forced to tolerate as diplomats abroad, who had embarrassed her. Once she had been asked, to her own mortification, why Mamie Eisenhower was called by that name, that *prenom*. And why she wore that hair style: bangs! Imagine! And God knows Bess had been no beauty. But now, the White House was an example and a challenge to any stuffy European corps of diplomats or court. No European could make her feel apologetic now.

The imminence of Cyprus' troubles were put aside, all the usual talk talk talk about them temporarily discontinued. There was too much talk about the open hostility between the Greek and Turkish communities, and Alicia was convinced that the fact of the talk was the underlying cause of the very hostility discussed. "But they both get on so well!" Alicia in-sisted. "Look at the success of the Charity Ball! If they'd let women run this country, we'd work things out, wouldn't we?" she said, nudging Mrs. Kuchuk, wife of the Turkish Vice Presi-dent, and smiling.

Kadir was there too, smiling and bowing, applauding the shrimp-on-toothpick-turkeys, drinking champagne like no true Moslem. And Glafkos and Lila—how Alicia loved to say "Glafkos" instead of "Speaker of The House." Her pink cheeks warbled names in her red mouth—her tongue enhanced them with the flourish of a laugh. Wasn't she a friend of Lila, who was not entirely accepted by the Greek Cypriot women, being Anglo-Indian as she was?

Alicia was sorry that her own ambassador had left so
early. He would have seen how well she could entertain, what
an asset she was to her husband's service. Two for the price of
one, she always said. How some women absolutely "loooved"
the foreign service, and how some loathed it. And how could
one possibly do well at the difficult job of hostess in several
countries, several languages, if one loathed it? She couldn't
imagine the incident which had happened (who could?) when
Hugh was present at a lunch for Gallo Plaza Lasso, Deputy
Director of the United Nations, and Hugh asked, "Say, why
do you know so much about Latin America?" he having been
reared in and a former president of Ecuador.

The telephone rang, but Hugh would get it. The noise
of the party was too loud, so he cupped his hand, shouting
back into the phone.

"Hugh, for heaven's sake, stop shouting. We have guests.
Here, take the phone into the kitchen!"

"Alicia!" he called from the kitchen. "Come here!"

Now what could he possibly want? She hoped that her
husband hadn't been called to the Embassy, as had happened
quite often lately. Too many guests would leave. "Alicia, look,
the Marine guard, he is notifying heads of sections."

"Well, about what?" Alicia was impatient.

"The President has just been shot—! Killed, In Texas."

"My God! That is terrible! But what are you going to
do about it? Do you have to go to the Embassy?"

"I have to make an announcement. I have to tell them.
Here. All the guests. It's what would be expected. That's my
job. I am head of the press, of public information."

"What do you mean it's your job?"

"Good God, Alicia! Don't you understand anything?
I'm head of the U.S. Information Service. I'm responsible to
the local press, the. . ." he looked wildly around him, searching
for words.

Alicia interrupted strongly. "Now look here, Hugh Strong. You are responsible to your guests as host. You are not going to break up a good party by some terrible news that they'll get in the morning's papers. They'll hear it soon enough, don't you worry."

"Alicia, do you know what you are saying?"

"I know what am saying. I always know what I am saying, and I tell you that your guests will thank you for sparing them. The bringer of bad news is unloved and unlucky here, don't you know that? I tell you, Hugh, bad news should be postponed. We are not going to be the bringers of bad news! Beware the bringers...don't you know?"

"But Alicia." Hugh was hesitant...

"Hugh, your guests will appreciate having this night, this evening, unspoiled. Come on!" She thrust her hand to his and pulled him behind her, but he, for once worthy of his responsibility, stood up against his wife and returned with his driver to the Embassy. Because he was never noticed, his departure was not either.

"Come on, Nikos!" she cried, holding up her glass. "To you!"

Nikos Sampson. She had invited him too. Most everyone disliked him, feared him, but one feeling bred the other, Alicia believed with vehemence. The British never stopped telling tales of his butchery during EOKA days, but he had nevertheless earned the grudging respect of Greek Cypriots. He had, after all, fought effectively for independence. He had helped win independence from the British Crown. He was a hero, well, to some people at least, brute that he was. And here he was, drinking champagne with her. She thrilled with pure excitement.

Nikos grabbed her by the wrist, looked into her eyes. Then shrugged, smiled, and kissed her.

"More! More!" her guests demanded. They could go

along with Alicia' s games.

"More champagne, you mean?" she warbled. "Jorgos, bring more champagne!"

"Aphrodite wasn't born here for nothing. Oh I loooove Cyprus!"

"Hear! Hear!"

"I drink to Jackie!" That was Kadir.

"To Friendship!"

"I drink to the independence of Cyprus!" That brought cheers. But they already had independence. Was someone playing with Alicia, who was not very informed on politics, on practically anything, except entertaining?

"To self-determination!" That was surely Nikos. Self-determination meant getting rid of Cyprus' constitution, hence the beginning of hostilities with the Turkish Cypriots. Nobody wanted it to happen, but nobody was doing anything to stop it. That subject was usually what everyone talked about, a subject Alicia tried so hard to subdue.

"Boo! No politics."

Her bubble nearly burst with delight. "What a 'bomb' you are, Alicia," someone cried. How everyone roared at the remembered "bomb."

"Jorgos, more champagne!" Alicia ordered.

Jorgos appeared, his white coat over his arm, wearing his street jacket. "No more champagne, Kyria."

"But Jorgos, there is another entire case in the basement chilling. Just in case. Get it quickly!"

"I go home, Kyria." His face was red and his mouth contorted. He turned to the guests and shouted, "And all of you ought to go home! Don't you know what has happened?" He pointed to the hall table. There lay a ticker tape message, under the roses, delivered long ago by a silent Embassy driver.

"What does he mean, Alicia?" The question stood still in the room. The guests stood guilty and silent, and did not know why. Only one advanced to the hall table, not eager to know what he would read.

He reddened, stared at Alicia and said two pale words, "You knew?" and was gone.

Each silenced guest straightened up and filed past the hall table. Alicia could not stay the sobered line of guests, which stiffened with the pause of reading, their assumed guilt still in the sullen air, written by the invisible hand in the visible air. They were all Belshazzars. All.

Alicia stared out into the emptied hall, and saw only white chrysanthemums.

# CHRISTMAS 1963

"By the way, we are invited to attend the annual Christmas party given by the children at the blind school," Frank said.

"What is so great about that?" I wondered.

"It is Makarios' big Christmas event. He attends, with Mikalakis, and Dolly Triantafyllides. They invited us."

Mikalakis was the Chief Justice of the Supreme Constitutional Court, and Dolly, his wife, was my good friend.

"When is it?"

"The twenty-second. About eight, I think."

"Well then, let's go."

"I knew you'd want to," Frank said. "We weren't invited last year."

"Why not?" I asked.

"Because we hadn't been here long enough. And then, there was the problem with our house — the Archbishop's house. That nearly wore out our welcome by the Archbishop before we had begun. Now we have passed muster. It's quite an honor for Mikalakis to ask us."

"So I will see the old boy first hand?"

"Not if you call him 'Old Boy.' You had better get used to saying 'Your Beatitude.'"

"Can the girls go?" I wanted them to go.

"Definitely not. This is an adult party. Except for the blind children, that is. Anyway, they got Makarios' autograph last Christmas."

So they had. And they could watch him again this year, when he visited the orphanage on Christmas Day, close to our house. Maybe, I added to my thoughts.

On the night of 20 December, two Turks were shot by Greek Cypriot police on Ledra Street, named *Murder Mile* by the British, which it had been during the days prior to Cyprus'

Independence. We all held our breaths. When now, would *it* begin, what we had been fearing, dreading, certain of its happening? Were the Turks shot for the Markos Drakos bombing? Two lives for a damaged statue?

The night of 22 December we went to the Blind School. We were introduced to Makarios. We shook hands; his were warm and grandfatherly, closing on mine in a firm comfort. His face looked directly at us: at Frank, and then at me, and back to Frank. His eyes were heavy-lidded, clouded in mystery. A Byzantine face. A secretive face. His unshorn hair wrapped into a knot protruded from under his headpiece, a stove pipe five inches high and draped with blue cloth which flowed down the back of his gown. He wore a heavy Byzantine jeweled cross suspended by a weighty gold chain, and another chain with a pendant, the enameled face of the Virgin. He held his sceptre in his left hand.

Frank and I sat behind Makarios, who was seated between Dolly and Mikalakis. His dark blue robes became his graying hair. Sitting behind him, listening to the blind children recite, dance, and play musical instruments, I only heard myself listening hard to Makarios, who sat so still, unlike a Greek. That is what was different—he was so quiet, calm, his face passive. Greeks weren't like that. I thought his breathing or his heart beat would tell me something. I imagined speaking to him.

*Your sceptre, Your Beatitude, is it the same one which was has been carried since the Fifth Century?*

*Your Beatitude, yours was an ancient civilization, sophisticated in arts, architecture, fine craftsmanship when our country's natives were in loin cloths, grinding corn with a stone.*

*You have spiritual and temporal power, in your hands, which your scepter symbolizes. Why, you could probably stop the wind from blowing.*

*Your Beatitude, listen. What if...if we, the U.S., the U.N., instead of paying for your consequences, what if we give every*

*Turkish family $50,000 and passage to Turkey? They could buy land. They would be rich. They are only 100,000 people. That could average 25,000 families, a generous estimate, considering the number of children they have. Five million US dollars. More will be spent before this war is over. Not counting blood.*

"You should propose that to the Turks."

Was that his answer to the conversation-in-my-mind? But he/I continued: *They wouldn't accept it any more than we can accept the Constitution as it is.*

*Why not?* My imagination pressed him.

*Because they would be admitting defeat, because they would be defeated, because they have lived here for nearly 500 years, and they consider this their homeland. Which, of course, we know that it is not. It is our homeland.*

*How many years do you have to live in a land for it to be "homeland?"* I asked, thinking of my grandparents, who had lived for generations in the south of Norway and who had emigrated to America in the late 1800's. Would America never be their home? Homeland? But we Americans made it ours in one or two generations. Could we possibly understand?

"When it is as long as the Greeks have lived here, it is sacred homeland. We can anoint ourselves with our earth. We call it sacred. Every stone belongs to us. We will not give up one stone. To anyone.

*Even if you may all die for it?* I didn't believe what I knew.

*Even if we all, men, women, children, all, die for it. We will be at home in our death. Our bones will rest in comfort. What does it matter that we die for it? We will be proud. We can die worse deaths than dying for our land.*

Reason could not, would not change what beat against the ribs of one's body, what was compartmented off in the brain cells: *Never to give up, give in.*

The cake was brought in. Was it a New Year's cake or

like the cake of Epiphany—Twelfth Night—when the Magi appeared with gifts? With the cake of Twelfth Night comes the end of the roaming of spirits let loose on All Saints Day, spirits seen by the villagers in phantasmagoric shapes, appeased by the simple homemade cakes dipped in honey and placed on peasant rooftops for them. Savvas told me about them. A New Year's cake is called St. Basil's cake, made of cream of wheat with sesame seeds on the outside. Somewhere inside the cake is a coín, bringing the same luck which a sixpence in a plum pudding brings to its finder.

His Beatitude rose, approached the cake, and from somwhere, seemingly nowhere, appeared a sword. Was it from the folds of his cloaks, was it handed to him on a velvet pillow, removed from the ancient relics of his ancient title? Taking the sword, he cut the cake, slowly, ceremoniously, as though he were administering to those potentially evil spirits roaming Cyprus, placating them. Here was a man with an American university degree, returned to his native folk customs.

As we departed, after our own handshakes and adieus to all, I could only think of the sword, appearing from nowhere, nowhere I had seen. A magically appearing sword to cut a Christmas cake.

I went to sleep, only to dream of a mythical sword that I was trying to pull from the middle of our small courtyard in the sea house. I was awakened by the telephone's rude ring and a voice I knew which said, "This is Wyatt Earp, reporting that there is gunfire outside of my house." Frank was on his feet and dressed in minutes. Dick Welch lived on the edge of the Turkish sector of Nicosia; we were well within the Greek sector.

I got up to put on a warm bathrobe and sheepskin slippers with the map of Cyprus embroidered on them. The floors were icy. We both opened the door of the upstairs terrace. There was the unmistaken sound of gunfire, rifles, in the distance, but coming from several locations within the walls of the citadel—our house had acoustical ears attuned to the walled city, on a hill as we were.

It was the morning of 23 December. One month after Kennedy's assassination. We were adrift and lost, sitting on a small island in the Mediterranean which had had nothing to do with our history and now everything to do with us.

It had begun...The powder had been ignited. The small Greek Cypriot armies were now engaged against the Turks, against their houses, their families, wives, children. A Turk was a Turk. Barbari! Infidel! Usurper of Greek land. And for the Turks, the same: the Greeks were the oppressors. Each side was on the offensive, and each side was defending what was its. His Beatitude, whose warm and comforting hand had closed on mine only hours before, had spent much of the rest of the night with that same hand on the cold steel of guns, handing out his arsenal to school boys and to the small armies formed by various Greek Cypriot groups and consisting of former EOKA heroes. Minus Markos Drakos.

The day dawned unlike any other. It was cold. Tomorrow would be Christmas Eve.

"Mommy, will Karakoumi be shot?" Kristin asked.

"Mommy, I'm worried about Tulay. She's Turkish. Will they shoot her?"

"No, Karakoumi won't be shot. She isn't a Turk, or a Greek," I answered. "No, Tulay will be all right, I am sure." I was not sure.

"But what about the Stellas?" Robin had two Greek Cypriot friends named Stella.

"They live far away from the shooting."

"But what about us? Will they come here?" Jeannie asked.

"No. They will not come here. We are friends."

The firing is heavy: Bren machine guns, Sten light machine guns, Frank told me, both with their rapid and regular cacophony; mortars crunching into buildings; rifles splitting the air; heavy machine guns, ominous and sullen with message—weapons made in every country, of every type, every age, collected by the little armies and now brought out and probably cradled with pleasure by impatient, heroic boys. We have learned the different sounds in the once-clear air, now weighted down by the heaviness of gunpowder and despair.

No one has entered the Turkish quarter of Nicosia, and the American trapped there, Paul Carlton, still has not exited. He works for Frank. We don't even know if Paul is alive. Judy is outwardly calm, which belies her neurotic state of nerves, but she won't come to stay with us. "Paul will/would have wanted me here," she insists, and changes her verb tenses. Past. Future. Present.

The News is Rumors and Rumors are the News. The number of dead is unofficial and the answer is simple: nothing is official, because there isn't any "official" anymore. The government, as it existed, is no more, the Treaty abrogated. But that is slightly incorrect: everybody is official. All the Greek forces were issued police uniforms until they ran out, everyone, that is, who was male and over fifteen, just as they were issued guns, which they didn't run out of. So they have guns and identification cards—if lacking a uniform—which state that the bearer is a *Policeman* or part of the *Greek Security Forces*, responsible, they go on to say, for quelling Turkish insurgents and murderers. These *Policemen* stand on every street corner with Sten guns; and in front of the boys' school opposite the Marble Oasis, they stand with rifles.

A *Newsweek* reporter was allowed into the Turkish quarter to photograph the bodies of three children and their mother thrown into a bathtub, "murdered by Turks," say the Greeks, to arouse sympathy for the Turkish cause. "They will stoop at nothing, even the murder of their own people."

"Cover-up by the Greeks for their atrocities," say the

Turks.

"Turkish Officer goes mad and kills family," the Greeks say, trying another tack.

Everything Western reporters send out is supposed to be censored, but we, even so, are not getting any Western papers.

All is rumor: Verified or Unverified.

Fifty bodies found buried in a mass grave, each shot in the back of the head, hands tied behind their backs. Are they Turkish or Greek? Turkish...Greek...

Back and forth, accusations, denials...Greek Cypriots won't come out of their houses, fearing Turkish massacre... Turkish Cypriots won't come out of their houses, fearing slaughter by Greeks.

The Peace Corps has been forced to recall all of its members working in villages. One Corpsman, a Christmas guest, has reported that, in his attempts to find temporary storage for cut-off villagers' food supplies, he has been told by a Greek shopowner that he cannot lend his ice-cream warehouse because it is occupied by corpses. Who knows in the outside world that there is no embalming in Cyprus and that bodies are required to be buried within 24 hours after death? Unless, of course, gunfire prevents burial, and there is an ice-cream warehouse.

Rumor rumor rumor, talk talk talk. The girls are worried about the Stellas, and Tulay, and Karakoumi and Charlie Boy, but they are stimulated by the social time in our house: the refugees, the children, the journalists. They do not know that children like themselves are being killed, their houses destroyed, that their parents are killing and being killed. How could anyone explain that?

The News of the Week:

Becky Toner is leaving Cyprus. Her husband is the head of US AID. She is leaving with her two sons. She has had her fill: her husband's driver, a Turk, was pulled from his car in Nicosia and shot on the spot. Verified. He was suspected of being a member of TMT, the Turkish underground. Not verified... He made Becky's life on Cyprus possible: he knew where to find candles for dinner parties, where to find a repairman for an inadvertently melted pewter tray, where to find everything which took most of the rest of us, wives without drivers, months to find. Becky rewarded him with affection and loyalty. He became a member of Becky's family.

The Turkish wounded are being taken to Turkey because the General Hospital will no longer treat them. Unverified... The General Hospital administration asked all Turkish nurses to report to a given room, where they were all shot. Verified... The fifty bodies in the mass grave are Turkish. Verified... The boys from the high school are in front of my house shooting at small birds: Ireni came screaming to tell me. I went out and told them that there were children in this house and that the house belonged to Makarios, and that if they didn't leave I would report them. Verified by me... All Americans should place small paper American flags on their front windshields to identify their nationality. Flags issued by the American Embassy. Verified... We feel safer...

Five American cars burned outside the homes of the owners/occupants (families of radio technicians who work at the State Department Radio Relay Station) by anti-American factions. Verified... Who are the anti-American factions? All Greek Cypriots. All Americans are ordered to remove paper flags from the windshields of their cars, so they will not be identified as Americans...

To be one hundred per cent *not* pro-Greek means one hundred per cent pro-Turkish, and hence anti-Greek. Arithmetic is different in Cyprus... Peace Corpsman accused of gun-running to Turkish villages. Accusation verified. Falsity verified: Corpsman was teaching a blind Turkish villager how to earn a living by weaving baskets... Greeks set fire to Turkish houses in Ormorphita. Verified... Turks raided a Greek monastery in retaliation, killing two priests and wounding others. Verified...

Try to stop the wind from blowing.

Try to stop the winter rains.

Be angry at the sun.

What do we do for Christmas?

Tally of Turkish dead and wounded: 300 dead, 400 wounded. Unverified... Greek Cypriot fatalities: 80. Unverified...

The nearby ruined monastery has a bitch in heat whose cycle has not been disturbed by the disturbances. Twenty-four male dogs (I counted them) are in hot pursuit night and day. Howling fills in between small and infrequent gun lulls. Verified.

The heavy firing lasted five days, Christmas in the middle. Now it has stopped, and only sporadic cracks of exploding powder rip the air, but they are more frightening. We do not know why. Everyone feels it.

We had a New Year's Party at the Marble Oasis and *Everybody* came. Everybody excluded Greeks and Turks, who didn't know what their attitudes were to the US, so Everybody was the Americans, the correspondents, Israelis, British—anyone who felt like venturing out at night and who had children who were my children's friends. Savvas made a beautiful suckling pig, apple and all, and we danced the Soft Shoe, the Charleston. "Yah Sas!" cried lanky Charlie McCaskill, "Yah Sas!"—Charlie, who had sincerely "regretted" that he had only one stomach to give to his country, when faced with his first little pickled bird, bones, head, and all. "Yah Sas!"

"Mommy, why don't you give parties like this always?" asked Kristin, who didn't have to go to bed, ever, I had said, if she didn't want to. Meaning, not like the boring diplomatic dinners when Savvas was being his best dignified self, proper and white-coated, gracious and meticulous in his butler manners.

Karakoumi, whose name I will nevermore be able to say because it is Turkish, is probably starving in her stable, or shot for foraging.

I cannot distinguish what I have learned in conversations from what I have read or heard on the radio from what I have thought. True, road blocks have gone up or down, wherever one goes. There are only a few on the road to Kyrenia, manned by Turkish Cypriots or the Turkish Army contingent. They stop us for identification and wave us on quite cheerily. I am wondering if they think us friends. I am wondering if we *are* friends. We have gotten used to the presence of guns everywhere. We have been to Kyrenia and found Karakoumi in good shape, wearing a strawbelly from being fed all straw and no grain, no greens, but alive. More than we expected. Fikret looked shattered. He was ragged, with a month-old beard. Fikret confided that he had spent six nights in our quiet sea house along with his son, each with a Sten gun, guarding the valley between our house and the Greek villages beyond it, one of which contained Marulla and her donkey. How could I ask him why he hadn't found grain for Karakoumi?

We looked for grain. None in Kyrenia, so we went to the village above it: Kasaphani, where the local merchant said that he could spare ten okes. Hassan's Turkish family with nine brothers and sisters never emerged from their tiny house for the entire five days of the Christmas attack.

The houses are shuttered and quiet, the streets empty in spite of the sunny weather. Our house, too, stands derelict. All the Turkish houses around us—Rustem's, Orek's, Muftizade's, even Kadir's—are empty. All is desolate. All hushed. They have not physically changed, but the space they occupy, the air they breathe, is a different color. Fear has changed the color: fear is no-colored, waiting to become recognizable, without ever becoming so. Our house will henceforth be filled with loneliness, and the sea will echo back long, lonely waves.

Charlie Boy did not appear. Life now would be confined to Nicosia. We might never see him again. Did dogs know about wars? The girls did not mention him. Had they forgotten, or was he relegated, already, to be a smaller grief in the face of those so much larger?

The Greek Cypriot press wrote this response to the *TIME* magazine publication of the photograph of the bodies of the Turkish mother and her three children in the bathtub:

*"In its issue of 10 January 1964 an American magazine TIME has published, in the form of a document, a macabre picture of a dead Turkish mother together with her three dead children in a bathtub, and under the picture the caption in capital letters: SLAIN TURKISH CYPRIOT MOTHER AND CHILDREN! and under this another caption in small letters which reads as follows: 'The price for a dog is three monks.' The publication of this picture is a journalistic immorality of the first degree...The young Turkish woman and her children were not at all slain by the Greeks...they were killed by the husband and father of his family after a maniac crisis...the husband of the dead woman, an Officer of the Turkish Army Contingent, had turned the house into a machine gun post, from which he was murdering Greek citizens.* [Who reading this would know that there would be no Greek Cypriots in the Turkish quarter?] *It is not necessary for anyone to be a Coroner in order to realize that a mother is not packed with her three children fully dressed in the tub of the bathroom...The position of the tragic victims is well-prepared in the tub, so that no one would think that the tragic victims had posed for this picture. The blood stains which are spread on the walls of the tub have evidently been put by the photographer...the publication of this picture tries to accuse immorally the Greek population of the island for an action for which civilization, morals and the history of the Greeks, completely exclude. The publishers of TIME Magazine, if they were to study the Greek*

*and Turkish history, they would have clearly seen which history of these two people contains such barbaric deeds. The Greek Cypriots know that there is difference between the war coarseness and criminal barbarity...The Greeks do not kill in cold blood in comparison with the Turks...The forged pictures unjustly poison world public opinion and are shadowing reality and distorting the history of liberal peoples..."*

# TARTUFFE

Robert and Maureen Pendleton, retired British tea planters from Malaysia who had settled in Kyrenia, called me in Nicosia two weeks after our last visit to tell me what I feared—the pony was not being cared for. Not fed or watered, nor ever taken out of the garage-made-stable.

Couldn't I have expected that Fikret, honest and faithful, had more important things to do than indulge a British-American fetish of kindness to animals? And that at a time when Frank had learned that *he himself* was one of the leaders of the Kyrenia TMT, according to Greek press reports. When people were being killed daily, houses bombed by ignited temperaments as well as bombs, hostilities mounting? The eighteen miles between Nicosia and Kyrenia were not occupied, but were half-Greek, half-Turkish, which meant that no Greek or Turk could travel those miles all the way and that, therefore, Kyrenia was forbidden to them both. Anyone else, probably, could travel the road—diplomats, certainly, although we were encouraged to use it only on a strictly need-to basis. No embassy wanted to encourage an incident.

I went to the Veterinary Clinic outside the bastion of old Nicosia to ask Mike Petris for a place to keep the pony. Certainly he had a special feeling for that little mare.

"Bring her here to the clinic. I have some stables. We'll find a place for her."

I didn't know where else to put a pony, except at the British bases that were too far for me to ride her, see her, and if I asked the bases to take her, she would have to be a gift horse. I was not ready to give her up forever.

Mike looked at me quizzically. "Look, you will hire a truck and bring her by way of Myrtou, of course? You're not going to be foolish, are you? I nodded, meaning yes, I guess, that I wasn't going to be foolish. But Myrtou was a three-hour drive. I could find a truck. I nodded yes. I meant no, I wouldn't be foolish.

"Frank Jones," I pronounced, at one of our rare moments together when I wasn't asleep, "I am going to bring Karakoumi to Nicosia. I have a place to keep her."

I didn't see Frank very often. Even mealtime now converged into one expression, which was chanted daily by the girls—"Soup's on!"—and was the signal for the telephone to ring and the summons: immediate attention required at the Embassy.

"Fine. But how will you get her here?"

"Ride her. OK?"

"As long as you get someone to check you out, now and then, along the way. Say, how about one of the Peace Corps boys? They're out of work now."

"What happened? Since when?" I hadn't heard.

"Well, you remember that one Corpsman who was accused of gun-running? The outcome of that incident is that because teaching handicrafts to a blind Turk was not part of his assigned job, he, and now the entire Corps, is accused of being partisan and receiving guns from Turkish ships and delivering them to the TMT. So they all had to be called in from their villages—no point in getting one of them killed. Now they are just waiting around to see what will happen, where they will go from here."

I found them through Petey's husband. The coming Sunday, two of them would be free from tidying up their reports. They would be departing the following week for Ethiopia.

Two corpsmen and I drove to Kyrenia in the inconstant January sun. I hoped the rain would wait.

We were stopped four times at roadblocks: two Greek, one at the outskirts of Nicosia, one at the entrance to Kyrenia. Two Turkish in between.

What was the reason for the blockades? Merely an

assertion of ownership, I thought. Of territorial rights? The
guards looked at the identity documents of those few travelers
on a once-busy road as though they really didn't know what to
do with them. Certainly the Turkish soldiers couldn't read our
passports, turning them upside down as they did. Were they
Turkish Cypriots, or part of the Turkish mainland garrison?
No way to tell. All of them wore the star and half-moon of
Turkey, in red, on their khaki uniforms.

When we arrived at the third roadblock, on the crest
of the Kyrenia Mountains, the indifferent sunshine had faded,
and the sea's clouds were not encouraging. It would rain, most
certainly. I had worn a warm sweater and brought a thin nylon
parka, used in other days for skiing in the Alps. It was red—a
useful color under the circumstances.

We turned down the muddy road leading to the beloved
sea house, but stopped first to greet the Pendletons, to thank
them for calling about the pony they'd looked after, and to in-
quire about their health.

The Pendletons had come to Cyprus too late. Too late
for the peace which the British had enjoyed for a century and
for their polo matches, croquet and teas on half-green lawns.
Too late also for Robert's health: he spoke with the forced air
moving over his absent, cancer-operated larynx. They had also
left Malaysia, then Malaya, too late—after British fortunes had
been lost, and Robert's with them. Where does one go when
the Empire dies? Back to Britain where they've never lived?
Maureen had never lived there, and Robert not since he was
at Oxford. So they had chosen Cyprus, with its benign climate
and healing sea. Now they were awaiting the much-discussed
Invasion perhaps only days, and yards away. The Invasion was,
of course, Invasion by Turkey, the Great Fear in the hearts and
on the tongues of every Greek Cypriot. Weeks ago, was it only,
that Maureen had questioned Frank: "If the Turks invade the
island, where do you think they will land?"

"Why, right here. One hundred yards in front of your house. Turkey is only forty miles away from here, you know."

"Oh, really! Do you think so?" Maureen had remarked. "Well, I must get some film."

"Color?" Frank had asked.

"Oh, most certainly. I've never seen an invasion before." She might have been speaking of the gulls' flight, or the rain coming down.

Whitewashed houses, though normally sun-dazzled, were cool in summer. In winter they resembled cold grey doves, huddled and lifeless, humped against the rain, knowing of nothing to do but wait. The Pendleton's house was such a one, and I knew the winter clamminess of its interior.

Maureen greeted us, wrapped up in her usual layers of "jumpers" and cardigans.

"Delighted you came. But we'll miss the pony. We got to be good friends... You are riding her, of course?"

"Yes, of course," I answered as matter-of-factly as I was asked. Our Anglo-Saxon temperaments *were* different from the Mediterranean.

I took nothing extra but the halter rope. Eighteen miles was a long distance for a pony confined for weeks without exercise or sufficient food. No extra weight to burden her. The Peace Corpsmen were to check me every five miles or so.

Out the muddy lane, past the shivering acacias, waving at Robert and Maureen, until Maureen's shawl and cardigans were as small as a gull's wing in the grey distance. Through the desolate village and up the long ascent to the mountains, a five-mile distance in no-man's land, being at that time claimed by neither Greek nor Turk. Nor guarded. The pony was not so certain of my directions—we had ridden always towards the sea, along the sea, away from Kyrenia. She looked back at me, wanting her stable already, after only two miles.

The road was entirely deserted. Up and up towards the

mountains, but the sea was the color of the sky, and it seemed as though we made no progress. Then it began to rain, quietly. A thin mist, visible only to the hand, and felt by the face. I put on my parka, the hood over my head. Red. Maybe I was wrong. Maybe I should have had a blue one. Or one of each. I was still closer to Greek territory than Turkish, and was wearing a red parka on a deserted road. Perhaps I could even be seen from the Turkish stronghold at St. Hilarion, the Crusader-built fortress where the eagles screamed into the sea wind. Then red would be right.

Startled by the broken stillness, I turned around to see a car, not mine with the Corpsmen but a small blue Morris Minor crawling like an ant in the vast distance behind me. On and on it came. Robert and Maureen appeared.

"We brought you some lunch. Something hot. It started raining." Was it also one last glimpse Maureen wanted of a parting which might be definitive? Who knew where one—I, she, Robert—went from here? "And we really wanted to see you," she continued. "It's too funny, you know. You really ought to have a bundle of sticks. Or something to carry. You look like an unpurposeful peasant, a peasant without a mission, in an Englishman's parka. Why don't you have a donkey? And that ridiculous English saddle—why not a wooden one!"

We all laughed. We *were* all ridiculous, standing there on the empty mountain road, eating sandwiches and drinking soup as though it were a perfectly normal day and we were here every day of our lives, pausing for our midday lunch, drinking soup in the rain on a deserted road, armed soldiers at either end.

"Good-bye! Good-bye!"

Five miles to the top. Pony lagging. Who was dead ahead, wondering who was occupying the middle of the road on a Sunday afternoon in a Turkish-occupied area in a country committed to hostilities? They, two soldiers, peered down the road at me, guns pointed in my direction. Sten guns. And two carbines crossed, standing beside them in the middle of the road. Their barrier.

I took off my hood and demonstrated, by indicating my hair, that I was *she*.

Not *he*. They peered, still. I peered back. Where were the Peace Corpsmen, I wondered. Stories of infidel Saracen Barbarians flooded my mind, the rape of women, the cutting off of hands, stoning women who were too free. No Turkish woman would be riding a pony, astride, in the midst of nowhere. I must be suspect, I thought, as I arrived at the barricade of crossed guns, on no dashing charger ready to strike them down as the horse of Artybius had been trained to do. I was mounted on a drooping pony.

They peered into my face, and then into each other's. Guffaws! Louder! They slapped their thighs, each other's backs! They roared! And gestured me onwards. Onwards I went, and then, suddenly, they stopped laughing. Wondering, perhaps, I was thinking, if they had made a mistake, not certain of what they had seen. Maybe thinking that I, Arlene Jones, on a simple mission of pony rescue, was really a Mata Hari in disguise. Escaping. Or the wife of Frank Jones, spy, slipping through the lines. Oh my God, I am the wife of a spy! I suddenly remembered. My stomach clutched.

Or, I could be one of Nikos Sampson's Tartuffes. He had written only yesterday in Mahki: *Those foreign diplomats and journalists were tartuffes, breathing fury against the Greek Cypriots for crushing the Turkish terrorists...these tartuffes want the Greek Cypriots to strew the path of the Turkish insurgents with flowers, and then allow themselves to be massacred.*

More and more possibilities came to my mind. Both sides could accuse me. I could be accused of being a gun-running Turk-lover. Without guns? And my accomplices, the already accused Peace Corpsmen, using my car... Damn.

Where *were* they? My Corpsmen? Why did I ever ask them? They hadn't even left Kyrenia. Or had they? They had vanished. Perhaps they were captured, and their, I mean *my* car was being filled with guns by the Greeks to prove that they were running guns to Turks. Oh God, I could see the headlines in *Eleftheria* now: "U.S. Diplomat Tartuffe, woman NATO spy, plots against peace-loving citizens, runs pony express through Turkish lines." And my color photograph in a red parka! Frank must have been crazy to let me come. Go. Whatever it was that I was doing. Why didn't I listen to Mike!

A shot! Then several more staccatoed in the distance. A machine gun. I could recognize them all: Bazooka, Sten, Bren gun sounds. And of course, the rifle. I consoled myself by thinking the sounds were normal. But here? On a lonely road, with no one in sight?

Two hours, six miles. Twelve more miles to go. I dismounted my unwilling beast bearing my burden, tied the halter rope around my waist. No good horsewoman would do that, I knew, but it would enable me to lean into the rope, to encourage the now-balking pony. Rest... The mist increased. Mount. Ride another mile, tortoise pace. Walk. The rain stopped. The sun slipped through, now and then. More rain. I saw my car arrive, coming from Kyrenia. I didn't ask the Corpsmen where they had been. Didn't want them to think I was worried. One offered to ride the pony. They were too heavy for Karakoumi. Even I was now. I tried to sit on the tailgate of the station wagon and lead her. The car overheated in maintaining such a slow pace. I couldn't drag her after the car. She stopped. Rest. Met after another mile. Tried to lead her from the car again. No go. Met them in another two miles.

How far had I gone? I had descended the mountain into the Mesaoria Plain. How many miles to the Turkish village of Geunyeli on the outskirts of Nicosia?

I remembered that I knew an animal rescue shelter two miles to the right, away from Geunyeli. Should I take the chance that they would take Karakoumi, that they had room for her? It would mean four more miles, if they wouldn't... I decided to take the chance. The Corpsmen had gone on to Geunyeli.

With relief, I came to the shelter. They didn't have room. My throat tightened more in pain than anger. I was afraid I would cry. Couldn't they understand? No! Very un-British. The woman snapped at me. Unbelievable.

On to Geunyeli. Mounting, walking, dragging poor Karakoumi, but I was angry with her as well. Why couldn't she understand I was trying to save her? I was stupid, I knew. I had to whip her with the crop. She wouldn't move. I was reminded of her colic.

Two more miles. The rain had stopped now. The sky had cleared. However, it was getting on toward dusk. Hurry. Hurry. I counted steps. Two more. Good. Ten more. Wonderful. And on we went.

Geunyeli appeared as a true oasis. Or mirage. No, it *was* Geunyeli. I could see the coffee shop was full, as usual. I could see my car, and the Corpsmen, playing backgammon, feeling comfortable in an element they knew. Maybe they *were* Turk-lovers. A coffee for me, the pony untethered, children gathering around, curious, but quiet. Normally wary, Karakoumi now would not have moved for a fire-bomb. I had another coffee, and was eyed only slightly by the normal-seeming Sunday crowd of men and boys. I had heard from Fikret that villagers thought a tired horse was a bewitched horse. Did that include me? Was it Greek Villagers, or Turkish Villagers who thought that?

The only difference from normal was the number of men in uniform. And the guns: a motley assortment, carried carelessly, deposited casually here and there. I was accepted in the coffee house as all Western women were accepted and their own women were not. The only thing I did not want to happen was to be seen by anyone in the American diplomatic community. Not that anyone I knew now went to Kyrenia. But there was always Elizabeth who had a driver, and could go to their rented house to collect things. But for the Turks, this woman on a pony was one of the many odd occurrences which went unquestioned, as the guns went unquestioned, and were, in fact, a return to something they had experienced before.

Dusk was fast coming on, and I was relieved to be only two miles or so from the stable. I had one more roadblock to pass, just on the edge of Nicosia. Off I started, with the reins tied around my waist, leaning forwards, dragging Karakoumi.

And then the distance was reduced to one mile. Dragging a staggering pony, mounting from time to time to no avail, I was all but standing still.

Car lights flashed in the semi-dusk. Why? Then I saw the American flag on the black Ford, and the Ambassador's driver. Elizabeth leaned out of the window: "Heavens, Arlene! Is that you? What on earth are you doing here? Are you crazy?"

"But you, too, Elizabeth, are here." Counter an attack with an attack, as Frank always said and the Greeks practiced. We confronted each other.

"Yes, I had to collect some things from my house. Who knows when we can go back and forth again," Elizabeth remarked, importantly.

"But I had to collect some things too, Elizabeth," I said.

"But what? What is so important? And what are you doing here on a horse, in the Turkish sector, in the dark? Answer me that!"

"I had to collect my horse."

Elizabeth paused. "Wait until I tell Frank and the Ambassador where you were. And at this time of day. You do know there's another roadblock, don't you?"

"He knows, Elizabeth. He knows. He may not know where I am at this moment, but he knows what I am doing. After all, I couldn't leave the horse to starve, could I?"

"You are ridiculous!" Elizabeth pronounced, and urged the driver on.

The only real hazard of the trip, oddly enough, I thought, was meeting an official American. And it had to be the Ambassador's wife. Just when I was nearly there. I had never been in Elizabeth's favor, having started off so badly by confusing the day of the luncheon given in my honor, and arriving late. The embarrassment of being reminded by Elizabeth's phone call and arriving after the soup to the head of table, the empty place of honor. I never regained my footing.

Elizabeth did not like her job and was, because of it, convinced that no other wife in the Foreign Service should. And she had been placed in that position by the whole apparatus of the State Department's Foreign Service: The Ambassador's Wife! A position eagerly hoped for, awaited, a position which would justify all the early years of Junior Wife, Junior budget, Junior allowances, Junior position, and always being at the beck and call of The Ambassador's wife. It was all so departmental: making calls within the proper time after being newly posted, *no matter who baby-sat your children*, even if they were homesick, crying, ill in a hotel; wearing white gloves; never sitting on the right side of the sofa *unless you were the senior wife, if you called in a group;* cowtowing to women not senior in age but senior in husband's rank. I remembered the advice from Washington prior to my first post: "A single strand of pearls and a black dress are appropriate at all times... A Foreign Service Wife *never* has an opinion which *could be* taken to be official; therefore, a Foreign Service Wife *never has an opinion. Such behavior would mar your husband's career.* I remembered a bit of information passed on to me in a previous post by the

Ambassador's Wife when Frank and I were invited to a farewell party for the Ambassador. Frank was out of town, and I was summarily disinvited: "*My dear, without your husband, you simply don't exist.*"

We simply could not be two women friends: she was the Ambassador's wife, and I was not even Foreign Service. I was an imposter because of Frank's position, given Foreign Service cover for the CIA. We could not be friends.

The Ambassador's Wife—of all persons to find me out, to find me leading a pony in the Turkish district, when I was possibly risking Official American Policy, flaunting the Ambassador's recommendations or orders. But to Elizabeth, I was always where I wasn't supposed to be. I knew how well the grapevine worked in Cyprus, remembering Sabri's knowledge of me, our pony, our search for a saddle. If I were to go to Kyrenia tomorrow and go to his Milk Bar, Sabri would surely say to me," Well, I hear that you were in Geunyeli in a coffee shop at dusk yesterday...on a horse." I even knew what I would reply to his remark: "Not on. With."

It was dark when I arrived at the veterinary stable. But I knew where to go, and would deposit the pony quietly. I would call Mike in the morning...

"Kali Spera, Kyria..." Damn, I thought, knowing the voice.

"You got a truck, did you? Quite a drive, wasn't it? More than three hours?"

In the darkness only his voice and not his face was speaking. I didn't know *how* Mike meant what he was saying.

"Who told you that I...?" But I didn't know what to ask. Mike interrupted me.

"You know that village where you had coffee?" And I nodded in incredulity. "Well, the pony called ahead. She's not so stupid as you are."

Mike was laughing. And then I was laughing. And crying. And Mike fed Karakoumi a hot bran mash, saying, "It's why she called. It's what she asked for."

Our laughter stopped and our ears were filled with the sound of munching jaws, a sound signifying that all was well, that a tired and hungry animal was eating and bedded down for the night in the security, the comfort of the stable.

I thanked Mike. Or I tried to. I didn't need to because we both believed in a simple need—shelter and food for a refugee, his refugees being animals—and in his wish that others' needs could be so simply satisfied. It was a small beauty in the face of so much ugliness.

"Don't thank me," he said hoarsely. "Courtesy of the Cyprus Government... It may be the only thing you'll ever get from them."

And we went our separate ways into an uncertain night.

# VALENTINES

*...Assassins of great presidents, murderers of Negroes, highwaymen, collabora-tors, imperialists and Fascists, following in Hitler's path...*

– Greek Cypriot Press

We have become the Enemy. Where will the first strike against us be? Against whom?

It is the fifth of February. The days are crawling by. We expect each one to be cataclysmic, and each day we are relieved to know that it hasn't been so, and we are also disappointed, be-cause the cataclysm would interrupt the endless game of wait-ing. We are waiting for the *Talks* to begin. When will the *Talks* begin among Britain, Turkey, Greece, and the United States? When? George Ball and British Foreign Secretary, Sandys, have arrived, conferring with the American and British Am-bassadors. Elizabeth gave a dinner party at the Residence for them. She had plans to show a movie after dinner.

"Mr. Secretary," Elizabeth addressed the British Foreign Secretary, Mr. Sandys, "What do you think about the diver-sion of the Jordan River?" Sandys looked at her with incredu-lity. She meant "division," but "diversion" was truly what she wanted, and all of us. The husbands present were there for an after-dinner meeting. Hence, immediately after an awkward, impatient dinner, they disappeared. We wives sat there, wait-ing for a signal from Elizabeth, who looked utterly defeated. I rose to go.

"Well, now, I suppose you too, Arlene, are leaving me. Don't you want to see a movie?" Elizabeth was trying harder than any of us to forget, to carry on with a life that could exist on a level other than Cyprus. But I couldn't rise to the occa-sion. I was weary of everything. But, particularly, I knew what Frank's reaction to me would have been.

"Tell Frank I have gone home, Elizabeth. I'm sure the

meeting will be late." That seemed to me the only thing I was certain of.

The next evening Frank had invited a newly arrived journalist for drinks. He was replacing the *Newsweek* correspondent who wrote, "The price for a dog is three monks," earning himself a *Persona Non Grata* from the Greek Cypriot Government. It happened to journalists for being too truthful and to diplomats for being too sympathetic to unpopular causes. Causes unpopular to the majority government, that is.

Minutes later, an explosion. As a unit we exited to the marble-floored verandah in time to witness the second explosion—a great red flash in the dark, the reverberating thunder causing the house to tremble under us. Then blue smoke visible above the red, and that was the end of all the guests. The target was the American Embassy.

"Mother! What happened?" The girls rushed out to the verandah with us, and I remember saying, "I think the American Embassy was bombed..."

"But who, who would do it?" they cried. How to phrase my answer. It would be, of course, the Greek Cypriots, who would, of course, blame it on the Turks. What it would do was set something in motion, the something I had always dreaded.

I put my arms around three little girls and said, "It was only some silly person showing off. It will really be nothing."

This something we hadn't and had wanted produced an instant consequence, even though only one American was injured—a Marine guard. The consequence: immediate evacuation of all American families.

Urged by his staff, the Ambassador finally made it voluntary. I breathed quietly once more. Six hundred women and children departed, women with small children and hurriedly packed luggage, all their dear things forgotten. They left behind pet dogs and cats, household goods, cars, and whatever could not fit into their allotted sixty-six pounds of luggage.

My mind is in overdrive: I do not know what I plan to do... I do not want to go... I do not know where to go... I do not want to live out of a suitcase for weeks with my children. I am not frightened to stay here. I am frightened to leave. What about a home? School? A semblance of a community? For myself I do not care. But I am four.

The refugee problem is growing now with a mass movement of Turks within the island to join larger concentrations of Turks. They have left their houses, their farms, their jobs for crowded, cold, unsanitary conditions of uncertain duration, and before too long there will be a real refugee problem. I mean that it is here now: the fields will not be tilled and planted, the grapevines will be untended, the oranges will rot on the ground. Cyprus cannot grow things year-round, and the season coming up is the busy one: by May the harvesting of wheat must be finished.

I seem to think in bits and pieces. The words which we have exchanged so endlessly with one another—Americans, Israelis, British, the few Greek-Cypriots who have remained our friends—these words have kept us together. Words have been our link, separating what we think is the real from the unreal. They have been our articulated, hopeless gestures, our way of understanding what is happening to us. They have kept us sane: blessèd and betraying words. But now words too are becoming broken.

The next day I went to the park near the veterinary clinic to ride Karakoumi after I took the girls to school. They went off so quietly. Even their words were stilled. I wanted to talk with the past: with Karakoumi...

The stable-clinic is next to the House of Representatives, and while I was cantering in the sort-of park, I heard a familiar sound: the roar of a crowd. Demonstrator-students were gathering around the House of Representatives, carrying anti-NATO flags, protesting the NATO peace-keeping offer. Mounted on Karakoumi, now my war horse, lively and recovered, I felt invincible, the only mounted person in a sea of pedestrians. I saw Makarios step out on a portico above a window to address the crowd. But thinking of a possible Incident, I retreated to the park. I was always making headlines in my head, placing them in the various newspapers. I knew which one fit where. This was for *Eleftheria:* "Woman Spy PNG'd for mocking meeting on War Horse."

For all I knew, Karakoumi, when faced with an approaching crowd, could rear and strike, or kick someone. I could not rid my mind of the story Herodotus told about Darius' general, Artybius, whose horse "reared up and killed his master's opponent with his feet and mouth..." when he was sent to Cyprus to quell the revolt against the Persians. I giggled a little at the ridiculousness of the thought.

When the meeting dispersed, most of the angry young men came seething through the park, and came suddenly upon a woman on a pony. They didn't know what to do. They stopped *en masse*, startled. Were they going to rush me, to seize me for spying? But whatever intentions they may have had, their angry purpose was dispersed. They looked sheepish, and started kicking their toes in the dirt. They put their hands in their pockets and were afraid to pass me. So I stayed, confronting them silently for a time long enough to please me, and then I turned my War Horse and headed for the stable.

A Greek Cypriot friend of Frank's volunteered to stay in the house with me, if I felt in any danger. The offer made me feel in danger: the people offering to protect me are the very ones agitating, spreading propaganda, causing the trouble, and killing Turks who are/have been, my friends... What is a friend?

Yesterday, pandemonium broke out downtown in the

walled city. Shops closed in a frenzy, the general hospital blocked off its entrance while the dead and wounded from the afternoon's fighting were brought in. But such an event is now commonplace. Was it yesterday? The day before? Certainly, it will be again tomorrow.

The streets are eerie, desolate and isolated. Americans have been spat on in the streets. Mainland Greeks have been ordered to remain indoors by their Embassy. There is a pit in my stomach I can't get rid of; this morning it had not gone away. I knew where it was exactly, could feel it resting quiet as a stone. It was a stone that told me it would stay, along with the grief I still felt for President Kennedy's loss and with it, our abandonment.

Reports from military sources on yesterday's raid on a Turkish village, in retaliation for the ambush of a Greek vehicle by Turks, are that Greeks pushed Turkish women and children ahead of them as protection while they fired on other Turks. Houses were burned, regardless of occupation. As usual, no accurate report of the number of Turkish causalities is listed. The Armenian dentist whose house is in the Turkish quarter called the American Embassy to ask if it could get a truck to rescue his grand piano. "If there is anything I love," he said, "it is my grand piano." He sent his Turkish wife to the house to collect valuables, and when she was there it was raided by armed Greek Cypriots. Naturally, she fled. "You mean you left it unlocked?" queried her shocked husband.

Fighting has broken out elsewhere, in scattered places. There are so many different groups within each community that each is unsure which is friendly, which is not. No one in the Greek community is actually in control any longer, not one of the organized small armies, nor the armed, uncontrolled civilians, all of whom have increasing numbers of weapons and responsibility to no one. All is confusion and chaos. The right hand does not know what the left hand does.

The house is cold, and the emptiness in me chills me even more. Savvas is grim, and the Marble Oasis grew empty long ago. I want to hear it again full of voices before I leave: the crying baby, the music, the "soft shoe," my children chattering.

Jeannie, Robin and Kristin went to school today, some of the few American children who did. Out of one hundred fifty pupils in the Middle and Upper school, thirty were present. First, all the Turkish children departed and now, many Americans. The British call their leaving "premature repatriation." We say evacuation.

Every day the girls ask, "Do we have to go to school today? When are we leaving? Julie and John left yesterday. There are only four Americans left in my class."

"Mommy, where are we going? Who is going to take care of Charlie Boy?"

"When shall we pack?"

"Mother, aren't we going away too? Everybody else has left."

"I am the last American in my class. Mommy, I'm scared."

Elizabeth is leaving. I have not yet been commanded to go, but life has gone from us anyway. We live in a ghost town. We are the last American family left. It is strange to be here now: suspended between action and inaction. We contemplate the knowns in numbness and perplexity. We really don't wish to understand what is happening. But we do know, and it seems too preposterous. The knowledge reduces us to nothing. It sweeps away the humanity of us, and we are as Nothing.

Mass Murder.

The Turks all know that they will be killed unless Turkey intervenes, and they know too that if Turkey does invade they may die before the Turkish army can save them from murder or starvation. Greek Cypriot news of the Americans is that they are evacuating wives and children because we have jointly arranged with Britain and Turkey for Turkey to invade Cyprus.

Their story is that the bombing of the American Embassy was done by the Americans themselves to prepare an excuse for the evacuation. I am sitting at home trying to understand what is happening to humanity.

I hear shouting going on outside—there are supposed to be more anti-American riots today because Under Secretary of State George Ball has arrived again. (How many times now?) But stepping out onto the balcony, I discover that it is only the poor suffering inmates of the mental institution, shouting and throwing their faded grey uniforms over the stone wall.

Much later. But it is the same day, I think. I have been to a meeting of the Junior School parents. In a summary report for the "year which began so well," the headmaster reported that "Out of two hundred ninety pupils, forty-four are left." First the Turkish children left, or rather, were *unable* to return, then the American children. Some Greek Cypriots fled the country. But the headmaster didn't go into that, because Greek Cypriot parents were present, along with the Israeli Ambassador's wife and a few British parents. That was all.

"What we had hoped would be the most successful year of all, making the school a true international community, has ended in sorrow. The teachers tried their best to keep the atmosphere from reflecting too much on the absentees. But there were the inevitable questions of the little ones that we tried to answer. Our conclusion is that the staff, built up for so many years, will have to be cut by more than half...as soon as possible," Mr. Bosustow continued.

"Well, why can't you fill the places of the absent Americans with those people on the waiting list?" asked Mrs. Aristides.

"There is no longer a waiting list."

"Perhaps," the headmaster continued, "the Turkish children will be back in some weeks..." Glances exchanged among Greek Cypriot women, whose husbands were leaders of the Greek Cypriot community, meant *If they ever do come back, there will be a uniform withdrawal of all Greek Cypriot children.*

The girls made Valentines this afternoon for all their friends, hoping they will come back. I am looking at them, my children and their Valentines, and I am thinking about them, and I wish I knew what I should do, what I should tell them. I can't say, "They don't mean it"— the endless brutal killings, children, mothers, all. Can I tell them that people governed by fear become hysterical and are no longer responsible? Can I continue to teach them that the world responds to the Golden Rule, that there is a Golden Rule which matters more than other Rules? That their lives will never experience violence? Turn the other cheek? And die? Or fight, and live? Maybe I should tell them that goodness makes goodness and violence makes violence

"Mommy," Kristin asked, as we sat around the kitchen table cutting out red hearts. "Shall I send a Valentine to Mr. Makarios, to thank him for our house?"

Now I know what I can tell them: I can say yes, I can tell them to make more Valentines.

# ANDROS

"Kyria, the telephone, for you," announced Savvas.

I didn't know who was left to call me. Georgia, I thought. How I envied her, living not far from her real home anyway, in Jerusalem, and not being asked to depart by her country's government. The Greek Cypriots had no bone to pick with Israel, and her family was not in danger. Her children were some of my girls' last remaining friends, although their ages and sexes didn't entirely correspond.

"Hello?" I said.

"Kyria, is that you? You are still here?"

My stomach's stone made its presence felt. "Yes, why is that surprising? May I ask who is calling?"

"Andros."

"Andros who?" My question was blunt. I didn't know anyone named Andros.

"It doesn't matter. But I think that it is rather late for you..." Meaningful pauses.

"Late for what?" I was feeling half-angry, half-panicked. Frank had gone to Kyrenia to get some of our things—bathing suits, in particular. Maybe something had happened.

"Late to leave. I...I'm afraid the Invasion is beginning." Panic replaced my anger. What did this man named Andros mean?

The *Invasion,* threatened many times by Turkey (begun once, and turned back because of diplomatic efforts) if it was beginning, would be landing on the northern coast of Cyprus: Kyrenia, most probably. No one would want to be in the way. Especially Americans, blamed for arranging this invasion.

"What do you mean?" I demanded.

"I am very *sorry* for you, Kyria. Very *sorry.* Too bad. Good-bye."

I sat down, stunned. If Andros was right, why then, why

then...what should I do? When would I know the truth? Shaking visibly, I thought I would call the Embassy. Dick Welch.

When I heard his voice, my body relaxed with relief. It had seemed as though nobody was *out there*. "Dick, Frank has gone to Kyrenia...and, well, someone named Andros called me to tell me, tell me that...that the invasion is on."

Dick paused, and the pause panicked me again. Our lives, mine and my children's, would be worth nothing if it was true, Makarios' house or not. To catch the American Chief of Station of the CIA and accuse him of supporting Turkish Cypriot gunmen would be a real *coup,* except that it would be false. Why didn't Dick say something...

"Arlene, look. I don't think this is true. It can't be true. Someone is only trying to harass you. Look, I'll get back to you immediately," and he hung up.

Minutes later, the telephone! I grabbed for it. "Kyria, the voice said..." It wasn't Dick. "Kyria, you must leave. Quick. You must leave today. I tell you for your good. You must leave. Goodbye."

It was the same voice. Why? Who was he, friend or enemy? Get hold of yourself, I told myself...You are OK. It is some crazy on the line...

The phone again. "Arlene, Dick here. Don't worry. The invasion is not on. I repeat, NOT. It is *not* on its way, I have confirmed that. It is not on.

"Dick, it was only my assassin calling anyway, to make sure I was home." I laughed a tight, high laugh. Not my laugh at all. But a laugh.

"Say, are you OK?"

"If I weren't I'd tell you. You know that. But I am a little jumpy."

"Arlene, look. I'd pack your bag. Just in case."

"Just in case what? You just said it was off!"

"It *is* off. Just in case something else, such as the evacuation order comes in today's cables. OK?"

"Thanks, Dick. Thank you for the *good* news. Keep me posted."

"I will. Remember what I said."

I added up the signs: phone calls, threatening or not; Dick's reference to evacuation; and Frank's name reported in the Greek Cypriot papers as giving direct orders to Denktash, leader of the Turkish Cypriot community. Frank Jones, American COS, arranging for the invasion of Cyprus by Turkey... Frank Jones, *in* Kyrenia for the Invasion. I was the last dependent (God, how I hated the word "dependent"). But it was, I decided, time to pack. I could no longer expose my children to the consequences: kidnapping, or... I would stop there. I didn't want to continue thinking along those lines. I would pack. And wait for Frank's return. Oh God-if-there-is-one, please let him come back, and let me get out of here, with my children...

And there was one more "sign," perhaps the most significant of all: I felt, for the first time in my life, murderous. I had learned an astounding thing about myself, a thing that shocked me: *I knew that I could take a gun and shoot people. In cold blood. Not just people, but any Cypriot with a gun in his hands. I could do it, and I was convinced I could do it without a qualm. That is why I should leave, go to Israel, Beirut, anywhere else but here.*

Jeannie heard my telephone conversations, bits of them at least. It was Saturday. "Mother, we *are* leaving, aren't we?"

"Jeannie, I guess we are. What do you think about leaving? What do you think about staying?"

"Who will take care of Pippa?"

"Daddy and Savvas will."

"You mean Daddy is going to stay here?"

"Why yes. Did you think he was going with us?"

"But Mother, I don't want to go without Daddy. I don't

want to leave him here." She began to cry.

I was ready to cry. I didn't even know if Frank was going to make it home today. If he did, I wouldn't care if I didn't see him for a year. Just let him come home from Kyrenia today. I couldn't tell Jeannie my worst fears.

"Jeannie," I said. "I don't know how you feel about being here, with all of your friends gone..."

"Alex isn't." Alex was English and lived close by. "I don't want to go either. Where will we live? Will I go to school?"

Jeannie was bringing up questions I hadn't wanted to face. I kept putting them in the back of my mind. Something to deal with later. All I could think about was Frank getting home safely.

"I don't want to go either, Jeannie. But we may have to."

"Who says we have to? Does Daddy say it?"

"Only if State gives orders," I answered.

"But how can they give us orders? How can they tell us what to do? They don't have any right to tell us to go away. We live here. And all my things? Mommy, I won't go."

Jeannie's tears changed to determination. She stiffened and stuck her familiar chin out. That chin would probably save her from bad moments, always, but it would also demand of her an unwilling compromise, which would not be a compromise if against her will. I remembered the dentist she went to for a toothache—before Mr. Nambian. He smiled at her and was so charming.

"And how long have you been in Cyprus?" he asked her.

"Just a week," she answered.

And the conversation went on. Do you like the Sea? Yes. Do you swim? Yes. Most of the Cypriots can't swim; we just bathe. Funny, Jeannie thought. Then the moment came.

"Now open your mouth," he smiled.

Jeannie sat there, without expression, with her mouth closed.

"Now open your mouth, Jeannie!"

Her jaw tightened.

He approached it with his hand, to squeeze the lower jaw. Her jaw clenched. His jaw clenched. He reached for a tool. Incredibly, he started to pry open her mouth... A mother always, I came to her rescue. We fled.

"I won't go," she said.

"Even if I go, Jeannie? With Robin, and Kristin?"

"Even if you go. I'll stay with Daddy. I'm not afraid." And I don't think she was as frightened as I. Stand firm, Mother, she was saying. My mind was racing to tell me what to tell her, how to explain why we were going to leave. I had decided that I couldn't tell her the dangers I had thought of. That was all. Isn't that what mothers were all about?

I remembered the dream I had had once, during our years in Poland, where the realities of Polish life during the War were always present in our minds: what our Polish friends had suffered, what the Jews had gone through, the mound of rubble that had been the Ghetto... I dreamed that the Soviets had *shot* the sun and that all life on earth was going to die. The sun had been *killed*, and although it would take a few days, maybe weeks, we would all die. In order to get out of Warsaw, people were scrambling through a turnstile such as those I remembered in the New York subways. It was the refugee situation again, which I so dreaded. Still, I knew that *we had a country*. But as we passed through the turnstile, my three little girls and I, we saw Frank executed by a firing squad. There would be no mercy from anyone, and I understood that. My dream-problem was this: could I bear to kill my children, since they would surely be killed if I did not do it myself? Or could I bear to have them understand what was happening by seeing me die? In my dream I made the decision I would have made in reality: I would ease them to their deaths, and keep the knowledge of death from them.

And now I would do the same: keep another knowledge from them. They were never to know what I was fearing: their kidnapping, to be used to make Frank confess his complicity in the Turkish invasion; Frank's torture, confession and murder. There were ways to make even the toughest confess. No, I would play it *straight State Department.*

"Jeannie, State is going to order our departure. Daddy must support that order. It's his job. And he can't leave, because there is nobody to do his job. His job is very important. He will help bring peace, so we can come back. You will have to understand that. Daddy will tell you the same thing, and he will expect you to be a brave girl and help take care of your sisters and me. You are the big girl. Don't make it hard on him. Jeannie, you know it *will* be very hard on him because he loves his family. He doesn't like to live alone."

"Mother, we never see him anyway."

"That's true. But he is a real soldier. He has been through war. He doesn't want one here. And he will do everything to prevent it. And even though you, we, haven't seen him very much, he knows that we are here. And it will be hard for him to think of our not being here.

This was my prayer for Frank's return. I was inventing my needed God rapidly. I could see His face. I could see Him listening. Please...I begged my still and very quiet god.

"Mommy..." Her calling me Mommy again let me know that Jeannie would try, that she would help me pack, that she would accept what we had to do—"will it be very long?"

I clasped her in my arms and hugged her. But I did not want to let her see my tears.

"Jeannie, maybe not for very long at all. Maybe a few weeks. But maybe more. We don't know. But we'll travel. We'll see lots of things."

"I'd rather be home with Pippa and Daddy and going to the sea."

"I know," I said. "So would I... But we will be back. Everything will be the same." But in my heart, I knew that nothing would ever be the same again. "Will you help me pack? Choose what you want to take?"

"We'd better tell Robin and Kristin. I'll help them pack, Mum." Jeannie hesitated. "But Mother, Daddy hasn't told us yet that we have to leave."

"He will have to, I fear. By tomorrow." How I hoped he would tell us. Tell us anything. Just come back.

I found the suitcases and presented a brighter face. Robin and Kristin were excited. They loved to go places. See things. Anywhere was home, as long as I was there. Weren't home and mother synonymous?

"Can we pack our Barbie bags?"

The Barbie bags! Small, box-like black vinyl bags, just the right size for packing little girls' most-loved small toys and games. Given to them by their grandmother one Christmas when we were in Poland, when none of us had known what/ who Barbie was: the rage of American commercial toys—a young lady doll, complete with breasts and brassieres, and at last a boy friend, Ken, each with endless, expensive outfits to buy. And when I did find out what Barbie was, and the girls found out, I wouldn't let them have a Barbie doll. So they only had Barbie cases. But the cases were perfect for traveling. I never questioned the contents—anything they wanted to have, so long as it fit in the Barbie case. Bless Grandmother. And surprising choices were made. Once a pine cone from Connecticut. Miniature stuffed animals. Card games. A *Stricklisl*, an Austrian knitting apparatus for children. Wooden toys from Poland. A post card from a friend. Gifts of avowed friendship. Miniature notebooks with remembrances. This time, I was certain that Jeannie would bring a snippet of Pippa's hair.

I was not really permitted to watch them pack their Barbie cases, which would be packed and repacked several times before we would actually leave. I would have to choose their clothes.

"Will it be hot?"

"Well, I don't really know." I didn't know how long...

"Then why has Daddy gone to get the bathing suits?"

"Is that what he went to get?" I asked.

"Mother, we heard you ask. You said we might need them, that it might be summer, you said, before we came home... Why isn't Daddy, back?"

"I'm sure he will be here soon. There are so many road-blocks, you know. And he probably went to see Fikret about the pony."

"Mommy! Fikret doesn't take care of her anymore! Don't you remember!"

I was preoccupied, it was true.

"And Daddy wouldn't go to see a Turk now. You know that would be dangerous," said Robin as she was busy with her case. I hadn't known how much they knew. How much they really did know I couldn't ask, without revealing things I didn't want to reveal.

"Tell you what," I said. "Let's have tea. Let's have Savvas make us tea, and we'll sit by the fire."

"And spin, Mommy," Kristin piped up, not that far from her nursery rhymes.

"That's a good idea. Do you have a spinning wheel?" I said.

"No, but I have what Ireni showed me. You just drop a bobbin and it spins from your hand."

So it did. That is the way the village women spun wool—the very simple act of gravity pulling a thread out of a mass of twisted wool and letting it drop with a weight. "Do you have one, Kristin?" I asked. And out from her case, buried under a tiny tiger, came her spinning bobbin.

My children were more resourceful than I. And knew more.

Savvas lighted a fire under the formica chimney and brought tea and lemon shortbread. Cambric for the girls, with lots of milk. Plain for me—as had become my habit ever since milk became so inconstant in Poland, arriving, if at all, from Denmark on Tuesdays, and being poured from forty-liter cans into our own containers on the street in front of our house. And without lemon, because lemons were never found on the Polish market, so I had gotten used to tea without lemon. Why was I thinking about Poland so often?

Kristin got up and pressed her nose against the French door leading out to the marble verandah. The rain dropped against it. Then she said, ever so casually, "Daddy is coming."

"Where? Where?" I jumped up and cried, giving the lie to my casual concern. And there he was—by the car, gathering an armful of things from Kyrenia. I stayed where I was.

"Daddy, want some tea? It's nice and hot."

I looked at Frank for some sign of what might have happened. He gave no response. Had he talked to Dick? I really couldn't dump my fears on him now, with the girls here. Maybe not ever, I thought suddenly, when Frank said, "Arlene, I have to go back to the Embassy. Dick has been there all day."

"Will you be home for dinner?" I asked, and I could feel my eyes begin to fill. "Well, let's hope. Soup's on, you know... I hope I got all you needed."

"Daddy, did you see Charlie? Did you see Fikret?"

"No. No Charlie. No Fikret. I didn't expect to," Frank answered, and then he was gone.

Frank was back from Kyrenia, through all the road-blocks, through attempts to pin a near-Turkish invasion on him. He was safe and sound, and now I was angry with him, all my promises to myself broken. I might have to leave by tomorrow, and perhaps I would never, never be able to talk with him before I left. Perhaps he would never know what kind of day I had spent. And maybe, maybe, I thought, he didn't want to know.

# NOMADS

It is Washington's birthday, light years later and another country later, but only a day has passed: we are in Israel. Four of us are in one hotel room because no one of us wanted to be away from the other. And Jeannie, who was eleven years old one month ago today, is very sad, and misses her dog so much that she puts her suitcase on her bed every night so that the weight will make her think that her dog, Pippa, is sleeping there.

The untainted and the tainting—the Peace Corps and the CIA—jointly are now "The Cyprus Touring Club," and our rented car contains five female children, two women and one man. We set off for the places whose names have been familiar to us for so long, the places of the origin of the world and its ways of goodness and wickedness: the Red Sea, the towns of Sodom, Jerusalem, and Nazareth, the Sea of Galilee. And Acre and Safed and Tiberius and Caesarea. And on to Beersheba in the Negev Desert and hopefully, from there to the tents of the Bedouin.

Anarchy was our status. We were defying all rules: no school, no uniforms, no schedules. And finally, no braces for teeth, because Kristin had left hers on the table of Lot's Wife's Inn on the Red Sea.

In the gritty and barren desert, oases appeared, but not of green palms and pools of water. Oases of rising concrete settlements. Ugly. Attempts to make the niggardly desert provident, in which only Bedouins had been able to survive. But their goats, the animals requiring the least vegetation, left more desert behind them, eating every root which might hold fast a bit of sand. There were many tents of the Bedouin, made of goat hair, woven into endless pieces, draped over each other on a frame of bent wood every few yards. The tents belonged to the desert: the concrete looked blasphemous.

"Robin, you pick which one you want to stop at," Med said. "And the Bedouin will admire me with two wives!"

"Yes, and five female children!" Petey said. "A man who can't produce a son, even with two wives! You will not make such a grand impression."

We laughed.

Med Bennett, was a tall, lanky American who could easily be taken for an Easterner, until you began to think him one, and then he would switch, and you would be convinced he was a Westerner. He liked to straddle worlds. Laconic, more self-aware than any cowboy could be, so that his Western mask had to fall off when you got to know him. But so did his Yale face: it wasn't there, except in his education. Everybody knew that Dick Welch had gone to Harvard; nobody knew that Med Bennett had gone to Yale. Med lived somewhere in the West, people said. Oh no, in New England, others said.

In truth, the world was his home. His beliefs were kept guarded, and what emerged from Med Bennett was his dry cowboy-self. Until you knew him. In this way, he and Petey were ideal to be with, to bounce truths off, truths which to me were rarely spoken.

"Well, Frank, Dick and Harry (and there was indeed a Harry in the Embassy) are back there, fighting a man's war. While I'm vacationing with the women. And I'd rather be here, about to enter the tents of the Bedouin," Med announced.

"Somebody has to take care of us," Petey said, her dark eyes laughing. Petey could take care of herself.

"And it won't be the dagger boys," Med added. "I consider that my war, taking care of the women and children, makes their war necessary. I mean, there will be something left to protect."

"What will you do if we all cry?" I asked, laughing.

"If I were you, I would," Med said, flatly. I didn't expect that sort of answer: "Let it all hang out. Cry! You know

Welch's favorite saying—that Greek song—'If you wanna cry, cry!'"

Did I know it? Yes, every weekend I heard it in the summertime, now so long gone. But its meaning was "Go ahead and do it and see what good it does you..." And what Med was driving at was really for me to cry, to let myself go, to behave as I felt. For once.

I knew what Med's war was: a war against ignorance, against poverty—he was for all the good, the ideal things, things not politically expedient. He couldn't speak seriously about his kind of war and still be Med. He was realistic about it, realistic about human nature. He didn't expound the Peace Corps as the answer to any country's problems, but rather as a benign, if minor way to address some of the small economic problems of the world, wherever they were felt. Its manner was not the manner of the great world economic organizations: US AID, the World Bank, the ILO. He didn't really have a great deal of belief in organizations that treated human nature as corruptible, even though he knew it was. So I knew what he thought about the CIA. He just couldn't see me suffering for it. Was I?

"Med, I'm having a free vacation, free travel. Who could ask for more?"

"Yeah," he said. And he decided to stop, right there. Or I would have cried, maybe. I could say "fight fire with fire," but what Med fought for was something much more basic: simple economic need treated with food and self-help. And after the Cyprus mess was over, it would really only be started, and organizations like his would try to pick up the pieces again. The political situation would unravel the fabric of the economy, and Frank was addressing the political situation; Med was addressing the economic. And over and over again, little or big wars came along and destroyed the efforts of good men. And Med knew it.

"But we would freak them out, if they—the spies and the politicos—knew that we were together, talking about *them*. We forbidden bedfellows! We have to sneak away to the tents of the Bedouin to have a chat," Med said. We were passing our third set of Bedouin tents. What each of us knew, however, was how much of us was still in Cyprus. Only our physical selves were traveling in the Negev Desert, looking for a friendly Bedouin.

"Mr. Bennett, here. This is the one. I want to stop here." Robin had chosen. "Will they be friendly, do you think? Will they like us?" We were familiar with being not liked. With being hated. Feared. Blamed. All those things together.

"We'll soon find out," Med answered. I think that none of us was sure.

We drove up a small hill to the series of tents. We weren't yet able to take in the herds of camels and goats, being too busy weighing the kind of reception we would receive, feeling like invaders, like gawking tourists. Approaching us was a tall man with a decorated dagger in his belted, flowing white robe, an Arab headdress, also white, held in place by a gold-threaded sort of crown. It looked nearly like those which were sold to tourists. I wondered if it was. But he was beyond our expectations, could have been Lawrence himself. We dismounted from the car and walked towards him, as he walked towards us. When we saw the dagger in his waistband, Robin squeezed my hand more tightly, and Kristin looked at me, fleetingly, questioning.

He bowed to us, courteously, and gestured with his arm to advance, then to enter his tent. In it were some of his men, barefooted, grizzly and shabby, but gracious and hospitable, with unself-conscious dignity and friendliness that said they did not care what nationality we were so long as we were gracious guests. The anti-American habit had not yet arrived at the tents of the Bedouin.

The men got up, and a rug was brought, rolled out for us to sit on, and we, one man, two women, and five female children, were invited to sit down. One charred log was desperately trying to keep alive a smoky brass pot of Turkish coffee. But they offered us tea, somehow in sign language and few words, just *Chai,* and sent an old woman, safely out of purdah, chadorless, to fetch a piece of brushwood to encourage the fire. Water for the tea came out of a tin can fetched from some probable oasis in the Negev, an oasis we hadn't seen. The tea, when it arrived, was sticky hot and served in tiny sugary glasses. The girls were about to refuse, and didn't know how. They looked to me to decline for them, but I smiled to them, and said with my teeth shut: "Drink it and shut up." They drank it, smiling.

Baby goats were the only ones allowed to wander freely behind the door-drapery of brightly colored, hand-woven wools, where a tiny baby cried, which we all longed to see. The mother peered at us through the draperies, and we saw only eyes that were beautiful and as young, possibly, as fourteen, her face draped and her hair draped, her figure extremely slight. And we wondered what these Bedouin women must think of these white women with their short skirts, sitting down so freely with their men—and the men, in turn, probably thinking *what* about these women with the different-colored hair and bare faces. And alas, we would never know because we couldn't speak Arabic, and even if we could have, there would have been those endless preliminaries to go through, and furthermore, we would have understood enough of their culture not to be sitting there at all, and without proper coverings. And the subject would have been forbidden anyway: to say what one really thinks and truly feels, especially with foreigners, is so rare among these people that the word "outsiders" is anathema. Indeed, it is that in most languages, which is why Cyprusses happen! *Barbari!* We were in the tents of the *Barbari,* and we were there as honored guests.

As the day drew into dusk and the camels made picture book silhouettes against the red desert sky, we left the tents. The cowboy, Med, tried to ride a young camel from the flock, jumping on him from behind. The young camel sat down and dumped him off. Then the camel turned its head around to see who it was that was so unaccustomed to the way to treat a camel, and muttered a camel expletive.

The Bennetts, on their way to Athens, left us in Beersheba. Maybe I would soon be allowed to return to Cyprus. Med would never go back: his Peace Corps had terminated its operation in Cyprus. He would be reassigned. But Cyprus was still our home.

We took a *sheroot* from Beersheba to Jerusalem. Waiting for it to collect us, I went into an antique jewelry shop in Beersheba, and spotted a collection of old silver coins, sewed together, row on row, onto red fabric that I recognized as belonging to the Bedouin. It was what a woman wore draped across her face; it was also her husband's bank account, along with her gold bracelets, if she had any.

"Where did you get it?" I asked the shopkeeper.

"A Bedouin woman brought it in only yesterday. If you want it, you should buy it. It is very rare to get one. This woman will be in trouble when her husband finds out. She sold *his* wealth.

"Not hers?" I asked.

"Not hers. Never."

I bought it. I felt little pleasure at her loss, her need to sell, but still, I felt a kinship with it, with her. And felt comforted. This headdress of ancient Arabic coins, worn thin from use, added to as new coins were found or traded in the desert would be my talisman, which I would never wear. But I would think of her, the Bedouin woman, and across the gap of our countries, our lives, we would clasp hands.

Sheroots were often rickety old Hudsons, once upon a time limousines, now used as taxis between cities, unscheduled door-to-door transportation anywhere in Israel. Ours was to call for us at our hotel, but it did not come, so that another one, nearly full, was sent to pick us up. It was a Packard of 1940 vintage with jump seats. As we entered, no one wished to make room for us. We finally squeezed into the seat farthest back, all four of us in space enough for two persons. But the general unfriendliness was worse than the lack of space. The girls were frozen into silence, and we clutched each other. Another passenger kept digging his arm into my side, without looking at me, and I kept my eyes sharp for any touching of my children.

After three hours of this, it was dark when we arrived in Jerusalem. At that moment, the fabled city meant nothing to us and we were dropped at the door of a pension near the King David Hotel. We went to bed without dinner, happy to be snug in a not-unfriendly bed, after such an unfriendly ride.

I learned that the sheroot is not recommended transportation for a woman with three young children, or a young woman—that it is guilty of all sorts of things as it moves along, the specialty being rape in the back seat, while the driver keeps insisting that the behavior of the passengers is not his affair. We had escaped.

We had friends in Jerusalem, Israelis who had been in Warsaw with us and took charge of us. But three little girls were not very interested in the monument of the Holocaust, in new settlements in the desert, in the industry and brains and drive and determination and self-imposed austerity of a new nation trying to carve out manna from a desert, or in tributes to slain Jews, the gigantic faces in red-blooded glass by Chagall. Nor was I. I wanted as much as they to know how Frank was, to know all about Pippa and Savvas and Ireni and Karakoumi and Charlie Boy, and if and when...

I was invited for dinner by friends, he a former minister

to the Israeli mission in Warsaw. I hesitated to leave the girls alone. I never had. "But your girls will be well-cared for in the pension. It is a good family who runs it. You need not worry."

"Ruth is teaching Hebrew to new immigrants in the Negev settlements. The Sephardim Jews," her father the Minister said. "Language is country, you know." Yes, I did know that language is country. Ruth was his daughter, now eighteen years old. "Miriam will finish gymnasium this year, and will begin her military service. She wants to work in a kibbutz, in agriculture... This is their room, which they share when they are home. We were lucky to find such a fine apartment..."

I stared into the tiny space of the rooms, remembering the Minister's spacious house in Warsaw, not understanding his words. But then, I didn't understand Israel. My mind wasn't on it. It was on my children, alone in a pension. Why was I here?

At ten P.M. I managed to get a taxi. I entered the still pension, climbed the stairs, and quietly opened the door where Jeannie and Kristin slept. There was no one there. I felt the thick, bloody muscle of my heart in my throat, gagging me. I flew to the other room, and opened the door. There, sitting on one bed, with the lights blazing, were all of my flesh—one, two, three—I counted them, alive, and mine. "But what are you doing up?" I gasped.

"Mommy, Mommy, Mommy," they all broke out at once, "The people were screaming."

"They pounded the door. Mother, they said awful things," Jeannie said.

"But who? Who are you talking about?"

"Someone across the hall. They were having a fight, Mother. And she wouldn't let him in, and he called her awful things and pounded on the door."

"But wasn't anyone here from the hotel?" I gasped, my fears fulfilled, my guilt pouring over me for leaving them.

"No. There wasn't anyone else. We just heard the fight. Kristin and I came to your room, in your bed with Robin."

My bed, I thought. That was all the comfort they had, because it was mine. I hugged them to me, all three, blinking back my tears.

That night, I thought about what I should do. Was there a *should*? I couldn't find one, but by morning, I had come to a decision. I would call Frank to find out if we couldn't come home. Life was less dangerous in Cyprus than in a pension in Israel, or any country. We were tired of hotels, hotel meals, suitcases, no school, visiting, traveling. We wanted *home*. If we couldn't go home, we would go to Athens. Back to Petey and Med. Maybe they would be there for some weeks. "We are coming home, Frank," I said to the crackling telephone. "We are homesick. We are..." *Please don't let me cry,* I said to the invisible air.

Silence in Frank's voice. And the silence, I knew, was no. "Say something," I said, and I couldn't stop the tears.

"Arlene, what can I say? You can't come home, that is all. I've had all the contents of the house packed up, even."

"But why, why did you do that?" My home I had worked on so hard to make it mine, ours, dismantled, paintings gone, objects of familiarity, eight months in shipping crates, now again in crates, warehouses, our lives packed up and put in storage. As we were, in storage in an unfriendly pension.

"Because of too many threats..."

"To you?" I insisted.

"Well, to Americans in general." Frank wouldn't tell me anything. Didn't he understand anything but war? What about us? We were also, by now, part of the refugee group. I couldn't talk—my throat was pulp. I would call back.

Back to the dining room where I had left the girls having breakfast. They had promised to stay there. "Can we go back to Cyprus?"

Why had I ever let them even think it was possible? "We were cut off," I said. What else could I do? I must get myself in order. What was I going to do?

"Madam, the telephone." The desk clerk was summoning me. It would be Frank.

"Look, Arlene. Why don't you go to Athens? I can arrange a house for you there, send the car. I'll arrange your tickets..." This was worse news than I had thought. A house? My car, shipped to Athens? This meant months before Frank thought we would go home. Maybe never. "OK," I said. "OK." It was all I could say.

We left Israel on 9 March 1964, on a plane which spent half an hour in Nicosia, where we greeted Frank and Savvas and Ireni and Pippa. We were not even allowed by the State Department to go home for a half day, so by the time we said hello, it was time to leave. Frank had to disentangle Jeannie's arms from Pippa, so that Frank and I didn't even have a farewell embrace. It was our wedding anniversary.

So we live in this flat of bare walls and minimum furniture and little girls crying each night because of homework they don't understand, and because of their homesickness. "Mommy, what do you think Pippa is doing now?" Jeannie asks.

"What's Savvas making for dinner, do you 'spose?" says Kristin, making me look at the simple chicken I have cooked and remember the hamburger of yesterday with frozen vegetables. Savvas would be appalled.

If there is March, then there is April, and if there is an April, there will be May, and it is certain that June follows May—however separate and distinct each month is and each week, and a single day, each is the same: they flow into each other in a steady, connecting filament as palpable as sunshine, transparent as rain. We let time pass, we try to connect to its connecting, to run our fingers over the impalpable thread. One day less, before our return to Cyprus.

We try to know where we are. We try, oh we do try to walk the stones of the Parthenon, to gaze at columns the color of wheat floating like dreams against a cobalt sky. Our dreams take on a shape. They are columns, beehive tombs, a massive gate of lions, or an amphitheatre, where Kristin, in the center of the stage of captured earth, can whisper to us in the topmost ring of stone, can say her dreams, and we will shout them onwards, from Epidaurus to Delphi, to Cyprus, to Pippa, to Daddy, to Charlie Boy and to Karakoumi.

We have been to Sunion, where Kristin found the name I said she could. She ran her fingers through the letters. "That's a 'B,' Jeannie said, as Kristin hesitated to pronounce it. "And then there's a 'Y.'"

"Mommy, let me do it. I found it," Kristin said. "The next is 'R.'"

"And then?" Jeannie pushed her on, impatient.

"Oh," said Kristin. That's easy. And then... 'N.' B-Y-R-O-N."

"Who is that?" she asked.

"An English poet," I said.

"Oh," said the girls, in unanimous disappointment. They were looking for a treasure, a piece of paper that said they were going back to Cyprus. Even on carved Greek columns. It made no difference.

"Mommy, if we got on a boat here, right down from this temple, would it take us to Kyrenia?" Robin asked.

"Well, the sea would take us there, if we found a boat that could, that would," I said, looking at that wine-dark sea. Everything once sailed to Cyprus.

And we visited Delphi, where we sat in the sun and spent a lunch hour with the Gods, who, I hope, smiled down upon us from their lofty perches there, overlooking the Gulf of Corinth in the distance, with the temples of the Gods above us and the wine and cheese and bread and olives of the country and the sun high in the sky. And I rubbed my talisman from the Bedouin woman, and I could hear the Oracle reverberate through temple walls that we who passed here now would not pass again.

"Mother, we are going back to Cyprus, aren't we, when school is over? We *can* go then, can't we?"

We had exhausted our excursions: they had become round trips to and from the heart. Now we only wanted to go one place: Cyprus. I didn't know how Frank's war was going. In Greece, the Motherland, Cyprus was a fly, an irritating one. Cyprus seemed self-contained, sealed off from the rest of the world, walled up in the hearts of a woman and three children. And Frank's absence was the negation of Love. Love was Presence.

We wanted to be our own country, our own continent, our own island. And despair was too close to the surface of us all—and not just for ourselves, but also for a world we had once known without it. But that is where it had to start, didn't it, with ourselves—and then it would grow and contain the world?

News Flash, 24 June 1964: WE ARE GOING HOME TO CYPRUS!

# HOME

We were home. Our excitement was quivering in the air. Each of us was Mole returning to the house abandoned so many months before. We felt traitorous to home, having been gone from all its dearness, funny house that it was with its marble expanses of floors, concrete canopies... Even the blue formica-covered chimney had become precious. It was home. The smells of home were all coming back to us. The smells of late June roses, now profuse in the garden, cilantro in the kitchen, and sweet pungent melon, already ripe, which Savvas knew we loved.

Jeannie's nose was buried in Pippa's smells, the wetness of his tongue upon hers. Did she care if she got his germs? She wanted to bring him inside her heart, wanted him to feel all the love she had stored, which had waited for him. Kristin wandered around her shared bedroom. "Where is Raspberry Black?" she cried, the teddy bear with the pink foot pads. Robin looked for "Baby Bunting," even though she had outgrown the doll that had accompanied her on so many journeys, a doll she once gave away in a seizure of growing up, but later asked for back. Running here, running there, looking for everything at once! "Where is my book about..."

The smell of the house was so different from the smell of marble dust in our Athens apartment, near as it was to a marble quarry. Its walls had smelled of emptiness, a damp smell like that of unused cellars, and the kitchen's odors had been foreign to me—the accumulation of families leaving telltale marks behind. And the tree roses in our Athens garden had smelled of loneliness because they were not mine.

For a day only, we were like guests come to visit without knowing quite where we were, insecure with Savvas and Ireni, and on our best behavior,

Savvas stood awkwardly, embracing the girls, wanting

to include me, remembering he was the cook and the everything man.

And then the flood of knowing where we were: we were home. Summer flowed through the doors and wonderful aromas from the kitchen—Savvas was outdoing himself. The bougainvillea was cascading from the second floor—it was already hot on the verandah, and the air was moistureless and smelled of heat. But the house was cool as marble, just the way it was meant to be. The glass in the front door which had been broken by the impact of the Embassy bomb had been repaired. Was it years ago?

"Frank," I said, as I wandered from room to room, "how did you remember where everything went, when everything was unpacked again? When did you decide to unpack?"

"Well, between me and Savvas, and of course, Ireni, we did our best. She's the one who dusts, you know. She really knew where everything went. And when you were really coming back, I decided."

There were the red crayon marks on the Polish painting, a remembrance from Tanya and the refugees of our previous Christmas. There was the magic of wonderful food that I didn't have to cook; there was a cool gin and tonic in my hand, the frosty sides wetting my hand, as Savvas reminded me to take a cocktail napkin. It was all coming back. It was easy to be waited on again. There was clean, fresh linen and ironed sheets smelling of sun. It all seemed the same.

But my study was now occupied by Ron E, who had lived here during my absence. I'd forgotten, and for a moment I had a flash of resentment that all I had been deprived of had been enjoyed by someone else. I remembered, suddenly, an unpleasant moment with Savvas before I left. Ron's trunk had arrived at our house before I had told Savvas that there would be another person living here. Surprises were not desirable. He was not prepared.

"For that you will have to pay more, Kyria," Savvas had said.

"And when I leave, with the girls, we will pay less," I responded. A mean thing for me to say. A mean attitude that I didn't really mean. One more adult in the house was much more work for him, and I knew it. I also knew that was the way to handle Savvas. I hated the word, *handle,* as though Savvas were a car, or a viper, or an unruly child. But it was the customary way, like bargaining, and Savvas had respected me for it, that I knew.

I was dizzy; things were happening too fast. I wanted change to come slowly enough for me to absorb everything, slowly enough to realize I was home. I feared my imaginings of home would be disappointed and make me cry, like feeding a starving dog too much too soon.

"Frank, I feel disoriented." The feeling of home that had flooded back was now leaving me. "I fear that somehow or other, I am going to be snatched away again. Or forced out. Do you think that is likely?"

"Arlene, do you think State would go so far as to bring you back, only with the intention of evacuating you again? Not very likely."

"Who is here, now, in the Embassy?"

"Well, you know, Kelleys and Dick. Ron is leaving next week. Toby, the Ambassador, you haven't met. But you'll love him. And Edith. You will be good friends, I'm sure of that."

"But how many families are here, in the Embassy, I mean."

"Kelleys. They returned from the States, you know. And McFarlands. And Ambassador Belcher's two boys. And you and the girls. That's it, Arlene."

"Will there be more coming? More families?" I couldn't believe it. "Dick's family?"

"Dick's family doesn't want to come back. They're

going to stay in England until Dick is reassigned. He has less than a year. As for other families, there won't be any more." Frank was matter-of-fact.

"Why not?" I asked.

"Well, most of the personnel have been reassigned, transferred, and those coming in aren't allowed to bring families."

I couldn't believe it. "Why not?"

"I don't know, really. Probably more will come later." Frank seemed uneasy.

"But I, we just came today. I don't understand."

"Yes, and I am so happy the girls are so happy. Aren't you happy to be back, Arlene?"

I kept forgetting I was back. "Of course, Frank. You know that. I am. We're home. Now what about the diplomatic community?" I asked.

"It hasn't changed very much, really. But there isn't a lot of mixing with the Greek Cypriot community. I mean, we Americans are OK again, to them, but there isn't the round of cocktails and dinners," Frank said.

"The Greek Ambassador?"

"A new one. He's OK. But you'll miss the Delivanis."

"And...The Slab?"

"Well, changed quite a lot. The people who are there, I mean. It's just less crowded. No Turks. No Greeks. Mostly our small American group."

"And our sea house? Looks abandoned?" It must, I thought.

"Well, actually, it was used quite a lot."

"By whom?" I asked.

"Everybody. Everybody from the Embassy. Visitors to the Embassy. Journalists."

There it was again, my resentment flaring. Everybody else was using my house, not a government-paid rental. My/

our house! While I was living in a barren apartment with five plastic plates, trying to get homesick children through homework which was too advanced for them.

"Well, damn it, I suppose it is a mess!" I said.

"Arlene, what is the matter? You wouldn't expect me not to use it, would you, because you weren't here? I don't understand you."

I thought I would cry. Tears kept forming, and I put my nearly empty glass up to my face, to feel the ice on its redness. "I'm sorry, Frank. "It just seems different. It has been, well, rough. Oh, I nearly forgot—have you seen Charlie Boy?"

"Arlene, I have seen him. But he doesn't want to see me, I'm afraid."

"Frank, what do you mean?" I asked myself if I cared so much for Charlie and answered myself at the same time: Yes, I did.

"He wasn't around for quite a while, and then, one weekend he came. But he wouldn't come close to me. I called him, but..."

"Is he all right? Why wouldn't he come close to you?"

"He is, but he doesn't look so well. As though he's been in a fight. Probably has."

"What does he look like?" Why did I have to worm things out of Frank?

Savvas announced lunch, and Frank was grateful. I was too. I didn't want too much bad news at once. The girls' chatter took away my throat's lump, and I felt more cheerful, remembering that I was home. What had I been thinking of? I was so happy to be home! To be taken care of, instead of being the caretaker: the maid, the cook, the father, mother, chauffeur, tutor, tour guide. And the censor.

In two days' time we were reacquainted with the parts of Nicosia that remained to us, and the girls had found all the left-behind playthings, books, school papers and the few friends still in Nicosia. I had to see Karakoumi—she seemed forgotten by the girls. And I had to see Mike.

I drove to the stable the next day and parked outside the city's walls, the space around it seeming terribly empty. I didn't see anyone near the stables. I had been gone for nearly five months—what if Karakoumi weren't there? But there was a quick step behind me, and a known voice, "Kali Mera, Kyria!"

"Mike! How are you? And where is..." In the same voice, two questions.

He answered me in his order of importance: "She is fine! Waiting for you. And I, as you can see, am also fine." We clasped hands. "But she's moved. Here," he motioned, "over here," and I followed him, hearing a whinny as I approached a stable door.

I hadn't cried since I'd been home, but these tears were joyful ones, and I rubbed them off on Karakoumi's face as she nickered and nuzzled me. "Sorry, Mike. I'm just happy to be back, that's all. Happy to see you, the pony. Now tell me about you, and Kiki."

"Kiki's having another baby. She's fine. She'll be happy to hear you are back. Get in touch with her, will you?" Mike was genuinely happy to see me.

We were waiting until Saturday to go to Kyrenia, when Frank could go. I had decided to wait to see Charlie and not press Frank with questions anymore. Charlie would appear, I was nearly certain.

We drove there in a silence as complete as when I had been on that road with a pony. There weren't any other cars on the road. Eerie, it seemed. But the Greek Cypriots wouldn't go, and the Turkish Cypriots couldn't. All the familiar sights greeted us, and the check points waved us on, used to Frank's appearances. The Mesaoria Plain was already harvested, turned to brown until the winter rains came. It was only the beginning of summer. Up, up to the crest of the Kyrenia Mountains and then the excited moment when the sea spread out before us—today it was glassy and quiet. What a beautiful day to swim. The greeny-gray of olives and the darker carob trees replaced the brown of the plains in the landscape. We drove slowly to take it all in. Butterflies were everywhere; the songs of finches and larks were the only sounds in the vastness, and the occasional lamb bleat. The stillness enhanced them.

"Daddy, where is Mehmet? Have you seen him?" Robin cried.

"No, Robin. I haven't looked for him."

"And Charlie?" Jeannie finally asked, sitting next to Pippa.

"Daddy hasn't seen him," I lied. "But I'm sure we will."

Down our lane finally, to the sea house, each of us conscious of the other's excitement, hoping all would be or seem the same. Hoping that nothing had changed. We saw some stray metal rods that had supported Ali Dana's fence by Rustem's house. We saw Rusten's shuttered house, and then we saw our familiar blue doors. We unlocked them and the girls rushed in, forgetting that each door within the courtyard was padlocked as well. Jeannie unlocked the door to their room with the platform and the girls rushed in.

"Daddy, what are all these things doing here? These clothes? Whose are they?" Jeannie asked, and each girl came out carrying the clothes that were strewn on their beds.

I went into the kitchen and dining/living room first, and found it filled with other people's books, the kitchen dirty, the refrigerator half full of old, unwrapped cheese, smeared butter plates, wrinkled fruits, rancid odors. Clearly Savvas had not been here in a long time.

"But why, Frank, why didn't you have him come? He could have taken the bus around to Myrtou. Why didn't he come, if you had so many people?"

"I didn't see why Savvas should look after all those guests who dropped in. He's not a maid."

"But someone here—Marulla? Where is she?" Marulla, whose donkey the girls borrowed before the birthday party, after which Jeannie thought she could handle donkeys, except that the donkey simply stopped to eat anything in sight. Thistles, stubble, anything.

"Marulla didn't want to come here anymore. She said the house was full of Turks, with guns."

Well, it had been, hadn't it? I couldn't blame her.

We set to cleaning it up. Bees were swarming around a large trash can in the courtyard, and wind had scattered its stuffed contents all over. Sticky wrappers, smelly meat paper, bacon, dirty diapers. There was no water. I turned on the pump, which pulled water from a well to a barrel on top of the house, listening for the familiar trickle of the water falling into the barrel. No sound. No sound meant no water. I looked on the wall in the living room, under the barrel. There were the telltale signs—the gray clay, put on the roof each fall to ooze into the interstices of bamboo and leaves, had run down the whitewashed walls, and the books on the shelf were soaking wet. Somebody had left the pump on, and the well had been drained. Then I discovered my little red polka-dotted *One Hundred Best Poems for Boys and Girls*—my first book of poetry, one that I had carried with me since I was a child. Its leaves were curled and brown, still wet. Home was broken apart.

"Frank, can we get a water delivery today?" I asked hopefully, trying to forget the debris, my book, and address the current lack of water. We would have to bring water in a large tank and empty it into the well, not potable water but sufficient for showers and dishes.

"Look, Arlene, let's all go swimming. It will make everything better, the sea will. OK?" Frank was right. I hadn't expressed my hopes of seeing Charlie. Perhaps after we swam.

Were we all looking for changes? Or were we pretending there were none? The sea was the same, the same in its infinite variety. Today it was glass; the waves heaved themselves without breaking, until they hit the shore. We walked down from the sea house, under a few branches of the gigantic fig tree. Kristin avoided touching the tree whose branches she had once been so much at home in, that house of leaves. Nahim Bey had left his mark: we knew that there was something sinister about the fig tree. No one should be in its shadow too long. One should never sleep under it, as though we would. But sit in its shade and contemplate the sea, contemplate the ancient galleons coming in? Why not?

We reached the sea—it was a great, glassy, undulating mirror whose surface, it seemed, we would shatter if we entered. We all seemed hesitant, as though some great nascent threat surrounded us. Maybe the shark sucker was there; maybe the surface would shatter and close over us again, like ice.

"Last one in's a frog," Frank said, sensing our hesitation. We all eased ourselves forward on our bellies, floating through the shallow water, out to where it was deep enough to swim. The sea was so calm that not a stone was rolling on the bottom, not a grain of sand moving. But we broke the surface, churned it up, let it settle back around our bodies as though we belonged to it, the surface tension of the water joining our skin without a seam. We could break it, and call it back at will.

"Mommy," do you suppose that some of this very water is what we touched in Nafplion, where the fishermen were?" asked Robin. This very drop she held in her hand? Did it connect her, us—did this whole great body of water connect us with Turkey, with Greece, with Lebanon, out through Gibraltar, on and on to any part of the world? Who knew? But we were at home in the sea again, lifting the sparkling magic through our fingers, watching it fall in its place of glass.

"Hey, I've never seen it like this! This is great!" And the

splashings and cries echoed far out into the sea that swallowed up every sound. Back in Cyprus. Back in Kyrenia. Back in the sea!

Hours later, rinsing off with the water deposited in the well and pumped to the roof, brownish water, we heard a whine at the door. "Ssshh!" I said, hoping it was Charlie, not wanting to scare him.

A brown and white face looked in from the door. But would not enter. "Stay here and don't make any noise," I said to girls ready to engulf him.

I was ten feet from Charlie... Was it Charlie? "Charlie Boy," I said to a skeleton of a dog. The hair that should have been white was dirty grey, the brown hair grayed and sparse, back and legs scarred, eyes sunken. His tail that was always a half circle above his back, wagging, was drooped and still. His tail and eyes had been his voice, and now they were dead. He stopped, he hesitated. But with my one step nearer, he fled. I turned back to Frank and the girls. I was crying.

"Mommy, what is the matter? Was that Charlie Boy?"

Charlie feared me, feared us. That is what hurt. Feared us because he was wounded, starved. Because he was homeless. I cried and cried. I couldn't stop. I couldn't. Charlie Boy was all our anger, and all our love and all our hate and all our desire to help and all our helplessness. Charlie *was* Cyprus.

Back in Nicosia, I noticed that Savvas, too, was different. Savvas was drinking. I asked Frank about it.

"Arlene, I didn't want to tell you. I had trouble when you were gone. He was very upset, you know—he missed you, he missed the girls. He missed the dinner parties, he missed being the distinguished cook, butler, all that. He never knew when I was coming home. He missed the order you brought to our house."

"Then why is he drinking now?"

"Are you sure that he is?" Frank asked.

"No. I haven't seen him. But he doesn't seem as quick. He seems sometimes even, well, even surly."

"I had a talk with him about this, and he asked me to lock the liquor cabinet."

"Yes, but he serves liquor all the time. What makes you think he couldn't have as much as he wanted, anytime? Just pour it into another bottle, a jar, measuring cup. Anything."

"But he really doesn't want to drink."

"Has he had a problem before, before he came to us?" I asked Frank.

"Apparently so."

"How do you know?"

"He indicated it, sort of."

"I guess I'll just have to keep my eyes open. I hate that, you know. Being conscious of spying, or trying to be unconscious of a habit of spying."

I had said it unconsciously, without thinking of Frank. But I wasn't going to apologize.

"Are you suggesting anything, Arlene?" Frank sounded hurt.

"Look Frank, it isn't easy for a spy's wife either, you know. I didn't belong anywhere, really. In Athens the Embassy community didn't know I existed. I met a few wives who asked what I was doing in Athens. And do you know what they more or less said?"

"What did they say?" Frank asked.

"They said, or asked, I suppose I should say—they asked *Who*? Then added that they didn't know *we* had any evacuated wives from Cyprus in Athens. *We* being the Embassy, of course. The *Embassy* would have taken care of its own, no matter where they were from. Look Frank, I am sorry. I just can't get it out of my system, I guess. The loneliness...the...even anger. At you, sometimes too. You didn't write. You hardly called. Is any god-damned job worth that? I had to pretend, all the time, that I was OK, that things were fine. What do you think would have happened to the girls if I had behaved as I felt? If I had had any brains, I would have chucked it all and gone to Austria, found a chalet and gone skiing, let the girls learn German.

"Frank, I think why I'm angry, why I'm upset, is because I think that our evacuation was unnecessary, that all my wanderings and our loneliness were merely because of Johnson's political campaign—that it would be unhealthy for his reelection if, by any chance, an American was killed in Cyprus... You know that, don't you?"

"Arlene, I think you are right. No other Embassy evacuated people. But in all fairness, you were in a special position. You know that I was blamed by the Greek press..."

"Frank, you don't have to explain. I have just been saying that I was, I suppose I *am* too, in a special position. And I suppose that, if the Turks ever threaten another invasion, the same thing could happen."

"Arlene, there are only five families here now. It isn't likely that anything will happen, even if the Turks do threaten. And by the way, there won't be any more. Not now," Frank added.

"What do you mean, there won't be any more?"

"Any more families. The day after you arrived, permission for families to arrive was withdrawn. Which means that had you waited for a week and gone on that cruise in the Aegean, had you even waited one day, you wouldn't have been allowed to return."

"And you, you wouldn't have let me come?" I was aghast.

"How could I? Don't you understand that I can't make exceptions for anyone, even for my own family?"

"Do you think that the guy who sent the cable, the guy back at State, moving us around like wooden chessmen, would be at the Nicosia airport saying I couldn't enter? Under what authority? Do you think George Ball, or Johnson himself, is going to come here and stand at immigration and... It is the Cypriot government, whatever that is, that stamps my passport. Not State!"

"Arlene. Arlene. You are here. You are back. Can't we forget what has happened? I wouldn't have felt comfortable with my wife and children here, under the circumstances. Can't you enjoy being back?"

"I'll get used to it." I knew I was being bitchy, that I was trying to punish Frank, that I somehow wanted to. Savvas was drinking, Charlie was starved, and I had vengeance in my heart! These were indeed *The Troubles*.

I hadn't even asked Frank about the "details," the "who-dunits," I used to say, of who was doing what to whom in the Cypriot government. All the *players,* as I used to call them. I didn't want to know that when he and Ron sat in the office of the Minister of Defense, his men, the Minister's guards, always placed a hand grenade on the table, the pin next to the Minister. In case anyone undesirable should find the Chief of Station in his office, and think ill of it, making it necessary to... pull the pin. Better to do it himself than let someone else assassinate him. At that point, to the Minister it didn't matter if the COS went with him.

I cared too much to know these disturbing details of people living with threats, giving threats. An eye for an eye. I wanted to go back somewhere into trust, openness between peoples and friends. I wanted to be valued, and to value. I wanted to be in a country where the Peace Corps could live, and where Fulbright scholars could work, where we could go among the towns and villages and be welcomed, or be unnoticed. I yearned for a community like that of the Bedouins or even a country like Greece, where Jeannie had accepted a beloved mouse pin from a child in Delos, given out of love, out of caring for a stranger. I wanted to live again in a time before I, all of us, became like them, like the Cypriots, feared and fearing. I remembered feeling murderous.

And so, the change in Savvas. His new habit made me realize all this. He too had changed. How could one not change when murder in the street was daily fare? When he, innocent even of ill will, could go to the market to buy cilantro, melons, and know that if he ventured too far, say near the Green Line, he could be, probably would be killed—for no reason other than the fact that he spoke Greek. And his inevitable changing was changing my relationship to him from trust to suspicion. That was all.

A. Jeannie, Robin and Kristin (l. to r.) on Marulla's donkey, 1964   B. Frank with the children   C. Ambassadors Taylor Belcher and "Three Button" eating sheep testicles   D. Savvas at lamb roast with two drivers

A. Archbishop Makarios   B. Monks & novices at Kykko Monastery, with
Charles McCaskill and Ambassador Belcher   C. Cathedral mosque, Nicosia
D. Youth marching to statue of Markos Dracos   E. Greek Cypriot armored
vehicles   F. Greek Cypriot military on parade

# SAVVAS

Our shrunken world had pathways to specific places: to and from Kyrenia, to and from the homes of the few close friends who remained, to the Ambassador's residence and back. Frank was right about Edie, the ambassador's wife. She was *one of us*. And we had shrunk to one family. We went to Kyrenia together, trying to avoid traveling alone across the Mesaoria Plain, through the many checkpoints between Nicosia and Kyrenia. We got used to the diminutions of our lives.

The girls and I both missed Mehmet the shepherd, who never was seen grazing his sheep anymore. We missed Fikret, and Kadir. We even missed Nahim Bey, old fox that he was— toad that he was (I couldn't forget the fig tree). And we missed Rustem—his house was now a square with big closed eyes. It was dangerous for us to associate with Turks, who were all virtual prisoners in the Turkish portion of Nicosia. Many never emerged from behind those dark, massive, medieval walls.

We missed Socrate and his companion drivers. Not that we had seen much of them, but now we couldn't. They were undoubtedly hiding in the mountains again, with their gang. I missed my rides through the countryside on Karakoumi. I hardly ever rode her anymore. Riding her in Nicosia was not the same as wandering with her by the seaside and to mountain villages.

While the Kellys occupied Kadir's cottage above the Slab, Edith and her two sons were in Tatli Sue. We got bored together, and were unhappy to have telephones that linked us to duty. Duty is the only telephone call one regrets. The wanted calls didn't come.

It rang and it wanted to know if I could I come to Nicosia that day. Why, I asked. "Because Edith wants you to come, but doesn't really want to ask you. So I am asking you." It was Frank.

"Why does Edith want me?"

"Because she has to give a luncheon for George Ball and Gallo Plaza Lasso."

"I'll come," I said. And I would. Edith was generous, keeping me from all sorts of social responsibilities. They fell heavily upon her, there being no one else. And she was good at it.

"Frank, I'll leave the girls here with Savvas. OK?"

"Sure. Why not?"

Nowadays, Savvas came by bus to Kyrenia, traveling only through Greek Cypriot occupied territory, spent three days, and had his day off in the middle of the week. Frank would come out in the evening and for the night. Social requirements weren't numerous with so few people around. And the Greek Cypriots weren't entertaining very much. The girls were always with John and Julie Kelley, or Tony and Mike, Edith's teen-age sons. But one mother had to be present, at all times in Kyrenia. It was Martha's turn.

"Savvas!" I called, hoping he'd be nearby—he often went to the beach with the girls.

He was on the patio, sweeping it.

"Yes, Kyria."

"I'm going to Nicosia for lunch. The girls will be here. Give them what you like for lunch. Whatever we have," I said, knowing he never liked to plan the menus. "And remember, they don't go swimming unless they are with Mrs. Kelley. But they know that."

Savvas, like most Greek Cypriots, couldn't swim a stroke. Didn't even bathe as Ireni did. And he wasn't really in charge of the girls, normally, but these were not normal times and his role sloughed over into other areas. Keeping an eye on the girls was one of them.

"But Mom, can't we swim with Kelleys?" Robin asked.

"Of course. You know the rules. But keep in touch with

Savvas. Let him know where you are. OK? And be here for lunch at twelve thirty. Be on time!"

When I returned at four o'clock, the girls were sitting on the patio, rather quietly. I sensed something wrong. "What's the matter? You all look sort of...funny."

"We're hungry."

"But didn't you have lunch, didn't Savvas give you lunch?"

"No, Mother. He didn't. He's in his room."

I went down to his room, the room with the sea view under our bedroom.

"Savvas?" I questioned. The door was ajar, and Savvas was sitting there, on his bed.

"Yes, Kyria," he slurred, his words thick on his tongue.

"Savvas, you've been drinking. Savvas, you haven't even given the girls lunch!" I was angry. I'd trusted him. He hadn't touched liquor since I had been back. And now...

"Kyria, you are young. You don't know a lot about a lot of things." His words ran together. He would never have said what he'd just said if he hadn't been drinking. Then I wondered, if...anything untoward had happened. I went back to the patio, and looked into the faces of my young daughters, angry at the inevitable, angry at myself for not having thought of it before, for leaving them.

"Jeannie, Jeannie, tell me exactly what happened." I clutched her by the shoulders.

"Mother, don't get so excited. It's just that Savvas is drunk," she replied, matter-of-factly.

"Then why didn't you get your own lunch?" I asked. Why hadn't they, I wondered.

Kristin didn't look at me. I didn't believe them. They were always ravenous when they went swimming. Maybe they didn't go...

"Did you swim with the Kelleys this morning?"

"Yes. But not very much, Mommy," Kristin said.

"Why not?" I barked. I was beginning to feel like a prosecutor, and maybe I shouldn't go on.

"Because we didn't want to!" Kristin answered.

"What did you do, then?" I tried to calm my voice. How could I think such horrible things? But, how could I not?

"We...we went to see Mehmet," Robin answered this time. They seemed to be taking turns, sharing the blows of my questions which I knew I hadn't softened.

"With John and Julie?" I insisted.

"No. With Savvas," Robin said.

"Look, I know that Savvas wouldn't go to see Mehmet. He wouldn't go to see a Turk for anything. You girls are not telling me the truth. Why? What did you do? And why didn't you have lunch?"

And why was I punishing them so? They wouldn't ever incriminate Savvas. Oh my god, I thought. What do I do? Treating Savvas, my own children, like criminals. They were guilty of...of something. Of deception, certainly. But what had happened?

"Come on," I said. "Let's get something to eat." And I started towards the kitchen, leading Kristin by the hand. I wasn't prepared for this, whatever *this* was. I know that children don't tell on parents, whatever they may suffer from them. And Savvas would be included in family.

The phone rang. It was a clipped English voice: "Are you Mrs. Jones'?"

"Why, yes, I am."

"I am Maureen Christopher. I am a real estate agent in Kyrenia." I hadn't known there were any. "I want to know what you are doing in my client's house. I have sent you several letters, and you haven't responded, I'm afraid."

"But why on earth should I? I'm afraid that you have

the wrong person." I was annoyed to be bothered over such a mistake, especially now.

"I'm afraid I have the right person. You are Mrs. Frank Jones?"

"Yes," I said, impatiently.

"And you rent the house from Nahim Bey?"

"Why yes. We do. This is our third year, and before that...

She interrupted me: "But it has been rented to my client for over a year. I have the contract from Nahim Bey himself. And my client is here with me, wanting to know why his house is occupied."

"Miss Christopher..."

"Mrs.," she said.

"If you would care to come here with your client, I will show you our contract."

"Could I come right away?" she insisted.

"All right. Now." I might as well get if over with. It would distract me from the present.

Mrs. Christopher's client was a British Brigadier General, retired, from Addis Ababa. Courtly, perfectly mannered. But upset.

"Sir," I said, "it is unfortunate that there has been a mistake. The wrong house, perhaps?"

But Mrs. Christopher was adamant, bringing forth her papers. She unfolded them on the dining room table, saying, "General Braithwaite has paid rent for more than a year, twenty Cyprus pounds per month. Here is the contract." And there it was, dated June, 1963. Signed by Nahim Bey. The signature was identical to that on my contract.

"Incredible!" I said. "The sly old fox! He knows he can't be brought to the Constitutional Court now. No one could expect a Turk to come. And the Greeks wouldn't process a case against a Turk now anyway. He has been collecting double rent, for over a year!" And he was legally untouchable!

Mrs. Christopher was astounded. But General Braithwaite quickly recognized that he had lost a year's rent, and a house to retire in.

"But did you, either of you, ever see this house?"

"We were brought here by Nahim Bey. But we couldn't enter. He said it was temporarily occupied. It was the location that General Braithwaite loved."

"I am sorry for you," I said. "The loss of the money is less than the loss of this wonderful place. I wish we could share... Perhaps when we leave, then you can rent it."

"Perhaps by the time you leave, I won't want it," General Braithwaite remarked. "Perhaps this...confusion will save me, in the long run."

"Save you from what?" I asked. "All the troubles here (I remembered that was the term the British had used, in the late Fifties, before independence) do not change the sun, or poison the sea. No one can destroy...all this," and I gestured around the courtyard, walked through the door of the patio, pointed towards Pentedactylos, towards Bellapais, then looked downward to the sea.

"Mrs. Jones, I have fought my wars. I was a Bengal Lancer. I...I want peace."

"But why not England, then?" I was, perhaps, being rude. But curious. Always the curious American.

"Because I am used to the sun. To a dry climate. I don't think I could bear the rain, the sometimes damp, chilling summers." The general was very sincere. I understood him.

"Yes, I do know what you mean. Molly and Robert Pendleton, retired from Malaysia, live near here." I wondered if he knew them.

"No, I don't," he said. "And I suppose that now, I won't meet them. Well, we shouldn't tarry, taking your time. I do thank you. I would never have believed what happened. But now I see." He turned, gave the suggestion of a bow, and parted briskly, Mrs. Christopher following, probably wondering if she should give back her agent's fee.

"Let's have some lunch, your lunch," I said to my listening daughters.

"Nahim Bey is a cheat," Jeannie said.

"Mommy, how could he do that? Do we have to move out?" asked Robin.

"No. There is an unwritten law that says if you already occupy a place, you can't be thrown out. Would you hate to move out?" I added, wondering what they thought.

No one answered right away. Instead, they looked at each other, thinking. Jeannie's turn, it seemed. "We have to go someday, don't we? I mean, aren't we going *home* sometime?" Where was that, I wondered.

"Won't you hate to leave this house?"

"Mommy, it's different. It isn't so much fun anymore. We can't go on donkey rides, or...or." Jeannie's mouth was quivering, her face tightening to keep back tears.

And I thought of Savvas, drunk, in his room.

"But I want to stay," Kristin piped.

"Let's get you some lunch. And Daddy is coming for dinner. We have...guess what?" I had gone to Pourgouris Grocer to collect what Savvas had ordered by phone. Good thing after all, I thought, to have a phone.

"*Padakia!* We have them all the time!" Robin remarked.

"You mean, you are getting tired of baby lamb chops?" Maybe we were all getting tired of everything.

"I'll tell you what. We'll get Savvas to make a chocolate souffle! This was unanimously The Ultimate Dessert, even in summer.

"But Savvas...?" No, I hadn't forgotten. I was pretending that everything was just the same. Going ahead, planning dinner. As though nothing had happened.

He'd be all right by dinner time, I was certain. But would they, my children? When Frank came... I'd wait until Frank came. And then we'd decide...

The girls ate the sandwiches I'd made, and then I said, "Let's go to the beach. I want to swim. Do you?"

"If we go to The Slab," said Robin.

"It's a deal."

Again, the sea washed away everything: Mrs. Christopher, General Braithwaite's disappointment, Nahim Bey's wily treachery. Maybe Savvas' drinking. But my leaving the girls again? I was remembering Jerusalem, although in the end nothing had harmed them. I would wait for Frank. It was wonderful to have him come to spend the night, during the week.

"Hey, you *are* good swimmers!" I hadn't concentrated on watching the girls swim for a long time. Nor watched them at all. They had grown a lot since we'd come to Cyprus, nearly two years before. They weren't small children anymore. Why did I think of them as little? Eight, nine, and eleven years.

I looked at Jeannie carefully as she lay on the Slab, stretched out on the warm cement in the six o'clock evening sun. The nicest time of day. Her long limbs were slim and filling out, and I remembered her skinny, knobby blue knees in the Polish swimming pool. She had changed in Cyprus. As had Robin and Kristin. They were muscled and tanned, with sun-streaked golden hair framing their faces, deepening the blue of their eyes—they were beautiful children, golden children. Children you wanted to touch. And again, I clutched at the thought of the afternoon.

We dawdled on the way to our house, the girls always looking for shards, always expecting to find some unbroken pot, a small marble statue buried in the earth. The fragments were piling up in the sea house, in Nicosia, in their rooms, in boxes, even in the Barbie cases. A small, carved marble acanthus leaf, a fragment with the head of a woman from a Byzantine bowl drunk from by bride and groom, then thrown down to be broken. Because of this custom, unbroken bridal bowls were rare.

We entered the blue doors of the house, saw the Moon Cactus framing the corridor from the courtyard. And then the corridor outlined the form of Savvas, who was calling me.

"Kyria, you are to call Mr. Jones. At the Embassy." He seemed perfectly normal. His drunkenness had passed.

But damn the telephone, I thought. Calling to say he will be late. If we didn't have a phone, he would make every effort to be here.

"Yes, Frank. You called. What's up?" I said.

"Arlene, you're going to be very disappointed." He paused. Why did he pause, why not out with it?

"Well, say it," I said. "I know. You aren't coming!"

"I'm afraid that's right."

"Oh damn! It's always like this. What now?"

"It hasn't always been like this, Arlene," he said, calmly.

"Like what? Like what?" I was always so insistent, expecting the worst. Like this afternoon.

"You know that Secretary Ball is here. And Gallo Plaza."

"Yes, I know."

"They want us to have a dinner meeting, with the Ambassador. I have to be there. I am sorry."

"So you won't come tomorrow night, either?" I was feeling sorry for myself. Whiny.

"I thought you should come home tomorrow. Savvas takes the bus back tomorrow anyway, doesn't he? He has to have a day off."

"He's had his day off, Frank."

"What do you mean?" How could Frank figure out what I meant? If I told him, Savvas would overhear me, and Frank would probably call me paranoiac.

"Nothing." We both paused in our conversation. I began again:

"OK, Frank, we'll come back tomorrow. I'll put Savvas on his bus. We're having chocolate souffle, and padakia," I said, in order of importance.

"I'll probably have spaghetti. You, or we, have the best cook, you know."

"I know. Well, goodbye, Frank. See you tomorrow evening. In Nicosia."

"If not before," Frank said.

"You mean, you might take a day off? Half a day, and come to the sea?"

"You never know. Well, bye for now. Sorry. Take care, OK?"

"Daddy's not coming," Jeannie announced.

"How did you know?"

"By the sound of your voice. You weren't happy."

It was true. I was forgetting to play my game.

# Erenkoy, the Village that Reached Happiness

*All joy is darkened, the mirth of the land is desolate... – Isaiah, 24:11*

Early the next morning, the telephone rang. I'd been dreaming I heard it from across the courtyard, from the dining/living room. Now awake, I remembered that I was in Kyrenia. Why so early, I wondered. It was seven A.M.

"Hello, Arlene?" It was Frank.

"Why are you calling me so early? What's the matter?" I said, trying to keep my heart from my throat, trying to keep from jumping to conclusions.

"Arlene, I'd feel better if you drove to Nicosia as early as you can today. There is a sort of uneasiness going on... Just to be sure? OK?"

"Frank, just to be sure of what? What are you talking about? What is happening?"

"Oh, the usual rumors. Invasion. That sort of thing."

"Look, Frank, you've always told me not to listen to rumors."

But I knew if Frank did listen, they would be serious.

"Damn, Frank. You know, this tension is crazy. OK. Never mind. We'll come as soon as we can. What shall I tell Savvas?"

"Isn't he coming back anyway, on the bus?"

"I'll tell him to."

I had planned to take him to the bus, feeling uneasy about his presence without Frank. We packed our few things, stopped to check with the Kelleys. Yes, they were going too. Back to Nicosia. Bill had called Martha as well, urging them home.

We could feel the unspoken tension rising. Would this be what we all had been waiting for, knowing, but not believing it would happen—the final, orgiastic bloodbath? Waited for by both Greek and Turkish Cypriots, by the American Embassy, the British Embassy. By Greece, by NATO. Waited for with dread by the UN troops, troops lacking adequate guns, with orders to fire only in self-defense. Troops lacking a right of search in a place where guns had been pouring in steadily since Independence, and even more since the Christmas hostilities that had caught each side "inadequately" armed, compared to now.

Somehow, we absorbed this news without reading; it permeated the air. The treetops witnessed the trucks unloading from the dock areas in Greek Limassol, truckload after truckload of weapons and ammunition, and whispered it from leaf to leaf, fig to olive to eucalyptus to pine. The fish carried the news in from the sea surrounding the little Turkish fishing villages whose ten miles of coast were about to be reduced by the Greek Cypriots and their present army supported by sophisticated military equipment. The fish slithered through and among the little fishing boats, counting smaller shipments coming from Turkey, whispering to each other and glad of their fins.

It would not be a case of His Beatitude, the Archbishop, handing out rifles to schoolboys, but of trained fighters issuing serious weapons to men trained in tough crash courses. Since January.

The trip back to Nicosia was wordless, until we reached the edge of Nicosia, near the Ledra Palace. I had already heeded a stop sign, when the girls cried, "Watch out! watch out!" and they all ducked behind the seat, shouting, "Mom, Mom, watch out!"

We all heard shots coming from multiple sources: there were shots from a helicopter, but they clearly were not meant for me. There were shots *at* the helicopter, and then I saw the *legal forces of the state* brandish their arms and start running, firing back, followed by the UN troops in their innocent sky-blue berets, soldiers in an ill-defined position. The helicopter belonged to the *legal forces* and it was clearly over the Turkish sector. I saw it!

"Get down," I yelled back to the girls. "Stay down." And I stepped on the gas... "OK, kids. All's well... Listen, they weren't shooting at us! Now believe me!"

The rest of the way home, across Nicosia, there were no people to be seen. I remembered without thinking that it had been a long time since I had seen children playing in the streets, and now there was no one at all. There were no shops open—they were all shuttered. Many were sandbagged. I seemed to see the sandbags for the first time, and when I noticed them, I saw that there were many. Where had I been?

When I got home, no one was there to tell us what was happening. We went to the Embassy.

Frank was in Toby's office, and we all filed in. "Daddy, they shot at us, all around us..." It was Robin.

"Frank, it's true, but not *at* us. At a Greek helicopter straying into the Turkish sector. Greeks fired back. The poor UN's could only watch. But what is going on? Another Invasion, I suppose?" I was weary of Invasion threats, shops shuttering down in seconds, people running around, frantic, terrified of others, terrifying. Frank clasped me, clasped us all to him. God, what was going on?

"It may be true, this time. But not by ship," Frank said.

"By what, then?" I couldn't think of what else.

"Air strike. Maybe. Then maybe, the Invasion."

"Frank, you must be joking. What are the UN Troops doing anyway? What are they here for?"

"A few hundred UN troops are supposed to stop an army, a navy, an air force? These poor troops have been warned by Makarios not to intervene. A UN helicopter was fired upon and told that the next time, they, the Greek Cypriots, would shoot to kill."

"You mean General Thimayya put up with that?" I said. But I already knew that Prime Minister Papandreau's appeal to Makarios to stop all attacks against Turkish villages had gone unheeded. Makarios had answered, "We will fight on till death!"

My wearied fears were rising again. Half anger, half fear.

"So now what do we do? Barricade ourselves in the Embassy? Thanks a lot. I think I'll go home."

"It's what you should do. If anything does happen, I'll come to tell you. Everybody is threatening. The Greeks threaten to kill all Turks because of..."

"Frank, you don't have to tell me what it's because of. It's because of Charlie Boy..."

"And the Turks threaten to invade, because of Makarios' attacks against those ten miles of Turkish fishing villages, Mansoura, Kokkina..."

Kokkina's Turkish name is *Erenkoy,* which means "The Village that Reached Happiness." It has only three hundred villagers, but the hillside caves around it are filled with refugees living in squalor, without water, with little food. Their supplies have been cut off in this "final phase" perpetrated by Makarios, Man of God, Archbishop of Kypros. Their fuel has been cut off so no bread can be baked. Without bread, the people starve. They have a few bags of flour which they cannot eat as flour. They do not dare go into the fields to gather untended crops, rotting grapes, bitter lemons...

And so we have gone home to wait.

To wait while Kokkina's neighboring villages of Mansoura and Alevga fall. Wait while Ayios Theodoros falls, all Turkish villages with Greek names. Wait while the Turkish Cypriots are pushed towards the sea and bombarded from the sea. And we wait to see if the UN Troops can get in to save the women and children. Which, of course, they won't be able to.

And so we wait for the Turkish planes that have held off so long. Words have gone from me but thoughts keep forming and will not stop. Isolated bits of facts. People I knew. Becky's driver. Two former Turkish drivers for the American Embassy. Assiz, shot through the face and mouth, losing an eye. Fikri, forced to ride a woman's bicycle, a loss of face in a country where women never even enter coffee shops. He is jobless, homeless, possessionless but is only one of the herded, bombarded, threatened Turkish Cypriots. Hattie, wife of a Turkish Cypriot Judge, and my friend so long ago, it seems, called me just days ago, awakened that day, she said, by the sound of gunfire. She expressed the hope that it would be the beginning of the end...just so *it* would be over, whatever *it* might be...

Turkish villages are surrounded and the villagers know they will be killed if the Invasion does not happen. The Greeks know that the Turkish villagers will be killed if the invasion does happen. This is Makarios' *final phase,* which he has so named. He expects time enough to gain victory, expects NATO members to keep the Turkish Air Force at home, while the Turkish villagers and Turkish refugees from mixed villages die from lack of water, lack of food, lack of shelter from the sizzling August sun—die in the ashes of their houses if they do not die from Greek Cypriot guns and mortars. They have circled together like threatened, hopeless, trumpeting elephants at the mercy of the modern world, or once westward-going wagon trains under Indian attack: people afraid, families afraid, animals afraid... Charlie...

So we, my children and I, sit on the marble balcony waiting for the Turkish planes. If and when. And wait for news of where they are. And then wait for news of when they will stop coming, as the Turkish fleet was once stopped by negotiations—news of the planes turning back to Iskenderun, the nearest Turkish air base, only minutes from Cyprus.

Polykarpos Georkadzis, Minister of Interior, has informed the American Embassy that, if Turkey invades, all Turkish Cypriots will be shot!

But they are being killed now, herded in their villages, their strongholds, all over Cyprus. As are Greek Cypriots, by Turkish Cypriots. My children are as silent as I, waiting. We wait to hear if Greek planes are coming, and Greek troops from the Mainland. And then we wait to find out if Makarios will call off his attacks against the Turkish villages of Kokkina and Mansoura. If he does not, Turkey says, they will strike by air.

Makarios did not. "We will not negotiate with the Turks even if this whole island should go to flames..." And then he demanded that all Turkish Cypriots lay down their arms. He must have been trying to provoke them, like a child poking a stick at a starving dog, believing it could not, would not *dare* to bite. It is an ancient insult to ask the enemy to lay down arms.

The final phase continued.

And we waited and waited and listened to the sound of sporadic gunfire. And I wondered where Mehmet was, and Yashar, and Fikret. I would have liked to comfort their children and I would have liked a chance to put my arms around the always-sad-faced wife of Nahim Bey, to forgive him, even, to say I loved him. And I hoped and hoped that Charlie was dead from a charitable stray bullet.

And then the telephone rang. It was Kiki Petris, Mike's pregnant wife, and she said, "Is it Kyria Jones?" Why should Kiki call me Kyria, I wondered, and I said Yes and then she said "It is very nice of you to send those American planes to bomb us, and you have children too..." And I slumped down in my chair.

And then, it got to be Sunday afternoon on August 9th,

and the day dragged on, and there was nowhere to go at all; we could only stay at home in the shade and drink gin with Edith and Martha or alone and wonder where shots were aimed this time and the next time and the next, and wonder what it would be like to talk about normal things: how nice or not that the weather was hot or cool, damp or dry, and whether or not to send for those records from Sam Goody and where to have Sam Goody send them.

Even the gunfire was boring by this time, and it sounded wrong if we didn't hear it. But the sun beat down as usual, and somewhere out in some poor little village, people were the victims of other men's pride and other men's age-old cruelty, and the victims of a man obsessed with desire to continue in power as head of state, praising those who died for the empty word of freedom. Freedom to starve and freedom to live without water in caves and freedom to choose self-determination in the heat of a Cypriot summer with horizons wavy with heat and passion and words of glory!

And then at six P.M. three Turkish Saber Jets buzzed Nicosia. They came in so low over the American Embassy and our house that I could see the faces of the pilots, and then the *firecrackers* started again like Greek Easter, and my children clung to me, silently, without tears, and I to them. I knew that the air strike was happening at that very moment, and that the *mopping up* was taking place and that there would be more mopping up after the mopping up. And we Americans would, of course, have arranged for the Turkish Air Strike and provided NATO planes and Napalm... And His Beatitude relayed a message to Ambassador Belcher that unless the raids ceased within a half-hour, he would order the systematic massacre of thirty thousand Turkish Cypriots, specifically including women and children.

Then, exhausted but sleepless, we went to bed knowing villages to be burning and ourselves to be safe, and at two

A.M. on August tenth, Frank came home from the Embassy and said to me, very quietly, *Arlene, you've got to go again,* and I said *Where?* thinking of Kyrenia, and Frank said *Beirut* and I said *I don't believe it and I won't go* and then he said *Edie is going and the Kelleys* and I said *By what time* and Frank said *Seven* and I cried.

# Newspaper Addendum

*During the summer of 1996 several Greek Cypriots were murdered in cold blood by Turkish-backed death squads. The present agony of Cyprus came about because of the betrayal against the movement for enosis during the 1950's by the British, who encouraged Turkish terrorism and expansionism at the expense of Cypriot Hellenes. Further betrayals occurred during the signing of the accords in 1959 when Cyprus was forced to adopt an unjust and unworkable constitution.*

*In order to refute the statement that "Turkish Cypriots were never held hostage by Greek Cypriots," it would suffice to look at the U.N. Secretary-General's report dated Sept. 10, 1964 (S/5950), which states that the restrictions imposed on the Turkish Cypriots in that period amounted to a "veritable siege." As far as the Turkish intervention in 1974 is concerned, the German newspaper* Die Zeit *put it best when it reported in its issue of Aug. 30, 1974, that "the massacre of Turkish Cypriots in Paphos and Famagusta is the proof of how justified the Turks were to undertake their second (August) intervention."*

– *Washington Times,* Letter to Editor, Suleyman, from Cyprus Blog

## It's time for Greek Cypriots to take part of the blame
### by Loucas Charalambous
#### Sunday, September 6, 2009

*"THE CYPRUS problem will be solved only when the Greek Cypriots admit and assume their responsibilities for its creation." The above observation, by university lecturer Alexis Heraclides, is probably the wisest view ever expressed in relation to the Cyprus problem. Its correctness is proved on a daily basis.*

*Because Greek Cypriots, with their behaviour, show that not only have they not recognised our side's share of the blame but*

*the denial of this gets worse with the passing of time. The obdurate refusal of the average Greek Cypriot to accept any blame for the mess we are in features triumphantly in the media every day. The story about the 1974 execution of the five Greek Cypriot prisoners, whose remains were recently identified through DNA testing, provided a perfect opportunity for an exhibition of this mentality. Everyone urged the government to report Turkey to the world and demand the setting up of war tribunals to try the Turkish government.*

*It is as if we did not know for 35 years now that all these unfortunate individuals listed as missing by our state were dead, many of them having been captured and killed either by the Turkish troops or the Turkish Cypriots. Now everyone is pretending to be surprised – our state, political parties and newspapers – by the revelations about the execution of prisoners.*

*But had not Rauf Denktash officially informed us, many years ago, that there had been executions of prisoners in 1974? Why are we surprised now?*

*It is important to note that while everyone is calling for the setting up of tribunals to try Turkey for the execution of prisoners and civilians, nobody is prepared to admit that we were responsible for similar 'achievements' during the 1963-74 period, another decade of bloodshed.*

*In fact, when one journalist dared to refer to a similar crime by our side, all the super-patriots of the country, led by the super-patriots of Phileleftheros, turned on him. According to our most patriotic newspaper, all Turks and the Turkish state were responsible for all the killings of Greek Cypriots, while if there had been some 'acts of extremism' (this is how it refers to the killings of Turkish Cypriots), a few 'extremist elements' were to blame.*

*The super-patriots of Phileleftheros had never heard Nicos Koshis, the chief of staff of the Akritas Organisation, stating on television that the late Archbishop Makarios had set up the illegal organisation and had chaired meetings at the presidential palace, during which he personally gave instructions about its running and operations. It was the 'fighters' of this organisation who were killing Turkish Cypriot civilians and dumping them down wells in 1963.*

*A few days ago, on a radio show, a woman caller, was hysterically insisting that all that happened in 1963 was that Makarios proposed the amendment of 13 points of constitution for debate and the "Turks got up and left". This is the only version of history that exists for most Greek Cypriots.*

*For as long as Greek Cypriots carry on living with their illusions, based on official myths, they will never be able to accept their share of the blame and the Cyprus problem would never be solved, as Heraclides correctly observed.*

# POSTSCRIPT

Richard Welsh (Dick) was assassinated in Athens in 1975, outside of his house, in front of his wife and driver. He was Chief of Station of the CIA in Athens and the first of thirty-four victims assassinated by a Greek radical group, members of which were not apprehended until 2003. They were tried and sentenced to life imprisonment.

In 1970 an attempt was made on the life of Archbishop Makarios, promoted by the Greek Junta, also known as the Greek Colonels, who took over the government of Greece in 1967 by a coup d'état. The Junta enlisted the services of Polykarpos Georgadis, by 1970 an arch enemy of Makarios, who no longer wanted Enosis, Union with Greece. Enosis was the primary aim of the Greek Cypriots' struggle with the British, and after independence, with the Turks. Georgadjis was gunned down, a week later by Makarios supporters after the unsuccessful attack on Makarios.

In 1974 the Greek Junta ousted Makarios in a coup, putting in place Nikos Sampson as President of Cyprus. (Sampson, during the EOKA period, 1956-60, posed as a photo journalist, shot British citizens in the back on Ledra Street, known as "Murder Mile," photographed their bodies and published them in a Greek Cypriot newspaper). His presidency lasted a week and was brought to an end by a Turkish invasion of Cyprus.

The Turkish intervention was upheld by the Standing Committee of the Consultative Assembly of the Council of Europe, which admitted the legality of the Turkish intervention in Cyprus, established by the Guarantor Powers of Britain, Greece, and Turkey. Afterwards, Cyprus was divided into the Turkish North and the Greek South. It remains so to this day.

Constant efforts to reunite, encouraged by the European Union and NATO, have remained a failure.

In 1976 Sampson was sentenced to twenty years imprisonment for his role in the coup. He was released in 1991 and died in 2003. Makarios died of heart failure in 1977.

# ABOUT THE AUTHOR

Arlene Swift Jones grew up on an Iowa farm where she "read books and rode horses." The most important constant in her life has been her writing, which she continued to pursue after marrying Frank Jones and entering the hectic life of a CIA wife and mother of three children. In that role, she was often obliged to pick up and move her households and children from one country to another. Finding schools was frequently a major problem, which she solved while living in Poland by founding a school, now called The American School of Warsaw.

In all of the countries where she has lived, Arlene has taught at some level, from first grade to the university lecture hall. She taught literature at the International School in Geneva and eventually became Assistant Academic Dean at the Ethel Walker School in Simsbury, Connecticut. Always her aim has been "trying to make young people more aware of the world, its history, art, geography, and politics." Her cultural, artistic and literary interests also led to her involvement in the building and operation of a new library in New Hartford, Connecticut, where she and her husband lived with their three daughters for many years.

Arlene Jones' first full-length poetry collection (*Deenewood, A Sequence*) was winner of the Tales Prize from Turning Point Press in 2004. A second book of poems, *Pomegranate Wine,* was published in 2005, having been a finalist for four of the country's most prestigious literary contests. Jones' poetry has often been anthologized and has been published in many journals, including *Prairie Schooner, Kansas Quarterly, Tar River Poetry,* and *Cimarron Review.* She has won several awards for her writing and has received fellowships from the McDowell and Ragdale Foundations. Her current project is a multi-generational work depicting the lives of Norwegian Quaker immigrants to Iowa, from whom she is descended.

This book is set in Garamond Premier Pro, which had its genesis in 1988 when type-designer Robert Slimbach visited the Plantin-Moretus Museum in Antwerp, Belgium, to study its collection of Claude Garamond's metal punches and typefaces. During the mid-fifteen hundreds, Garamond — a Parisian punch-cutter — produced a refined array of book types that combined an unprecedented degree of balance and elegance, for centuries standing as the pinnacle of beauty and practicality in type-founding. Slimbach has created an entirely new interpretation based on Garamond's designs and on comparable italics cut by Robert Granjon, Garamond's contemporary.

To order additional copies of this book
or other Antrim House titles, contact the publisher at

Antrim House
21 Goodrich Rd., Simsbury, CT 06070
860.217.0023, AntrimHouse@comcast.net
or the house website (www.AntrimHouseBooks.com).

•

On the house website
are sample poems, upcoming events,
and a "seminar room" featuring supplemental biography,
notes, images, poems, reviews, and
writing suggestions.